CHINA CEO

A CASE GUIDE *for* BUSINESS LEADERS IN CHINA

CHINA CEO

A CASE GUIDE ·—· *for* ·—· BUSINESS LEADERS IN CHINA

JUAN ANTONIO FERNANDEZ

SHENGJUN LIU

BICENTENNIAL
1807
WILEY
2007
BICENTENNIAL

JOHN WILEY & SONS (ASIA) PTE LTD

This publication is designed to provide accurate and authoritative
information with regard to the subject matter covered. It is sold with the
understanding that the Publisher is not engaged in rendering professional
services. If professional advice or other expert assistance is required, the
services of a competent professional person should be sought.

Other Wiley Editorial Offices
John Wiley & Sons, Inc., 111 River Street, Hoboken, NJ 07030, USA
John Wiley & Sons Ltd, The Atrium, Southern Gate, Chichester PO19 BSQ,
    England
John Wiley & Sons (Canada) Ltd, 5353 Dundas Street West, Suite 400,
    Toronto, Ontario M9B 6H8, Canada
John Wiley & Sons Australia Ltd, 42 McDougall Street, Milton, Queensland
    4064, Australia
Wiley-VCH, Boschstrasse 12, D-69469 Weinheim, Germany

Library of Congress Cataloging-in-Publication Data:
978-0-470-82224-1

Wiley Bicentennial logo: Richard J Pacifico
Cover design and page layout by Alicia Beebe
Printed in Singapore by Saik Wah Press Pte Ltd.
10 9 8 7 6 5 4 3 2 1

I want to dedicate this book to my parents, Laly and Eugenio, and my sister Laura. Despite the enormous distance between us, I want you to know that the heart can travel through time and space much faster than light.

Juan A. Fernandez

To those I love and those who love me.

Shengjun Liu

Contents

Introduction

Welcome to *China CEO: A Case Guide for Business Leaders in China*. The book that you have in your hands is the result of more than five years of work with companies in China. It includes a collection of cases on international companies doing business in this country. These cases have been used in the course Managing in China that Juan has delivered to international executives from all over the world.

The objective of this field guide is to complement *China CEO: Voices of Experience from 21 International Business Leaders*, my previous book with Laurie Underwood, published in February 2006 by John Wiley & Sons. While *China CEO* introduced a number of important themes and was based on interviews with CEOs of multinationals in China, this new book presents case studies on the same topics.

Every chapter in the field guide follows the same structure:

1 A short introduction to the topic covered by the chapter.
2 A case study tailored for that topic.
3 Commentaries on the case studies by a professor at the China Europe International Business School (CEIBS) and at least one practitioner with years of work experience in China.

Our purpose with this new book is to offer new information not included in *China CEO*. The case studies included in the collection are:

CASE STUDY 1: EMERSON ELECTRIC (SUZHOU) CO., LTD

This case deals with the communication problems experienced between US and Chinese management on the operation of the multinational company in Suzhou (China). The general manager from Taiwan resigned after one year in the position, leaving the new general manager with the difficult task of regaining control of the organization. He will need to create a culture of trust and open communication among its members.

CASE STUDY 2: ELI LILLY & COMPANY, CHINA AFFILIATE, WAR FOR TALENT

Eli Lilly and Company is a global, research-based pharmaceutical company with a history of over 126 years. Lilly China had more than 50 representative offices and about 500 medical representatives in 2003. Compared with its key global competitors, Lilly's presence in China is still very small. To facilitate Lilly's expansion strategy in China, Lilly China had an urgent need to recruit and maintain a pool of top medical representatives. However, Lilly China had high employee turnover for three consecutive years. Obviously, the company needed to strengthen employee retention. Should Lilly maintain current recruiting practices or switch to better options? Human Resource Director Mary Liu decided to ask a consulting team to help out with the whole problem. The case describes Lilly China's background, its human resources concept and structure, and the Chinese labor market.

CASE STUDY 3: GUANGZHOU PEUGEOT AUTOMOBILE CO., LTD

In 1985 Peugeot established a joint venture in South China. Peugeot introduced its management system into the joint venture, controlled key decisions and helped Chinese employees learn French and Peugeot culture. Before 1992, the joint venture enjoyed glorious days. With the increase in competition, however, many problems emerged, including unsuitable car designs, outdated car models, high prices, bad quality and poor service. Its production dropped so quickly that it almost ceased operation by 1996. Moreover, the serious cultural conflicts and interest fights dimmed the future of the joint venture. Finally, the Chinese partner lost patience until the joint venture ended in divorce.

CASE STUDY 4: PICANOL CHINA

Picanol was founded as a family business in 1936. It manufactures weaving machines for the textile industry and is headquartered in Belgium. Picanol hired a new CEO with the mandate of preparing the company for the competition in the global market. As part of the changes, the new CEO introduced a new business unit structure. Picanol China, under the leadership of expatriate manager Hans, is in a dilemma as to whether to implement the new structure rigidly or to be more flexible. The case traces the development of the new organization, together with the problems that ensued. It also discusses how an expatriate manager works with headquarters.

CASE STUDY 5: GM VERSUS CHERY, DISPUTES OVER INTELLECTUAL PROPERTY RIGHTS

Chery, a Chinese domestic car maker, launched a new mini car model, the QQ, in July 2003. This was several months earlier than the planned launch date for General Motors' (GM's) new mini car, the Chevrolet Spark. The QQ looked very similar to the Chevrolet Spark, but was much cheaper. GM claimed that the Chery QQ was a knockoff of the Matiz, a model owned by GM Daewoo. The QQ turned out to be a real hit with consumers, while Chevrolet Spark sales were much lower than expected. To make matters worse for GM, Chery was aggressively expanding into other countries where GM had a presence. Intellectual property rights (IPR) disputes were common in China's automotive industry; several multinational car makers had also brought infringement cases forward. GM had its hands full: it had to compete with Chery head to head in the market while deciding what actions to take with regards to its IPR infringement claim.

CASE STUDY 6: MERCEDES-BENZ AND WUHAN WILD ANIMAL PARK

In the morning of December 25, 2001, many people in Wuhan, a large city in middle China, were surprised to see a Mercedes SLK230 sports coupe being towed by a water buffalo in the street. The next day the car was wrecked by five strong men in Wuhan Wild Animal Park (WWAP); this publicly humiliated Mercedes. After the negotiations between WWAP and Mercedes failed, WWAP threatened to smash another Mercedes car. Why did such a terrible incident occur? What makes the car owner resort to such an extreme solution? How will Mercedes handle this situation? Could Mercedes avoid this incident happening again? No matter what Mercedes plans to do, the threat of another incident means that they have to act fast. This case will be particularly useful in discussing the company's public relations strategy and crisis management skills.

CASE STUDY 7: CARREFOUR CHINA, REVAMPING BUSINESS TO FOLLOW LOCAL RULES

China was a market that tempted the MNCs (multinational corporations). However, it set strict restrictions to protect domestic retailers. Though China did have a plan of opening the domestic market to foreign retailers step by step, it seemed to be beyond the patience of retail giants like Carrefour. As a result, many foreign retailers managed to expand in a secret but illegal way in China. Carrefour found that local governments had a strong motivation for introducing foreign retailers for the sake of employment and taxation benefits. With the help of local governments, Carrefour quickly established footholds in China's major business cities and developed into the No. 1 foreign retailer. It was not hard to imagine that the illegal expansion irritated local retailers and the Central Government. After this the Central Government issued circulars and regulations to warn foreign retailers and local governments, who just turned a deaf ear to the warnings. In 2001 rumors spread that Carrefour would be shut out and the Central Government would not appease it any more. Carrefour would have to do something to solve the crisis.

CASE STUDY 8: THE LOLLYPOP THAT TURNED BITTER, THE EXPERIENCE OF AN EXPATRIATE COUPLE IN CHINA

This case describes the experience of an expatriate couple in China. Alain, the husband, decides to take a challenging assignment in China. Montse, the wife, follows, but has to give up her own career. Once in China, things don't go as expected.

CASE STUDY 9: PERSONAL REFLECTIONS OF THREE FOREIGN ENTREPRENEURS IN CHINA

In this case three *real* stories are told by foreign entrepreneurs in China. The first protagonist was an expatriate who became a supplier to his previous employer. Later, he started a successful new company. The second protagonist started her China experience as a diplomat. After trying a low-risk, small business, she made a new move with help from a venture capitalist. The third protagonist went to China attracted by its culture. He learnt the language and even studied in a Chinese university. He later founded several companies with his classmates. Though these three foreign entrepreneurs had different growth paths and met different challenges in their ventures, they did share a lot of best practices and lessons for doing business in China.

Each case study covers one specific topic that is connected to the previous book *China CEO: Voices of Experience*. The relation between the two books is presented in the following table:

China CEO: Voices of Experience		China CEO: A Case Guide for Business Leaders in China
Chapter 1 Qualities of a successful international leader in China	<···>	**Chapter 1** Leadership in China: Putting the heart where the mind is Case study: Emerson Electric (Suzhou) Co., Ltd
Chapter 2 Managing Chinese employees	<···>	**Chapter 2** Human resources in China: Chasing the runaway bride Case study: Eli Lilly and Company, China affiliate, war for talent
Chapter 3 Working with business partners	<···>	**Chapter 3** Joint ventures: Dancing the Chinese tango Case study: Guangzhou Peugeot Automobile Co., Ltd
Chapter 4 Communicating with headquarters	<···>	**Chapter 4** Dealing with headquarters: The art of juggling Case study: Picanol China
Chapter 5 Facing competitors **Chapter 6** Battling intellectual property rights	<···>	**Chapter 5** Counterfeiters in China: Catch me if you can Case study: GM versus Chery, disputes over intellectual property rights
Chapter 7 Winning over Chinese consumers	<···>	**Chapter 6** Chinese consumers: The new kids on the block Case study: Mercedes-Benz and Wuhan Wild Animal Park
Chapter 8 Negotiating with the Chinese government	<···>	**Chapter 7** Government relationship: Playing Chinese poker Case study: Carrefour China, revamping business to follow local rules
Chapter 9 Living in China	<···>	**Chapter 8** Expatriates in China: Lost in translation Case study: The lollypop that turned bitter, the experience of an expatriate couple in China

The case guide includes a Chapter 9 that has no corresponding chapter in *China CEO: Voices of Experience*. This chapter covers the topic of foreign entrepreneurs in China and it caters to the request from several readers for us to include a chapter on small companies and their challenges in China.

The guide can be used in two ways:

1 **As a self-study book.** We recommend that our readers follow the following steps:
   - read the corresponding chapter in *China CEO*
   - read the cases and try to decide what you would do in such a situation
   - compare the commentaries in the cases to your own reflections
   - read the introduction to the corresponding chapter in the field guide.

2 **As course material.** You can follow the same procedure used for self-study, except that you can add group discussions after your own reflections on the case study. Basically, the steps to follow would be:
   - use the corresponding chapter of *China CEO* as pre-reading
   - refer to the cases in the corresponding chapters of the field guide
   - participate in a group discussion
   - ask the participants to read the case commentaries and see if they can add something new to what they have discussed
   - refer to the introduction to the chapter in the companion case guide as the conclusion by the instructor.

We wish to thank the commentators who so generously shared their experiences with us. Each case study received comments from a professor and at least one practitioner. A big thank you for your generosity.

Contributing professors

Bala Ramasamy is Professor of Economics at China Europe International Business School (CEIBS), Shanghai, China.

Dingkun Ge is Professor of Strategy and Entrepreneurship at CEIBS.

Dongsheng Zhou is Professor of Marketing at CEIBS.

Gerald E. Fryxell is Professor of Management at CEIBS.

Howard Ward is Professor of Management at CEIBS.

Per V. Jenster is Professor of Management at CEIBS.

Thomas E. Callarman is Professor of Operations Management at CEIBS.

Willem P. Burgers is Professor of Marketing and Strategy and Bayer Healthcare Chair in Strategy and Marketing at CEIBS.

William H. Mobley is Professor of Management at CEIBS and the Founder of Mobley Group Pacific Limited.

Contributing practitioners

Angeli Kwauk is Area Director of Human Resources of China Grand Hyatt Shanghai.

Bettina Ganghofer is Deputy General Manager of Shanghai Pudong International Airport Cargo Terminal Co. Ltd (Lufthansa JV).

Doug Ho Song is Managing Director of Doosan Leadership Institute, Doosan Group.

Gary An is General Manager of Amphenol East Asia Electronic Technology (Shenzhen) Co., Ltd and Amphenol Commercial Products (Chengdu) Co., Ltd.

Guosheng Zhu is Operation General Manager of BOC China.

Hans-Peter Bouvard is Business Development Director of Northern Asia Reichle + De-Massari Far East (Pte) Ltd.

Sergiy Lesnyak is Chief Representative of Ferrexpo Group in China.

Shaun Rein is Managing Director of China Market Research Group (CMR).

Wei Joo Chai is Factory Manager of Shanghai Kerry Oils & Grains Industries Ltd.

Xiaotong Li is HR Director of Shared Service Organization at Henkel (China) Investment Co., Ltd.

Xuezheng Li is Global Sales Director of Beijing BOE Optoelectronics Technology Co., Ltd and former Chief Public Relation Officer of BOE Technology Group Co., Ltd.

Yufeng Zhao is General Manager of Progress Strategy Consulting Co., Ltd.

Most of the cases have been written by the two co-authors of this case guide, sometimes in cooperation with others. We want to thank all of you:

George Chen, former Research Fellow at CEIBS.

Jacqueline Zheng, HR Manager of Eli Lilly China.

James G. Clawson, Professor at Darden.

Linda (Dongmei) Song, Research Assistant at CEIBS.

Wei (Wendy) Liu, Darden MBA 2003.

A special thanks to **Lydia J. Price**, Professor of Marketing and Associate Dean at CEIBS, and Dr. **Junsong Chen**, Research Fellow at CEIBS, for allowing us to use their case Mercedes-Benz and Wuhan Wild Animal Park.

Finally, we want to thank all the companies that have contributed to the case studies. Without them, this book would not have been possible.

Acknowledgments

There are many people to thank. First, the companies that so generously allowed us to write cases about them. Second, the professors and practitioners who gave their time to work on the case studies. Dr. Jianmao Wang, Director of the Case Development Center and Associate Dean at CEIBS, gave us great support. We also thank CEIBS for allowing us to use the cases. Linda (Dongmei) Song, our extremely competent assistant, gave assistance that was fundamental to the preparation of this book. Finally, Joan Draper took the time to read the manuscript and make suggestions. Thank you all.

Chapter 1
Leadership in China: Putting the heart where the mind is

INTRODUCTION

One question frequently asked by foreign managers in China is whether there is a most appropriate leadership style to use with the Chinese staff. Behind that question there is some expectation of a silver bullet or magic formula. Unfortunately, that formula does not exist. In our experience, most of the things that work elsewhere also work in China, with certain differences that we will explore later in this introduction.

Leadership is basically about influence, and influence rests on two pillars: results and respect for people. John C. Maxwell in his bestselling book *Developing the Leader Within You*[1] presents a model of leadership based on the development of influence.

The first step in this model is influence based on position, at the lower level of the stairs. This clarifies a frequent confusion between power and leadership. In a certain way, leadership is also power, but it is a power that emanates from the person and not so much from the position they occupy. Actually, you can have leaders with little position power but a great influence in the organization. The next step up is that of relationships: people follow because they like you. Results is the next step: people follow you because you get things done. Now, when you combine relationships and results, you start getting the influence that makes others want to follow with their hearts and minds. Development follows; this means that you help the people around you to become leaders themselves – you develop other leaders. Finally, on the last step is respect: people follow because of who you are. This is the top level of the model where true leadership is placed. According to Maxwell, real leadership is achieved after a life of helping others and organizations. We could not agree more.

The basic tenet of this model is the idea that a leader has to go through all these steps. The target to aspire to is gaining the respect of others, which also confers an important ethical component to leadership. Leadership is about influence emanating from a well-rounded person who considers others' needs, including those of the organization. This model presents an excellent road map for gaining influence and becoming a wholesome leader. It is appropriate in the West as well as in the East.

However, if we have to stress one important leadership practice in the Chinese

EXHIBIT 1.1: THE PATH TO LEADERSHIP

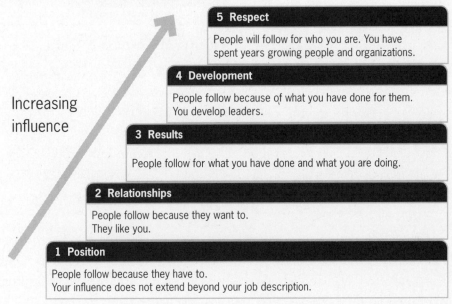

Increasing influence

5 Respect
People will follow for who you are. You have spent years growing people and organizations.

4 Development
People follow because of what you have done for them. You develop leaders.

3 Results
People follow for what you have done and what you are doing.

2 Relationships
People follow because they want to. They like you.

1 Position
People follow because they have to. Your influence does not extend beyond your job description.

Note: adapted by the authors from the original model

cultural context, it would be social skills. Daniel Goleman developed the Emotional Intelligence Model[2] in which social skills is one of five elements (self-awareness, self-regulation, motivation, and empathy being the other four). Goleman defines social skills as the proficiency in managing relationships and building networks. It is an ability to find common ground and build rapport. This concept of social skills is certainly related to the concept of *guanxi*,[3] so popular and, somehow, misunderstood when talking about business practices in China.

Guanxi in our view has two very different sides: negative and positive. Negative *guanxi* is frequently linked to corruption, getting private benefit by using company or public resources. The positive *guanxi* is about facilitating business transactions and it is more equated to the idea of social skills by Goleman.

As the following model depicts, *guanxi* can be represented as a number of concentric rings. The core is formed by the family. Next comes friends, classmates, and workmates. The outer ring is formed by connections or, in other words, the *guanxi* of my *guanxi*. Outside of the system we find others, people with whom we interact but are not part of our *guanxi*.

EXHIBIT 1.2: THE *GUANXI* MODEL

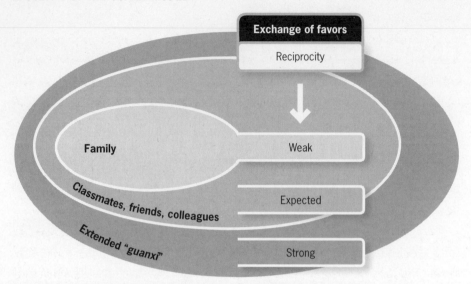

Guanxi is basically an exchange of favors and is maintained by reciprocity. At the family cycle reciprocity is not expected, although loyalty and trust are key elements for its maintenance. In the second ring – friends, classmates, and colleagues – reciprocity is stronger but not necessarily immediate. People do favors for each other and expect reciprocity in some unspecified time in the future. Finally, in the external ring – the *guanxi* coming from the first and second ring – reciprocity is expected and is usually immediate. The force that keeps the *guanxi* together is the threat of exclusion. When somebody uses or abuses the *guanxi* without due consideration to reciprocity, they will be excluded and it will be hard for them to have new business with any of its members.

It is clear that one needs to adapt to the local culture. The term in use that tries to capture this idea of adaptability is "global leader." However, in our opinion, this term does not capture the richness of the concept. It seems to imply that you have to develop a kind of rootless leadership style valid to any culture. However, to be a successful leader in China one does not have to stop being who they are or abandon their cultural roots. We rather prefer the term "cosmopolitan leader," which implies a respect for your own roots and at the same time openness to other cultures. A cosmopolitan leader possesses a practical and sagacious understanding of human affairs. It is about adaptation, openness, and capacity to learn. It is about having an open mind, accepting that the way you look at things is not necessarily the only and correct one.

Cosmopolitan leaders try to understand cultural differences without prejudices. It is very easy to fall into cultural stereotypes when confronting a different culture: the Chinese are not loyal to anyone, they only care about money and status, they lack creativity, and the list can go on. This may be true in certain cases but it cannot be taken as a general description of all Chinese people. There are 1.3 billion plus inhabitants in China and we would be very surprised if every one of them fits into these types of descriptions. China is a mosaic of cultures but, even more, beyond the cultural identity that everyone possesses, each individual has a distinct personality.

Finally, we would like to introduce the concept of working styles. There are certainly cultural differences that affect the way people behave in the work place. However, it would be a simplification to consider culture as the only factor influencing behavior. We prefer to use the term working styles. It is the result of the interaction among national culture, organizational culture, and individual personality.

EXHIBIT 1.3: WORKING STYLES

A foreign leader in China must be able to understand and work with different working styles. They must have highly developed emotional intelligence, which includes interest in others, listening, understanding, and accepting different viewpoints. They must also have clear ethical standards in personal and company matters, and be able to manage under a climate of uncertainty. On top of that, they must have proven professional savvy and knowledge of their organizations. Successful international leaders welcome diversity around them; they are driven by a sense of adventure and a desire to see and experience new things, and a sense of humor, so as not to take themselves too seriously.

The case study included in this chapter is a good illustration of different working styles and how they can negatively affect the good management of an organization. Eddie Turrentine, the new general manager (GM), is facing a critical situation in which the organization is divided into two camps: the Chinese and the Americans. The previous GM, a Taiwanese, was selected by Emerson to lead the Suzhou operation. The advantage, as they saw it, was that Mr Wang Wei could serve as a bridge between the two cultures. Wang spoke Chinese, was educated in the United States, with an MBA from Harvard, and had worked for Emerson for some years. He certainly appeared to be the perfect candidate. After one year in the position, Mr Wang resigned and recommended Turrentine as his successor. Turrentine, without previous international experience, had the daunting task of bringing together an organization that was breaking apart.

Following the case, you will find two commentaries: the first by Howard Ward, Professor of Management, CEIBS; the second by Guosheng Zhu, Operation General Manager of BOC China. Both commentators focus on the importance of creating a culture of trust and understanding as well as the pivotal role of Turrentine as the leader of this change.

CASE STUDY
EMERSON ELECTRIC
(SUZHOU) CO., LTD[4]

Eddie Turrentine was very surprised when his GM invited him to be his successor in March 2000. Turrentine was at that time the Procurement and Material Manager of Emerson Electric (Suzhou) Co., Ltd, a subsidiary of US conglomerate Emerson (its products are sold under the brand name Copeland, a major Emerson division). The GM, a Taiwanese named Wang Wei, told Turrentine that he would offer his resignation the following day and was planning to recommend him to be the new GM. Turrentine remembered Wang saying:

> *I have been thinking about this for several weeks and made my decision. I want to propose you to be my successor. You have the necessary experience and knowledge to run this operation. You are the right person to keep this organization together.*

These words were totally unexpected for Turrentine:

> *I had never planned to be the GM. I remember how surprised I was when he told me this. At the beginning, I was a little bit hesitant to accept. I had never been a GM before. Mr Wang Wei, the Taiwanese GM, was a very honest man. He told me that he truly believed I could do a better job than he did and that he was going to support me. I finally accepted when I was officially offered the position.*

Turrentine knew he was facing a difficult challenge. There were many issues to tackle in this organization, especially those regarding people. As Turrentine said:

> *So, there I was, the new GM. To tell you the truth, it was difficult to decide where to start with my new job.*

Copeland Corporation

Edmund Copeland founded the company in the United States in the early 1920s. Copeland patented and produced the world's first electric refrigerators and helped make them a household fixture in America. After participating in various other markets, including war materials during the 1940s, Copeland Corp. moved in the second half of the century to concentrate exclusively on its core competence; that is, the manufacture of air conditioning and refrigeration compressors. At the time of writing, Copeland employed over 10,000 people in more than 20 facilities worldwide, achieved annual sales of more than US$2 billion, and was one of the world's largest manufacturers of HVAC[5] compressors (see CS Exhibit 1.1). Throughout the early 1980s Copeland enjoyed its status as the world's No. 1 compressor supplier in HVAC markets, although it was serving customers primarily with 20- to 30-year-old technology, reciprocating (piston-driven) compressors. However, at that same time, the industry was on the brink of making a shift to more efficient and reliable scroll (orbiting) compression units. Copeland already possessed a significant developmental advantage in this new arena and also owned a number of patents in relation to the new technology, but lacked the capital base that would be required for the expansion needed to sufficiently penetrate even the US unitary (new home) market. Additionally, existing factories were not attractive candidates for conversion to this latest innovation in the industry, so it was not difficult to concede that these facilities would continue to serve the declining reciprocating compressor demand until their eventual phase out. The company had the potential to become the market leader, but it was in need of strong corporate support and funding to stimulate growth (see CS Exhibit 1.2).

Acquisition by Emerson Electric

In 1985 Emerson Electric, a US corporation with more than 75 divisions, purchased Copeland Corp. from individual ownership. The integration into this huge corporation provided Copeland with the necessary financial backing to expand its horizons globally. Emerson is regularly ranked in America's Fortune 100 and is usually listed approximately 250th–350th among the world's largest corporations, with US$15.5 billion in sales in 2000 (see CS Exhibits 1.3 and 1.4). As the new

CASE STUDY: EMERSON ELECTRIC (SUZHOU) CO., LTD

CS EXHIBIT 1.1: COPELAND'S WORLDWIDE OPERATIONS

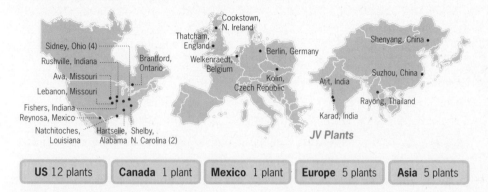

US 12 plants   **Canada** 1 plant   **Mexico** 1 plant   **Europe** 5 plants   **Asia** 5 plants

CS EXHIBIT 1.2: COPELAND HISTORY

Edmund Copeland:
Copeland Products, Inc.

Ohio (1937)

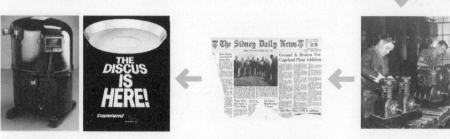

The 1970s

The 1950s and 1960s

The war years (1941)

Emerson Electric
and the scroll

• 1986 Emerson
  purchased Copeland

• 1987 Scroll was
  launched

CS EXHIBIT 1.3: EMERSON'S MARKET SHARE

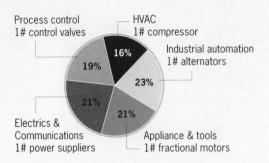

largest division in Emerson, Copeland garnered the lion's share of the corporate capital investment budget and aggressively constructed scroll-manufacturing facilities around North America.

With the financial support of Emerson, Copeland prepared to attack the global markets via manufacturing in regions where demand was buoyant and where investments were of relatively low risk. The company was already exporting approximately 25% of its production abroad. While European investments were successful and Asian joint ventures provided adequate returns, the company had routinely baulked when confronted with proposals for any large-scale, wholly owned initiative in the Far East. Finally in 1994, a 500,000-unit-per-year scroll factory was built and opened in Thailand. The company soon realized that the vast majority of the market served from this location was actually in China; further, importing products into China was not as simple a task as was originally perceived. Clearly, the company had not done its homework prior to making this investment. Emerson Electric had fallen into the same trap as so many other Western companies before it: it assumed that the Asian market for its chosen product was so vast and so virgin that careful analysis was not entirely necessary prior to moving into the arena.

Emerson Electric comes to China

Having learned this valuable lesson, the company conducted an exhaustive, two-year feasibility study, and the decision was finally made to move forward in its largest investment initiative ever outside the United States, a US$180 million

CASE STUDY: EMERSON ELECTRIC (SUZHOU) CO., LTD

CS EXHIBITS 1.4: EMERSON'S GLOBAL PERFORMANCE

IndustryWeek.com

EMERSON NAMED AMONG WORLD'S 100 BEST-MANAGED COMPANIES FOR 5TH CONSECUTIVE YEAR

Emerson is a world leader in innovative management strategies...

eWeek

Emerson Electric Co. E-Business Network Ranked Among The Nation's Best By eWeek Magazine

"Emerson is leading the way into the networked world of the new economy."

Goldman Sachs

"Emerson is one of the four most aggressive companies in e-business"

Business Week

"... a 'great divide' developing among companies like Honeywell, General Electric, and Emerson Electric which are integrating the Internet into their operations and those companies that 'don't get it'."

Bear Stearns

Emerson Electric Jump-Starts Itself

"The 110-year-old company now looks to be repositioning itself...the potential for Emerson is huge."

facility to be located in Suzhou, China. Emerson had already established multiple manufacturing facilities in China (see CS Exhibit 1.5). The feasibility study concluded that customer demand, competitive environment, labor market, local supplier capability, and other contributing factors were reasonably favorable, making the decision attractive enough to proceed.

The project was to be completed in three phases over a two-year period, all in accordance with Copeland's Plant Technology Franchise Guidelines, a gate management system used in implementation of the company's facilities (see CS Exhibit 1.6). The factory was also tasked with shouldering the additional burden of representing Emerson's commitment to excellence in Asia, functioning as its flagship enterprise in the region. Should the venture prosper, the company would be likely to invest even more heavily in the near future. Failure, on the

CASE STUDY: EMERSON ELECTRIC (SUZHOU) CO., LTD

other hand, might limit such activity for years to come. Needless to say, many eyes were intently watching the project.

Located only 70 kilometers from Shanghai, China's largest city, Suzhou was known to have a modern but relatively empty industrial park, completed in the 1990s. The Park's Singaporean management team was eager both to lure investment projects and to grant the necessary concessions to interested parties. The Park management was also well connected with local employment agencies and

CS EXHIBIT 1.5: EMERSON'S GREATER CHINA MANUFACTURING PRESENCE (AS OF JUNE 2000)

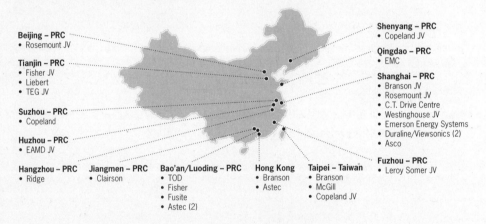

Beijing – PRC
• Rosemount JV

Tianjin – PRC
• Fisher JV
• Liebert
• TEG JV

Suzhou – PRC
• Copeland

Huzhou – PRC
• EAMD JV

Hangzhou – PRC
• Ridge

Jiangmen – PRC
• Clairson

Bao'an/Luoding – PRC
• TOD
• Fisher
• Fusite
• Astec (2)

Hong Kong
• Branson
• Astec

Taipei – Taiwan
• Branson
• McGill
• Copeland JV

Shenyang – PRC
• Copeland JV

Qingdao – PRC
• EMC

Shanghai – PRC
• Branson JV
• Rosemount JV
• C.T. Drive Centre
• Westinghouse JV
• Emerson Energy Systems
• Duraline/Viewsonics (2)
• Asco

Fuzhou – PRC
• Leroy Somer JV

CS EXHIBITS 1.6: EMERSON'S GLOBAL ORGANIZATION

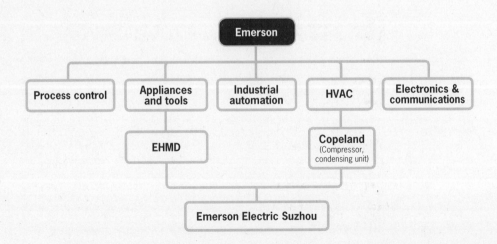

provided Emerson with reports indicating that labor was available in sufficient quantities and at lower rates than could be found in more metropolitan areas like Shanghai. Relatively high unemployment rates seemed an early sign that retention of hourly associates might not be of immediate concern. Several local vocational schools offered a steady supply of young, talented individuals for development in a cooperative learning environment. Also, a fair number of state-owned enterprises (SOEs) with unstable futures located in the area had some experienced engineering talent who might be made available. Overall, Emerson management deemed the Suzhou area an attractive environment for building a diverse and high-performance work team (see CS Exhibit 1.7).

As far as identification and development of a local supplier base was concerned, Suzhou's proximity to Shanghai was a definite advantage, as it granted accessibility to the businesses currently serving that city's expanding automotive manufacturing industry. While capable stamping and, to some extent, casting vendors were present in Suzhou, Shanghai firms complemented the forging shops and precision machining enterprises. Initial on-site surveys provided promising results for all of Emerson's needs.

Other less significant factors that played a part in the decision included presence of English-speaking schools, reasonable proximity to most customers, a competent subcontractor base, and a stable, well-developed infrastructure in communications and transportation.

CS EXHIBIT 1.7: A COMPARISON BETWEEN ST LOUIS AND SUZHOU

	St Louis, US	Suzhou, China
History	224 years	2,500 years
State/Province	Missouri	Jiangsu
Population	2.5 million	5.7 million
Attractions	Commercial center and road center, Lacelede's Landing, Gateway Arch, Old Cathedral of St Louis France, Old Courthouse, Wainwright Building	World of gardens, capital of silk, and land of abundance, Mysterious Taoist Temple, Panmen Gate, Hanshan Temple, Flat-top Hill, Delicate Rock Hill, Heavenly Pond Hill, North Temple Pagoda, Twin Pagodas
River	Mississippi	Yangtze

CASE STUDY: EMERSON ELECTRIC (SUZHOU) CO., LTD

CS EXHIBIT 1.8: EMERSON SUZHOU PLANT CHRONOLOGY

March 1996	1997	June 1998	August 1999	February 2000	March 2000
Business license	Asian Financial Crisis	EMR Board approval	First employee on Board	Pilot approved	First shipment

Recommendations resulting from the feasibility study approved at the corporate level included the following strategies:

- Target initially large OEMs[6] using 3.0–5.0 Kbtu/hr compressors as the major market segment.
- Include investment capability for the manufacture of larger compressors in the factory's capital plan, but to hold investment for smaller capacities.
- Phase in investment in three parts to reduce exposure in case of failure and to roughly match demand.
- Identify and hire bilingual Asians to champion the project, staff top management with one local Chinese and the balance with half overseas Chinese expatriates and half US expatriates.
- Utilize a temporary workforce to respond to the anticipated seasonal swings in demand.

Although the Asian financial crisis prompted Copeland and Emerson to hesitate for some time, the project was launched in June 1998. Production began in early 2000 (see CS Exhibit 1.8).

People and cultural issues at Emerson Electric Suzhou

Meanwhile, the staffing procedure began with the acquisition of a Taiwanese GM in March 1996 who would also serve as the project leader. Soon after, he began to seek out and hire key staff. The hiring plan did not include the identification of a human resources manager, at least not in these early days, and thus the process possessed no real guidelines or framework to ensure that any form of standardization was present for similar positions. Many offers were made and deals were struck by a variety of methods. These resulted in a variety of

June 20 2000	June 23 2000	July 17 2000	July 27 2000	December 29 2000
ISO 9002	Grand opening	Franchise audit passed	Advanced technology enterprise status	ISO 14001

compensation packages, contractual agreements and promotion expectations for the future.

This activity, the GM's hiring of staff at all levels at various wage scales and with wide ranging competency levels within each level, represented, in retrospect, the beginning of a situation that would soon manifest itself as a large problem potentially endangering the success of the investment.

The corporation mandated that at least one local Chinese manager be placed on the GM's team. The hiring of the plant's human resource (HR) manager, a local Chinese, fulfilled this mandate. In making this move, the GM used as a selling point to the other directors the notion that this individual would be capable of understanding and reporting important but difficult-to-detect behaviors among the factory staff, which might otherwise go unnoticed. The new HR manager was in his fifties, coming from a local SOE. As Turrentine mentioned:

> We hired a Chinese to be the HR manager so he could help us to form the local
> organization. He was a Suzhou local with many connections. You know, he had good
> "guanxi".

Many middle-management staff, primarily supervisors and engineers, were required to attend four- to six-month training programs in the United States and were subsequently required to sign lengthy service contracts with the company, purportedly to ensure the company's return on investment in the cost of the training. Turrentine added:

> We selected a lot of new people and trained them. We even sent 20 of them to the
> States for training. It was a six-month training program. We signed a three-year
> contract with those people. The idea was that if they left after the training, they would
> have to pay back the cost of the training. We had one case of an employee that left

17 months after the training. He had to pay back all the training cost, which was an amount almost equal to all his salary during those 17 months.

As the facility was still in a start-up mode, the team in place was, for a time, under little pressure to perform. Cost allowances had been planned well in advance for start-up inefficiencies; the company's sales forecast included only a small percentage of input from the new facility; and employees were kept comfortable to ensure that all had sufficient time to adjust to new responsibilities. During this first year of relative calm, however, the real storm was brewing just below the surface. The market began to grow at a quickening pace. Corporate sales commitments were quickly raised, and pressure on the facility to produce doubled and then tripled. Customers who were thought to place the bulk of their emphasis on long-term value were suddenly demanding lower prices and threatening to shift allegiances to competing suppliers. All of these issues were occurring just as the large group of middle management began to realize that the opportunity for upward mobility promised to all might actually be available to only a selected few. To make matters worse, this source of employee dissatisfaction went largely unnoticed by top plant management, as the HR manager had tried to keep this information from them.

During the production ramp up, several cultural differences between the US employees, the overseas Chinese, and the local employees became apparent. The results of these differences ranged from small, even trivial misunderstandings to those damaging enough that they might even endanger the stability of the plant staff. These basic cultural differences, coupled with predictable resistance to change demonstrated by both sides, would require skillful management to resolve.

Early in the project, during the facility construction phase, it became evident that the result-oriented US style would definitely clash with the personal relationship management style exhibited by the Chinese. For instance, US managers were seen as being unnecessarily eager to push the production system even before installation was complete. In fact, these managers were among the few who had been informed of the changes in the external business environment and the implications these changes would have internally. While the vast majority of the workforce thought it prudent to methodically test each individual piece of equipment prior to actual use, the few Westerners felt a need to force through the first few pieces of product. These US managers, thinking they might teach others a lesson in manufacturing principles, actually forced their will on the others, creating no small amount of strife.

The middle-management staff were persuaded to work throughout the night just to push the factory's first 20 pieces of product through assembly. The Chinese saw this as needless, as the next day was spent mostly idle, awaiting the test results from the samples. This was the first of many such incidents that would begin to tear the organization apart before it really even had a chance to form. Soon, it became obvious that the different levels of conflict avoidance within each group would also play a role in the unfolding story. As actual production piloting began, the Americans demanded an early morning meeting to outline the day's activities and goals, as well as a late-afternoon wrap-up session in which any responsible parties with incomplete action items were criticized for poor planning or execution. The Chinese, preferring to avoid conflict whenever possible, generally agreed to the daily schedule, even when acutely aware that the agreed schedule could not possibly be met.

Naturally this silent conflict was quite detrimental to goal achievement, as the Americans, blind to the differences, merely pushed harder. In fact, as due dates for deliveries drew near, these managers found themselves performing the work of engineers and supervisors, ignorant of the fact that the quality of their work was only tolerable. Although these managers eventually recognized that some differences between the two cultures were already negatively impacting the group's performance, their reluctance to change led to a belief that whatever behavior was most comfortable to them was always the best way to do business.

On the other hand, the Chinese also contributed to the worsening situation. To many in this group, it was obvious that the expatriate group was pressing too hard. In fact, many of them had even had similar experiences with other Westerners in previous assignments. Like their US counterparts, these Chinese middle managers saw no need to change their own style.

In building his management team for the plant, the GM originally planned to accommodate only one local Chinese and, as he assessed his needs, he elected to fill the HR department manager slot with this selection. Everybody agreed that this appointment would help to ease communication between the Americans and the Chinese.

CASE STUDY: EMERSON ELECTRIC (SUZHOU) CO., LTD

Furthermore, as the number of staff grew, there was an increasing need for an effective personnel management system. Unfortunately, cultural differences and a lack of awareness of these began to undermine the well-intentioned original plan. The HR manager, being a long-time employee of an SOE, had strong beliefs in the Chinese idea of maintaining power distance. In staff meetings the Americans almost always regarded his silence as agreement, when it actually often represented something very different. While US managers felt quite at ease to express their opinions and to attempt to sway group decisions their way, the HR manager thought it best to wait to hear the opinion of the GM and usually merely agreed with his ideas. Thus the original intention of getting the local Chinese perspective was largely never realized (see CS Exhibit 1.9).

Soon the entire organization found itself mired in indecision and one-sided decisions. The Americans continued to push, albeit with little result, and the Chinese continued to plod, methodically checking every item to the finest detail. The result was an inefficient, unmotivated employee base that witnessed endless bickering at all levels of the organization.

Next, a quite unexpected phenomenon occurred, strangely jolting the entire employee base into a survival mode that had started the improvement initiative. The Taiwanese GM decided to quit the team to join a telecommunication company. Unrest among local employees immediately became a major concern for all, as the sudden vacancy led most to believe that something was terribly wrong and that maybe they should all be considering a career change. The prevailing notion was that the boss was abandoning a sinking business.

Coupled with these personnel issues, suddenly the peak season was upon the industry, and the facility was, of course, ill equipped to handle the rapidly approaching demand. Clearly, quick and decisive action was required to right the ship and secure the investment's future prosperity. Given the attention the factory was receiving at top levels in the corporation and in the industry, it was also imperative to give the Board and stockholders a reason to feel confident that the situation was stable and that the decision to invest had been well advised. There existed a number of issues that had to be tackled urgently to ensure a truly successful venture, namely in the areas of people and cultural issues.

CASE STUDY: EMERSON ELECTRIC (SUZHOU) CO., LTD

CS EXHIBITS 1.9: EMERSON ELECTRIC SUZHOU'S ORGANIZATION CHART BY THE END OF 1999

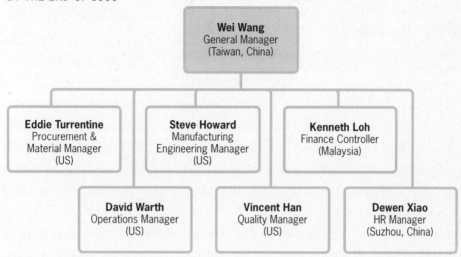

What to do?

Turrentine was really worried about the complexity of the situation. He saw the need for quick action in order to improve the situation. One long-term solution to the people issues could be the development of a company culture that would allow for the growth of employees while also supporting the business goals of Emerson. Turrentine recalled:

> *Our company has many high-volume manufacturing facilities with a lot of people; we have a lot of experience in managing high-volume operations, but we don't have much experience in managing multicultural organizations. We have to improve in that aspect.*

In some respects, Emerson currently had a strong management team, but it needed to further develop managers of the future to assure the company's long-term success. Turrentine saw this as his main task for the near future:

> *If we fail in China, it won't be because of the Chinese. It will be because I have not been able to create the right environment for people to cooperate, whether Chinese or American. I want to be very clear about that.*

CASE STUDY: EMERSON ELECTRIC (SUZHOU) CO., LTD

Annex 1: Comments by the US managers

Eddie Turrentine,
Procurement and Material Manager and current GM

We had some conflicting styles in our organization. For instance, the Chinese are focused on relationships while the Americans are focused on results. A second difference is the way we set objectives. I remember the first management meeting to set the objectives for the year. The Americans were very aggressive and ambitious with their objectives, while the Chinese were more conservative and prudent. Our Taiwanese GM asked: "How many defects do you think we will get?" David, our operation manager, said zero. The GM couldn't accept it and plugged in a number himself. Another difference is what we understand by respecting people. We wanted to be the preferred employer in Suzhou. What a preferred employer means to an American is totally different from what it means for a Chinese. For me, it means really caring about them and giving people the chance to grow. For a Chinese, to be a good employer is quite different. Hierarchy is very important to them. I'm the manager and you do what I tell you. Too often, they don't listen to their workers. You don't do this in America. I would not want to work for that type of employer.

Our previous GM was from Taiwan, could speak Chinese, and had an MBA from Harvard. He was a very smart man. He was in his mid-thirties, very young.

I knew Mr Wang already; we had worked together for five years in Alabama. When he invited me to come to China I was excited, because he knew a lot, and I had no doubt that I could learn many things from him. He was asked to stay three years in this post, but when the unit was ready to run, he decided to leave. I think he was afraid of failing.

The Chinese love meetings. We had meetings all day long and every day. They are used to solving problems in meetings. I respected my GM, but I don't like to waste my time with so many meetings. One day I told him: "I have a job to do. If you want to see me, you can see me after hours. You want to meet me at five in the morning, no problem. I must run a factory and I've got a lot of things to do here. That is my job."

He created a very hierarchical organization. We had one supervisor for each production line. Each line had 12 people on average. There were too many bosses.

David, the operation manager, and the HR manager had an awful fight. David said: "I don't know why we hired all those people. We have too many bosses here."

China has an old culture. They have their own way of doing things. For instance, they don't like to talk openly to each other. They keep problems to themselves. No one tells you what is going on. As Americans, when we don't like something, we tell you directly. We don't have problems with that.

I remember when we produced our first compressor on November 12, 1999 (see CS Exhibit 1.10). This first unit had to be shipped back to United States for a three-month test. My boss was very afraid that something might go wrong. That's one reason why he presented his resignation. He got out of here before the results came back from the States. Finally, nothing went wrong. Our first compressor was perfectly OK, but he was already no longer here.

CS EXHIBIT 1.10:
EMERSON ELECTRIC SUZHOU'S FIRST PRODUCT: A SCROLL COMPRESSOR COMPLETED IN 1999

David Warth, Operations Manager

Communication was difficult when I arrived here. First, it was just the language problem. We didn't understand the Chinese language. A lot of the Chinese people we hired didn't speak English either. But a bigger issue was the cultural problem; we were mixing people with different styles. Some of the Chinese managers we hired were very traditional. By that I mean to say that they preferred to tell people what to do. We had problems of understanding each other, and we had some conflicts between the two groups, especially when it came to discipline or personnel issues. The way I work is to confront the issue directly, face to face. It seems to me that Chinese managers don't like that.

Chinese managers believe that knowledge is power. Our idea is that knowledge should be shared and transferred to the other members of the organization. We want people to share knowledge. That is our way.

Chinese supervisors just care for how many people they have under them, to get a nice computer and an office. But that is not a supervisor for me. The supervisor has to be engaged in the business. He is also another worker with more responsibilities. He has to be productive and help his people to be productive.

The Chinese are sometimes very confused with the way we Americans do things. They don't understand our rules. We cross hierarchical lines when we need to; we don't care about that. They are very careful with the hierarchy and not to offend their boss. We Americans just want to get the job done. That is what matters for us.

Chinese managers are very attached to power. They like to control people and they like to be asked for permission all the time. They also love meetings and making speeches in meetings. That model doesn't work too well for us.

In China, if you have an idea or you want to do something different, you must get the permission of your boss and get many signatures. We tend to believe that this practice only serves to slow things down. Probably neither group's way is really best; I imagine that somewhere in the middle is the right thing for China.

Steve Howard, Manufacturing Engineering Manager

The Chinese are used to following a leader; doing what the leader says. They want clear directions and don't like to make decisions. That is surprising to us.

We expect people to learn and be able to solve problems independently, to have initiative. If somebody just repeats what I already know, then I don't need that person. I want people with their own ideas.

If I ask my engineers their opinions about a problem, they will look at me wondering why I am asking them. They think I am the boss so I must have all the answers and tell them what to do.

I had to take into account this idea of "losing face" when managing my Chinese subordinates. Chinese people say: "This is my territory, this is my area, and nobody can come to it. If you interfere, I will lose face."

They seldom ask others for help. For example, I have five engineers. Each of them is responsible for a different area. If somebody were in trouble, he would never ask for help from the other engineers. He thinks if he asks for help, they are going to think he is stupid because he cannot do his job.

Our previous GM was from Taiwan. He expected everybody to follow him. He was very smart, and intelligent, but different from us. He was educated in the United States, an MBA from Harvard.

At that time, the communication among the people was not very good. We didn't talk to each other. Everything was channeled through the GM. There was a lot of tension among some of the managers.

Another problem we had at that time was unclear expectations. We didn't know well what his (the GM's) expectations of our jobs were.

Chinese people are more worried about hierarchy than we are. For instance, in China, a supervisor has a higher position than an engineer does. In the United States, they are at the same level. Our Chinese engineers want to be promoted to be a supervisor. They don't want to stay as engineers. They all want to be bosses.

I would say to somebody from the States coming to work in China to be patient. Try to be a patient person. We are not used to being patient in the States, but that is a talent we have to acquire here.

Annex 2: Comments by the Chinese managers

Judy Zhang, Material Buyer

I had been working for 10 years in an SOE in the fiber manufacturing industry and was even promoted to the position of R&D manager. I had another two years of experience in a foreign company in charge of purchasing mechanical products. That was before joining Emerson Suzhou. My previous experience was always in well-established organizations and I have been used to following clear leadership.

American managers have a different style. They are very straightforward. They care about results more than maintaining good relationships. To many Chinese, they are too assertive.

The Americans set very tight deadlines that were beyond our usual capabilities and then pushed the deadline and made everybody very stressed. At first we were unfamiliar with this. But after some time we gradually got used to it and our standard improved. They call it "shoot before you aim." Now through our communication, we gradually got used to the American way of management. They also started to learn the Chinese way, which is more conservative and also more focused on details.

You know, we were brought up and educated to follow the leader's instruction. When we were children, the highest praise from our parents was "this kid is so obedient (tinghua)." So we are used to behaving in the same way to get positive appraisal from our leaders.

In our mind, a good leader should be someone who can set a good example, show integrity, and make correct and smart decisions. The management team should be united, speak in one voice, and have a long-term commitment to the organization. They should give us the right direction and win our confidence and trust. As long as the leadership is clear and the commitment is there, we Chinese can learn and adapt to the leader's requirement.

We don't have problems in changing to the American style. To me, I have learned a lot from the Americans. I like to learn. I like to make changes. Otherwise I would have stayed in the SOE.

Some foreign managers came to China only on a short-term assignment or because they didn't have a position in their home country. They use China to get a promotion. To be honest we were afraid of that, especially when we saw our GM resign. I hope the new GM can really pull the team together.

Jonas Chen, Production Supervisor

I had spent several years in a large SOE before joining Emerson Suzhou. I didn't like the work in the SOE. They behave as bureaucrats, not as professional managers. The organization was too hierarchical and inefficient. Before you put forward any new suggestions, you needed to think it over to see whether you might offend anybody, either your managers or your peers. That's why I wanted to make a change.

I felt puzzled when I found that there was also cultural conflict here. We could clearly feel the different and conflicting cultures in our company.

The departments under the Taiwanese GM were very formal, with strict reporting lines and orders to follow, a bit like in the army. Whenever any task was to be done, they had meetings to discuss the various possibilities to do it, compared pros and cons, and then chose one. Every step was in accordance with the rules.

The ones under American managers, like us, were active, open with each other and enthusiastic. We cared about the results more than the system. And in fact there was no system yet. Our managers just gave us the objective and direction. It was our job to find the way to achieve results. If it worked, then let it be the "system" for next time. If it didn't, we tried another way. The problems were solved on the floor, not in the office.

HR was the only department under a Chinese manager. The whole group was silent and just listened. The HR manager only followed the GM without independent input. I think they just did not have any experience of key personnel issues in a foreign company, so they were not prepared. Whenever any decision was to be made, they just reported to the GM and asked for his instruction. They didn't want to have trouble with the staff. They wanted to "keep order."

I know the Taiwanese GM tried hard to be the "bridge" between the Americans and the Chinese, but it seemed he was not successful. I don't know why. I just felt shocked when I heard of his resignation. He had made many verbal commitments to us, saying if we did well we would be promoted or would have the chance to go to the States. When he left, we had a strong crisis of trust. We wanted to know what would happen, and we wanted to have a say in it.

Xiao Dewen, HR Manager

It is not unusual for any organization to have problems at the beginning. It is important to solve those problems as a team and learn from each other.

We learned from the Americans, from their advanced management experience and their technology. They also learned how the Chinese think and behave. So far, we have worked together very well. We all have to learn and we have accumulated many valuable lessons. We will do better and better.

Some of the practices that have been successful in the States may not be that successful in China. Successful management in China must be based on strict policies and discipline. At first, we didn't have well-established policies. But we were improving. During that process, we had debates and those were acceptable. One example was about attendance control. We, in China, are used to punching in and out at our work place. Our salaries are based on that. We deduct money on a pro rata basis from those who often come late or leave early. In this way we encourage people to be punctual. This is normal to us. The Americans didn't accept that at the beginning. They thought that such control was the responsibility of the line managers through a process of disciplinary action: verbal warning, written warning, and termination. However, there were times when attendance became a problem and different managers dealt with that in different ways. Some were strict, while others were not. HR should ensure internal equity, so through discussion with the Americans we came to a compromise: operators needed to punch in, while office staff didn't. And it worked well.

We need to be open-minded with each other. We now do much better, and we will continue to do so in the future.

CASE COMMENTARIES

COMMENTARY 1
HOWARD WARD,
PROFESSOR OF MANAGEMENT
CHINA EUROPE INTERNATIONAL BUSINESS SCHOOL (CEIBS)

The basic problem

The experience of Eddie Turrentine and his team at Emerson Suzhou clearly illustrates one of the classic problems facing all foreign invested enterprises in China – to what degree do we need to change our culture to adapt to the Chinese situation? It is the eternal debate over globalization versus localization. The Americans want to run the business the American way and the Chinese want to run it the Chinese way. This led to a situation of two cultures in Suzhou:

> *Whatever behavior was most comfortable to them was the best way to do business.*

Sadly, what is most comfortable to us is not necessarily "the best way." Unfortunately, this type of situation often leads to a debate over the superiority of one national culture over another. It is the least intelligent way to tackle this problem. Experience of such problems in China and elsewhere leads me to believe that the only effective way forward is to avoid debates over national cultures and base discussions on "business culture." The basic problem facing Turrentine and his team is therefore *how to build a single strong Emerson Suzhou culture that will help the company to achieve its business goals in China.*

This single culture is rarely the result of a compromise. We are often confronted in China with the statement – "you can't do this in China." My answer to this is always – "which China are we talking about, the old China of the centrally planned economy (CPE) or the new China of the market-oriented economy (MOE)?" Many of the practices perceived as unacceptable by foreign-invested enterprises (FIEs) stem from the CPE "Tie Fan Wan" culture – though it is also true that others stem from the older Chinese culture based largely on Confucian values. Many of the older generation of Chinese employees have experience of working in only state-owned enterprises with their Tie Fan Wan culture and so interpret values of efficiency, quality, and service in very different ways compared to employees used to working in market-oriented enterprises.

Carlos Goshan, former CEO of Nissan, once said he was not trying to change the Japanese culture, but only Nissan culture. This then is the challenge facing Turrentine and his team: how to create a culture that is acceptable for his Chinese workforce and will enable them at the same time to give a satisfactory return to the Emerson Board in the United States on their investment in the Suzhou operation.

Establishing a single coherent culture for Emerson Suzhou

STEP 1: LEAD FROM THE FRONT
This challenge will be a vital test of Turrentine's leadership qualities. In times of change, leadership is all you have. He will need to establish the new direction, guide and inspire the employees, and maintain a policy of open communication throughout the whole change process. One thing that will help him is that there is little need to create an awareness of the need for change. Pretty much everyone is aware that the company is facing a crisis: the GM has left, the clients are making new demands, and there is low morale among most employees. The time is ripe for Turrentine to step up to the plate and show the way forward. The Chinese above all respect strong leaders with a clear vision.

STEP 2: ESTABLISH MISSION, VISION, AND VALUES FOR EMERSON SUZHOU
The basis of an appropriate business culture for Emerson Suzhou, as for any organization, is a set of norms and values that bind the organization

together towards the achievement of the business goal. It begins with an agreement over the business goal and the establishment of a set of behaviors and code of conduct that will help to achieve this goal. Turrentine already has a pretty clear vision in his own mind of Emerson Suzhou being an organization that has the twin goals of people development and business growth.

STEP 3: AGREED NEW MANAGEMENT BEHAVIORS FOR EMERSON SUZHOU

No matter how strong a leader you are, it is very difficult to bring about change of this magnitude. If you don't have a core of people who share your vision and values, it is difficult to implement change – but you don't need many. Turrentine needs to sit down immediately with his top team to develop the new mission, vision, and values (MVVs).

Agreement with Chinese partners over MVVs is often not a difficult process. What is problematic is how to translate the mission and vision into clear strategic goals for the short term. Even more problematic is how to translate the core values into behavioral norms. Values have no value unless all employees understand the behaviors associated with the values and are made fully aware of disciplinary procedures to be taken against those who do not follow "The Emerson Suzhou Way."

For example, what do the following values mean to the Chinese and US managers?

- We care for our employees.
- We believe in open communication.
- We believe in team work.

How as a Chinese/US manager do you expect me to behave? These are the sort of questions that will create a lively debate among Chinese and US managers, but agreement needs to be made and, equally critically, performance management systems should be set up to measure and reward the new behaviors.

STEP 4: SET UP PROFESSIONAL HR SERVICE

Many of the problems have arisen due to the fact that there has not been an effective HR department with appropriate policies related to recruitment, development, training, pay, and disciplinary procedures. It is essential for Turrentine and his team to recruit a professional HR manager – preferably of Chinese nationality – to replace the existing HR manager. It would be his/her responsibility to set up the new HR procedures and oversee the communication policy outlined below.

One of the key features of any successful change strategy is to develop reward systems that benefit the employees who change, and penalize those who don't. If you want people to change their behavior but leave the reward systems the same then nothing will happen.

STEP 5: DEVELOP A COMMUNICATION STRATEGY TO SUPPORT THE CHANGE

Unless employees feel they are involved in the process of change, unless they are kept informed of the implementation process, it is very likely that it will fail. Turrentine, together with his new HR department, will therefore need to set up new communication systems to inform employees of how and why changes are being made – these include the intranet, regular briefings, and the company policy manual.

Conclusion

The key success factors in developing a coherent single culture for Emerson Suzhou are:

- Turrentine's leadership skills enabling him to provide an attractive vision and demonstrate the new management style for the organization in the future.
- The setting up of change agent teams to formulate and implement the change strategy.
- The appointment of an effective HR professional who can develop the new HR policies.

In this situation Turrentine is not trying to change an already long-established culture, but to build a new culture for his company. To do this he will have to reconcile three different cultures: the Emerson US culture, the Tie Fan Wan culture of the older Chinese employees, and the more open-minded culture of younger Chinese managers.

Over the past 25 years, the Chinese have demonstrated that with the right leadership and an appropriate change strategy they are capable of enormous change.

As Turrentine quite rightly states on page 19 of the case,

> *If we fail in China, it will not be because of the Chinese. It will be because I have not been able to create the right environment (culture) for people to cooperate, whether Chinese or American.*

COMMENTARY 2
GUOSHENG ZHU
OPERATION GENERAL MANAGER
BOC CHINA

Emerson Suzhou is a very typical example of how a poor organization can look if there isn't an integrated company culture in which all the people can work effectively. As we know, a company culture is formed by the common behaviors and underlying assumptions shared by the whole organization. It is the way we conduct our business and deal with people. The diversity of working styles in a company should not be in conflict with its company culture.

I would say the problems that Emerson is undergoing are the consequence of a vaguely defined company culture. That is the main challenge Turrentine is facing: to create a company culture based on trust and understanding among all employees. Since the culture should be linked to the external environment, Turrentine should start with a good understanding of the business and its competitive advantage in the market, and therefore get a clear picture on what kind of culture they need to promote in the organization.

I would recommend the following:

1 Facilitate a communication forum with the senior management of the division to develop an action plan. This initial team should incorporate both US and Chinese managers. The senior team must be united when it is time to implement the necessary changes. Turrentine should be open minded and promote free communication during the forum. He has to show visible leadership and support for this process. The team should avoid getting caught into the old issues/problems and direct their attention to solving the problems in a positive way.

2 Once the senior team has reached consensus on the business vision, strategy, and objectives, it is time to set up a number of integration teams to work out the specific business objectives for each department, review and optimize business process, and simultaneously share information and create bonds among the members of the organization. During this period, teams should agree on a common working style. Each team should combine Chinese and US employees and managers to foster mutual understanding.

Turrentine should regularly check each team's progress and commitment to provide any necessary help and support. He also should ensure the proper working style is developing in each team.

Some training should be made available to the teams in order to develop common working styles such as project planning, to respect others' opinions, mutual responsibility, and so on. These guidelines should promote the integration of the team.

Turrentine should identify some small wins that can serve as an example to other teams. He must show visible support to the change effort and to encourage the involvement of the whole organization. Change management processes need to be well looked after.

3 Once all integration teams have worked out the business targets for the different functional departments, they should communicate those targets to the rest of the organization. They should make sure all individuals understand their role in the business and that they feel being part of the organization. A balance scorecard is a helpful tool at this stage. They should establish the proper performance measurement. Making everybody understand the connection among business, department, and individual objectives will help to create the necessary team spirit at organizational level. Routine review on the performance of business and individuals should be mandatory to address any issues and take corrective actions if necessary.

4 Turrentine also needs to establish leadership development programs to identify talented people. One of the objectives is to bring more native Chinese to the senior management team. At the moment, only the HR manager is from mainland China. Developing more local leaders will send a powerful signal to the organization. Managing people is always a most important issue in any GM's agenda.

5 An important issue is what to do with the HR manager. Turrentine should seriously think of replacing him with an HR manager with work experience in multinationals. This person could be hired outside or from inside the Emerson group. He should look for the support of his head office on this issue. This new HR manager must play a key role in establishing modern HR systems within Emerson Suzhou.

6 Turrentine should organize social activities, team-building training, and set up a company staff club to enhance mutual understanding among US and Chinese employees and managers. This will help to build personal relationships among them and promote team spirit.

Eddie could hire a qualified external consultant to help him on this process. This consultant can provide him with the tools and objective perspectives of the situation, and he/she could be very helpful in facilitating the process.

No doubt, Turrentine's actions and example are critical for the success of the transformation of Emerson Suzhou. To a great extent, his leadership skills will determine whether the organization can succeed or not. It is very important that he is well aware of this fact. However, it is the people at Emerson Suzhou that must take the ownership of the process. As the *Tao Te Ching* says:

> *The leader doesn't talk but acts.*
> *When the work is done, the people say,*
> *"We did it all by ourselves!"*

NOTES

1 John C. Maxwell 1993, *Developing the Leader Within You*, Thomas Nelson Publishers: Nashville.
2 Daniel Goleman 1997, *Emotional Intelligence*, Bantam Books: NY.
3 *Guanxi* is a Chinese term difficult to translate. It refers to the network of contacts a person has that can help him or her to obtain personal and organizational benefits. Frequently, it has a negative connotation.
4 This case was prepared by Professor Juan Antonio Fernandez and Research Fellow George Chen at CEIBS. The case was prepared as the basis for class discussion rather than to illustrate either effective or ineffective handling of an administrative situation. Certain names and other identifying information may have been disguised to protect confidentiality. The case was originally published by CEIBS in 2002. Published with permission.
5 HVAC refers to the heating, ventilation, and air-conditioning industry.
6 OEM refers to an original equipment manufacturer.

Chapter 2
Human resources in China: Chasing the runaway bride[1]

INTRODUCTION

The three basic tasks of human resources management (HRM) – recruitment, retention, and compensation – are as fundamental in China as anywhere else. However, these tasks become more critical in China due to the imbalance between the demand and supply of talent. The high growth of the Chinese economy needs not only natural resources but also people, especially high-skilled employees and middle managers. For many companies this lack of middle managers can certainly become the main obstacle for growth. One has to admit that this is a situation not unique to China; it also affects other rapidly developing economies. In the words of Barlett and Goshal,[2] "It is the limitation in human resources – not unreliable or inadequate sources of capital – that has become the biggest constraint in most globalization efforts." This situation has not changed since they wrote these words.

Chinese professionals are in high demand, not only by multinationals but also by Chinese companies. As a consequence, Chinese skilled employees and middle managers have developed high expectations on career progression and pay. They have the mentality that a better opportunity is always waiting just around the corner. It is very difficult to be loyal to one organization when they frequently receive new job offers with a substantial salary increase and a flamboyant job title. Besides, there is the perception among those who stay that they are somehow punished for their loyalty. As one Chinese manager told us, "Those colleagues that left had substantially improved their salaries while I only get 10% or even less. It is not fair."

Companies react to this situation by developing retention plans that usually focus on high achievers and high potentials. The chosen few feel flattered while those excluded wonder what is wrong with them or with their companies. They feel disenfranchised and most probably start looking for job opportunities in other organizations. Besides, those who have been singled out as high achievers raise their expectations even more and wait for the next stimulus. When this new stimulus does not come, they also feel disappointed and ready to leave. It is a never-ending story.

There is not a magic wand or silver bullet to solve the retention problem. As long as the imbalance between supply and demand continues, salary inflation, poaching, and high turnover will remain. However, companies are not totally powerless. They can implement certain measures not to eliminate, but to minimize turnover.

With this idea in mind, we present a model that gives some elements aimed at creating a more loyal and stable workforce. The model starts with selection and recruitment, followed by three basic HR tools strongly linked to retention: training, career opportunities, and compensation. Finally, there are two more elements to the concoction: people and company policies. The objective is to engage the employees. Engagement can be defined using the 3S model[3]: stay, say and strive. Engaged employees will *stay* in the company, *say* good things about it, and *strive* for best performance. Engagement is the goal, but not an easy one.

Let's now revise the different parts of this simple model.

EXHIBIT 2.1: THE HR MODEL

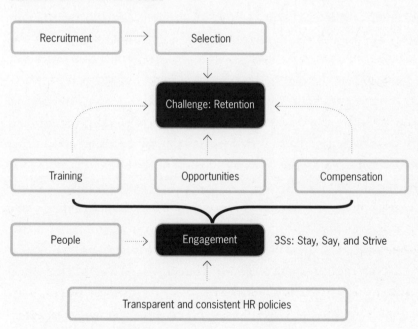

Selection and recruitment

In order to solve their recruitment challenge, some companies go for numbers. The logic is that the more candidates they attract, the greater the chance of finding good ones. The problem of this practice is the high recruitment costs without the guarantee that the candidates selected will fit into the organizational culture and stay, say, and strive (3S model). On the contrary, a smart recruitment policy tries to attract the right people from the very beginning. In that sense, companies should start by asking, "who are the right type of employees for us?"

It becomes critical to send signals to the right pool of candidates. An important means of achieving this is to leverage on the brands. Well-known multinationals have an easier time attracting good people, while small- and medium-sized enterprises (SMEs) and relatively unknown big corporations have a harder time. It is well known that the Chinese value public image. It generates admiration and respect for people when they show business cards with the IBM or Microsoft logo and with a nice job title.

However, it is impossible for every company to develop a well-known brand. To do this requires a substantial marketing expenditure over a prolonged period of time. Those companies can instead focus on building their brand image in the target groups they want to attract. Among other things, companies can grant scholarships to college students, offer internship opportunities, give executive talks in schools, and participate in case studies and research programs conducted by the universities and research institutions.

Compared with other sources of candidates, internal referrals can be a cheap and effective way to acquire new employees. Those recommending candidates should be rewarded after the new employees have proven their performance and loyalty to the organization.

In the hiring decision the degree of fit of the candidate to the company culture is important. The 360-degree interview is an excellent way to ensure this. Besides the interviews with HR and the direct boss(es), candidates can be interviewed by future subordinates and peers. A reference check is especially critical in China where fake certificates and inflated achievements in résumés are common.

An interesting situation is the importance given by many foreign companies to English as a precondition for hiring. The problem with this is that the company may reject excellent candidates due to their absence of English proficiency. Knowledge of the English language, no doubt, is important for an international company, but it can be learnt – instead, leadership and the right attitudes are difficult to learn.

Once the hiring decision is made, organizations need to make the entry passage as smooth as possible. They have to make the new employee feel welcome. A person-to-person approach is the most appropriate at this stage. Frequently, senior managers try to meet every new employee whenever possible. They answer their questions about the company and their future while presenting an image that the senior management cares. In this sense, it is important to go beyond the formal orientation process that many companies have in place and add a personal approach to it.

It is after the honeymoon period when the battle for retention starts. Selecting the right competent people who fit into the organizational culture is not enough to guarantee they will stay. Some important factors that help to minimize the retention challenge include compensation, training, and career development.

Compensation

Compensation is effective only when used in combination with other tools. Money alone is not enough to gain hearts. When considering what is important, you must take into account the age of your staff. In general, young people are mainly focused on cash. Job stability and family benefits are more important for older employees. Not all employees have the same needs. In a survey conducted by the German Delegation of Industry and Commerce in China,[4] they found that the main factors for leaving an organization, besides money, are lack of opportunities for promotion, not enough recognition of individual contribution, and few benefits for the employee's family, among others. They also found that while young employees (<35 years old) value recognition, cash, and quick promotion, more mature employees (>35 years old) value clear hierarchies and benefits for their families.

Training

The value of education is very much ingrained in the Chinese culture. Historically, the way people in China went up the social scale was through education. Social status was very much linked to the educational level of the person. It has been like this for centuries.

A good practice is to link your training and education programs to your employees' career development. It is also important to make clear to those employees that their training is an investment not a mere reward. They should understand they have to return it to the company by increasing both their performance and that of those reporting to them. A powerful practice is to ask participants in any training program to become teachers themselves. That is, to transmit what they have learnt to the members of their teams. This will not only help them to better absorb what they have learnt, but also it will help to improve the performance of their people.

Career development

It is important to tailor your development plans to the individual needs of the employee. It is also advisable to include high-touch elements into career development, which implies personal attention and frequent feedback by the boss. Elements of a development plan are rotation programs and overseas assignments. Companies should avoid the super-star syndrome and pay more attention to average employees who in the end may prove more stable and valuable than the stars. You should deal with employee expectations by giving them realistic career paths.

* * *

Compensation, training, and career development can certainly help to engage your people (say, stay and strive), but it is not enough. You will also need clear and fair company policies, and a positive company climate, one in which employees feel respected and valued.

Clear company policies and transparency

Traditional Chinese HR is mostly focused on administration; it rarely participated in the strategy formulation of the company. Its core tasks were dealing with paperwork and control. In that setting, HR departments provided little information to employees to avoid complaints and difficult questions. In contrast, the Chinese expect and value a very different treatment from foreign companies. They want clear policies and transparent and fair regulations. Sharing information helps to develop trust in the organization and it is a clear sign that the organization treats people with respect.

People

The Chinese value relationships with their direct bosses and other members of the organization. This is the ultimate and most powerful tool for retention when the other elements of the model are in place. A personal relationship with bosses is critical anywhere, but even more so in China. Employees want to feel appreciated, respected, and cared for by their superiors. One way to convey the importance of this point to the organization is by making the rate of retention part of the evaluation of any supervisor and manager in the organization. Companies can make the retention rate part of their evaluation and a criterion for promotion. Supervisors with an excessive turnover rate among their subordinates should be questioned before being considered eligible for promotion.

Finally, we should stress the key role to be played by the HR managers. HR as a career is relatively new in China. Chinese universities have just started to produce the first graduates in this field. The scarcity of talent also affects HR professionals. Many companies employ HR managers who were formerly performing other tasks with little relation to HR. Such professionals have to expand their functions and go beyond the mere administrative tasks. This requires a new breed of HR professionals able to act as a strategic partner, as well as fulfilling their roles as administrators. This implies a fundamental transformation in the roles of HR directors in China.

The case study below illustrates the problem of retention in Eli Lilly. It highlights the challenges for talent retention in China. Eli Lilly is a global, research-based pharmaceutical company with a history of over 126 years. Lilly China had more than 50 representative offices and about 500 medical representatives in 2003. To facilitate its expansion strategy in China, Lilly China encountered an urgent demand to recruit and maintain a pool of top medical representatives. However, the company suffered high employee turnover for three consecutive years with the consequent costs and disruption to their operations. Obviously, the company needed to strengthen its employee retention capability. When trying to improve the situation, Eli Lilly needed to pay attention to the Chinese context and work out solutions accordingly.

Three commentaries follow the case study. The first is by William Mobley, Professor of Management, CEIBS; the second by Angeli Kwauk, Area Director of Human Resources, Grand Hyatt Shanghai; and the third by Xiaotong Li, HR Director of Shared Service Organization, Henkel (China) Investment Co., Ltd. In the first commentary, key factors for attracting talents are discussed in detail. The second commentary provides insightful recommendations for attracting and retaining youngsters in China. Effective means for recruiting and retaining are the focus of the last commentary.

CASE STUDY
ELI LILLY AND COMPANY, CHINA AFFILIATE, WAR FOR TALENT[5]

It was the end of October 2003 and Mary Liu, Human Resource Director of Eli Lilly China and Hong Kong, was preparing the 2004 HR recruitment plan.

Compared with key global competitors such as Pfizer, AstraZeneca, and Glaxo-SmithKline, Lilly was a small organization with 500 medical representatives around China and it was relatively less productive. Preparing to initiate a series of new product launches in China during the next five years, Lilly believed that it would grow to be the top pharmaceutical company in China. It was Lilly's intent to double productivity while maintaining the size of the team. One critical requirement was the company's ability to recruit and maintain a pool of top medical representatives at Lilly.

According to Chris Shaw, President of Lilly China:

> *Lilly's company philosophy is to promote from within. Expansion to us means that we will need more leaders in a shorter period of time. We must be even clearer about how we are going to staff. We should ensure that we can obtain as much talent as possible with leadership potential and with the willingness to stay in the long run.*

However, Lilly had high employee turnover for three consecutive years. Especially in 2003, nearly half of those who resigned from Lilly had only stayed with the company for about one and a half years. Although the industry turnover average in the same period was higher than that of Lilly's, there was a need for the company to strengthen their employee retention pool.

Liu had to make the decision of whether or not to maintain current recruiting practices. She would have to make the decision by the end of 2004 when there would be a launch of some new products, which required additional staff. She commented:

> *The people who come to us should be able to make a difference and lead our organization to a higher level. It is an issue we must solve now. It's critical for the implementation of our strategy in China.*

CASE STUDY: ELI LILLY AND COMPANY, CHINA AFFILIATE, WAR FOR TALENT

Eli Lilly and Company is a global, research-based pharmaceutical company founded in May 1876 by Colonel Eli Lilly in Indianapolis, Ind., in the Midwestern section of the United States. Over the past 126 years, Eli Lilly has been at the forefront of many significant medical breakthroughs, most notably in the treatment of infections, diabetes, and depression.

Famous products include the world's first commercially available insulin product for the treatment of diabetes, Iletin®; the world's first mass-produced penicillin, Prozac®; the first major introduction for treatment of clinical depression, Zyprexa®; the world's top-selling anti-psychotic for treatment of schizophrenia, Prozac®; and a drug for the treatment of pancreatic and non-small-cell lung cancer, Gemzar®.

Relying on breakthrough products, Eli Lilly has successfully expanded its business. By the end of 2003, its workforce amounted to more than 46,000 employees worldwide, 21,667 from the United States. Approximately 8,800 employees were engaged in research and development (R&D). The company has R&D facilities in nine countries, 27 manufacturing plants in 15 countries, it has conducted clinical research in more than 60 countries, and markets its products in 138 countries.

Globally, Lilly was organized in a matrix (see CS Exhibit 2.1). At global headquarters, five functions (Quality, Science/Technology Administration, Manufacturing Operations, Corporate Administration, and Pharmaceutical Operations) reported to the CEO. Pharmaceutical Operations was responsible for the marketing and sales of Lilly products worldwide, including China.

The company also received recognition for its accomplishments and contributions to the community. This included the "100 Best Companies to Work for in America" award for five consecutive years by *Fortune* magazine and the "Top 10 Companies for Working Mothers" award by *Working Mother* magazine five times in nine years.

In 2003 Lilly global sales were over US$12.58 billion and it had the policy of investing 19% of sales back to R&D, a percentage much higher than that of other industries like electronics (6.4%) or aerospace (3.9%). Compared with other competitors, Lilly was ready for the following decade of expansion. It owned a rich pipeline of new breakthrough products ready to be launched on the market.

CASE STUDY: ELI LILLY AND COMPANY, CHINA AFFILIATE, WAR FOR TALENT

CS EXHIBIT 2.1: LILLY GLOBAL ORGANIZATION

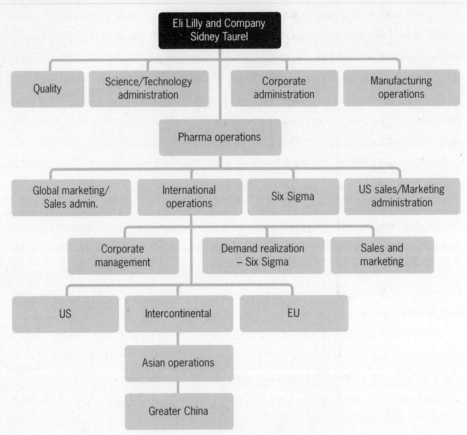

China's pharmaceutical business environment

Since the Chinese policy of reform and opening up in 1978, pharmaceuticals in China has been one of the world's fastest growing industries due to a huge potential unmet demand accumulated over 30 years.

Everyone, except farmers, joined the national medical insurance system. However, with a growing aging population and little social savings left from the planned economy, the social benefits fund was actually facing challenges. Pushed by the government, state-owned hospitals (the mainstays of Chinese hospitals) were exploring ways of reducing costs and raising profit. State-owned distributors, the legacy of the planned economy, remained prevalent when MNC or large local pharmaceuticals were looking for distribution partners. However, none of these distributors had the

CASE STUDY: ELI LILLY AND COMPANY, CHINA AFFILIATE, WAR FOR TALENT

capacity to cover several provinces or the whole of China. Drugstores were booming with chain stores available in the country's larger cities.

The fundamentals of the pharmaceutical industry were good. There was an increasing demand for better healthcare and improved economic capability. These included population size and life expectancy. An example of how this affected the market is that people in more developed regions had longer life expectancies than those in less-developed regions. People with longer life expectancies used more drugs later in life to preserve health and maintain an active lifestyle. Developed regions tended to have more complex diseases such as depression and diabetes. Both of these were critical drivers of business, especially for Lilly.

However, the external environment for healthcare was changing throughout the world, not only in China. There was increasing resistance by governments, payers and patients to pay for rising healthcare costs – hospital care, diagnostics, and pharmaceuticals. At the same time the costs of bringing new innovative products to the market kept going up, fueled by increasing regulatory requirements on safety and efficacy.

Competition was becoming even more dramatic. Compared to two or three medical representatives in the 1990s, more than 10 can now be found in hospitals waiting for the reception of target doctors in 2004. The time for the sales presentation was reduced from 15 to three minutes while the amount of information to transmit in that shorter time was the same.

Ultimately, in terms of Lilly, the genomic revolution was very exciting and very promising. It guarantees a future in which Lilly could have new improved drugs, but the cost of relaying that genomic revolution into medicines is still very high, in the order of US$1 billion.

Lilly's exciting product pipelines were ready and there was low risk of patent exposure until the next decade. These presented great opportunities for employee growth and development.

Balancing high cost with high demands from customers was becoming tougher. There was only one answer – to be more cost-effective. That is to say, pharmaceuticals should look into their current work processes to stop carrying out low-value-added work and focus on increasing productivity. Maintaining the current size of the sales force, while introducing breakthrough drugs, was a wise decision to ensure survival and even the development of the company.

Lilly China

Lilly China's early history dates back to 1928 when a sales office was opened in Shanghai. In 1995, Lilly set up a JV plant in Suzhou, investing up to US$28 million. By 2003, Lilly had a presence of more than 50 representative offices in China's major cities, covering areas from Hei Long Jiang province in the north to Hainan Island in the south, and Shanghai on the east coast to Xinjiang Province in the west.

The product pipeline of Eli Lilly included seven existing products such as Ceclor, Gemzar, Zyprexa, Prozac, Humilin, Evista, and Vancocine. Five new ones were on the waiting list for release. At the time of writing, Eli Lilly had 800 employees in China among whom more than 500 were medical representatives. According to IMS's[6] 2003 data, Eli Lilly ranked eighth with respect to sales volume, and it was rated number one in terms of annual growth rate. Overall, the two largest competitors to Lilly were MSD and Pfizer. Within each therapeutic area, Lilly has two to three local or foreign competitors, such as Novonortis and Tonghua Dongbao in diabetes care, BMS in cancer, and GSK in antibiotics.

Eli Lilly China was structured according to functions such as marketing, sales, HR, and finance. Sales functions were further divided into three areas, which were led by three general managers (GMs) (see CS Exhibit 2.2). Under the GM, there were regional managers (RMs) and district managers (DMs). The medical representatives (MRs) reported to the DMs who then reported to the RMs.

Each MR was responsible for promoting one to two products within a specific therapeutic area, such as antibiotics and oncology. The medical representatives usually served customers in several hospitals of a city. Their role was to advise doctors of the various therapeutics that Lilly was a leader in. Their daily job was to deliver key medical messages about Lilly products, as well as to ensure that doctors prescribed them properly.

The DMs usually covered all hospitals of the city, and RMs covered up to two provinces. District and regional managers shared the responsibility of recruiting people to fill job openings in their district, but the RMs and the HR department were the ones to make the final decision regarding recruitment.

Although Eli Lilly China was a small division within Lilly Global, it attracted huge attention due to its fast 10 years of growth (see CS Exhibit 2.3), especially with the huge China market behind it. Lilly China was heading for US$100 million

CASE STUDY: ELI LILLY AND COMPANY, CHINA AFFILIATE, WAR FOR TALENT

CS EXHIBIT 2.2: LILLY CHINA ORGANIZATION CHART

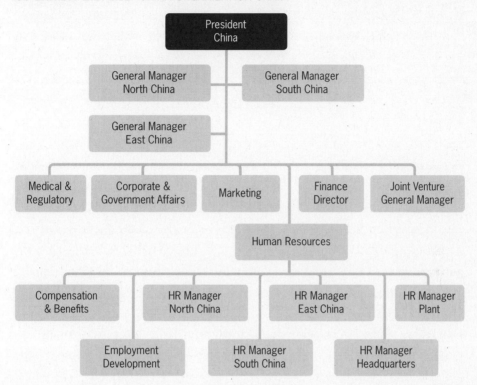

CS EXHIBIT 2.3: LILLY CHINA GROWTH

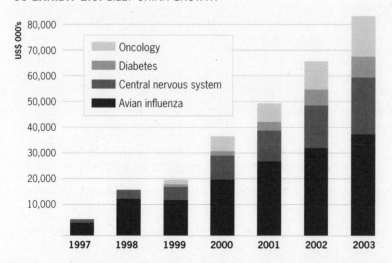

CASE STUDY: ELI LILLY AND COMPANY, CHINA AFFILIATE, WAR FOR TALENT

sales in 2004, while Wall Street estimated Lilly global sales to be US$13.5 billion. Lilly China was endeavoring to become one of the top 10 affiliates in Lilly Global within 10 years by putting more breakthrough products into the China market.

Lilly's culture

The "Lilly way" is characterized by what Lilly called the three values: integrity, respect for people, and excellence (see CS Exhibit 2.4). Many examples are available to demonstrate and affirm these values every day. For example, management were used to define "value" as one of the criteria in making tough people decisions such as who to promote, who should succeed, and who to fire. As people interfaced with Lilly during the recruitment process, Lilly interviewers communicated with candidates openly and honestly, and also expected honest information disclosed on the candidates' side in return.

CS EXHIBIT 2.4: ELI LILLY CORPORATE CITIZENSHIP

	Mission
Why we exist	We provide customers "Answers That Matter" through innovative medicines, information, and exceptional customer service that enable people to live longer, healthier, and more active lives.
	Strategic intent
Our overarching goal	By providing for the unmet needs of our customers through a constant stream of innovation, we will outgrow all competitors.
	Vision
Our promise	"Answers That Matter" is the foundation of our promise to our customers. We will deliver on our promise by listening to and understanding the needs of our customers and providing unmatched value.
The culture we strive for	We are guided in all that we do by our long-established core values: • Respect for people that includes our concern for the interests of all people who touch – or are touched by – our company: customers, employees, shareholders, partners, suppliers, and communities • Integrity that embraces the very highest standards of honesty and ethical behavior • Excellence that is reflected in our unsurpassed focus on quality and a continuous search for new ways to improve everything we do.
The winning outcome	As a result, customers around the world will increasingly choose our products, enabling us to generate a superior financial performance that benefits our shareholders, our employees, and the communities where we live.

Candidates who disclosed false information were regarded as unreliable and automatically rejected.

In 2000, Sidney Taurel, CEO of Eli Lilly, reinforced the culture by introducing the seven leadership behaviors (see CS Exhibit 2.5). He wanted to change the old culture rooted in a business environment of relative stability to a culture adapted to an environment of rapid, constant, and discontinuous change (periods of stability followed by periods of rapid change). According to Taurel, "We need a culture to carry our ideas to action, implement plans clearly and decisively."[7]

In 2003, Taurel once again reinforced one aspect of the seven leadership behaviors – create external focus – after he found that Lilly people were more self-oriented. In his article "Why branding matters," Taurel said that, in the past, Lilly people were more internally focused, rather than customer-focused. The pharmaceutical industry used to be a high-risk, high-return industry, now it was becoming tougher and tougher for the industry to maintain high returns due to the changing business

CS EXHIBIT 2.5: THE SEVEN LEADERSHIP BEHAVIORS

Sidney Taurel, CEO, Eli Lilly and Company

1 MODEL THE VALUES
Demonstrate the Lilly values (people, integrity, excellence) through daily conduct.

2 CREATE EXTERNAL FOCUS
Know how what you do fits into the bigger picture and compares with the competition. Create and leverage key relationships, outside your area and outside the company, to create conditions for success.

3 ANTICIPATE CHANGES AND PREPARE FOR THE FUTURE
Anticipate future events, challenge the status quo, and establish goals and requirements for competitive advantage.

4 IMPLEMENT WITH QUALITY, SPEED, AND VALUE
Make decisions and execute work plans to achieve results.

5 EVALUATE AND ACT
Evaluate results and adjust course as needed.

6 ACHIEVE RESULTS WITH PEOPLE
Enable and energize yourself, others, and the organization to deliver results.

7 SHARE KEY LEARNING
Seek and share knowledge; apply what you've learned from successes and failures.

environment. The only way out was to maximize customer value by closely focusing on customer needs and becoming more productive (see CS Exhibit 2.6).

From three values to seven leadership behaviors to an emphasis on creating external focus, Lilly was geared toward the direction of making itself more publicly recognizable in stakeholders' minds. Lilly people needed to change to the expected behavior model by becoming more proactive listeners and responding to external stakeholders.

Lilly HR: Organization, roles, and philosophy

HR in Lilly was organized into two groups: field HR and functional HR. Field HR directly reported to the GM and dotted report line, or informed but not received

CS EXHIBIT 2.6: QUOTES FROM ARTICLES THAT REFLECT LILLY CULTURE

> *Values, as my father understood so well, are really the heart of the matter. They tell us who we are, how we should behave, where we should be going. They help us to interpret the world and thus, ideally, to anchor the self in a larger reality. Values are, quite simply, the core of both men and institutions. Without a clear-cut system of values, people lack independence and will often grab at almost anything to fill their emptiness or solve the uncertainties of their existence.*
>
> "Values for a Second Century" (March 1976)
> Author, Eli Lilly

> *I believe that if we all share a common set of beliefs about why we are doing what we are doing, then the odds of continuing to successfully turn strategy into action will be greatly improved. Indeed, a shared set of beliefs about the "why" may well be the most critical ingredient in successfully empowering our employees and our organization.*
>
> "The Best Days Speech" (April 1995)
> Author, Randall L. Tobias, Chairman and Chief Executive Officer (retired)

> *The culture that we need therefore is one that allows us to harness the brainpower of all our abundantly talented individuals so as to raise the organizational IQ. We don't want that precious resource to be wasted by continually reinventing the wheel in routine chores. We need to design simple, efficient, universal processes for that purpose, allowing us to focus our thinking on finding and developing the best new opportunities for our business. Above all, we need a culture that allows us to carry our ideas into action, implementing our plans clearly and decisively.*
>
> "Leadership White Paper" (February 2000)
> Author, Sidney Taurel, Chairman, President, and Chief Executive Officer

orders, to the HR Director (HRD). Field HR was composed of individuals dedicated to each business area that provided expertise in multiple HR areas; for example, career development, coaching, and counseling. They had three roles: service, business support, and employee relationship (see CS Exhibit 2.7).

CS EXHIBIT 2.7: LILLY HR ROLES

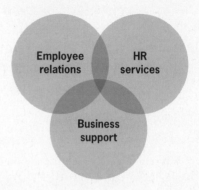

The first role was to provide essential services to support the corporate, affiliates function or team strategies, and to design and implement services to support business units and employees.

The second role was to identify the HR implications of the business strategy and the potential solutions. It required a knowledge and understanding of HR services and how they could be applied to meet the business objectives.

The third role was to understand and communicate the issues and needs of employees to management and offer solutions.

On the other hand, functional HR only reported to the HRD and played a role as internal consultant to design programs and offered information or support to field HR about any of their hands-on problems. The compensation and benefits (C&Bs) and Employee Development Manager were in this category.

Thus, in Lilly China there was not a centrally controlled recruiting function within the HR organization. Instead, field HR was responsible for delivering recruiting services to the local sales organization.

There were altogether 10 HR people in China; five were field HR managers to serve five sub-organizations: East China, North China, South China, the administrative department, and the Suzhou plant.

Lilly regards employees as partners to build businesses and is committed to treating them fairly. Therefore, the company was very selective and always hired people primarily for a career and not just for a job. Lilly would invest significantly in new staff to develop their career paths and promote them from within as the first choice to refill openings.

Lilly always did as much as they could to keep valued employees within the company to ensure continuity of their employment. Over a year, almost all key positions were promoted from within. In return, the company also expected employees to maintain flexibility and willingness to learn, and to continuously re-tool for the future.

Competitive labor market in China

The position as MR was not a highly regarded position in the organization; however, it played a critical role in the link between the company and the customer with respect to delivering medical information and building brand image.

In research-based pharmaceuticals like Lilly, companies even positioned themselves as the leading expert in their specialized therapeutic area. This image was built due to their daily interactions in communication and consultancy with doctors. It was normal recruiting practice to hire individuals with a medical background.

During the earlier stages of the pharmaceutical boom in China in the 1980s and 1990s, it was a popular profession of young doctors and graduates to be a medical representative. It paid well, offered training opportunities, and it was an easy way to earn money.

In addition to the improved incomes for doctors, there was severe competition within the MR position that made the industry turnover rate reach 30%, demonstrating the dissatisfaction that doctors felt towards a sales career.

In recent years, non-pharmaceutical industries emerged to absorb top medical representatives. The medical instrument industry was one example. In addition, state-owned enterprises (SOEs), after years of development, were now entering the stage of dramatic growth, at a rate much higher than that of foreign companies. They had huge demand for talent and could also pay competitive packages. The SOEs felt it was good to "buy" mature representatives directly from foreign companies. The medical representatives from joint ventures and wholly foreign-owned enterprises (WFOEs) were their hot targets.

What should Lilly do with their staffing system during this expansionary period? Were there any hurdles in the current system that prevented Lilly from being the most competitive in winning the war for talent? What is the ideal staffing model for Lilly China? Who are the targeted talents? How do you attract them? And how do you select them? According to Liu:

> *These days, I have been looking into next year's recruiting plan given that there will*
> *be a lot of changes in the industry, and we were going to introduce a new product*
> *portfolio in China. I had a discussion with our sales general managers and won alle-*
> *giance with them in terms of the necessity of doing a systematic diagnosis on our*
> *current recruitment system. I am eager to see the results.*

With this problem in mind, Liu thought that she might be better off to invite a consulting team to help explore the problem. She asked ABC Consulting Company and the China–Europe Consulting Group to present their project proposals on how to address the problems she was facing.

Current recruitment system and practices

The cost of losing a medical representative was very high. Possible expenses may be in placing recruiting advertisements, training, administration, transportation, time spent on interviews, and even the opportunity cost of having an opening for a long time. A wrong decision concerning annual pay for a US$12,000 job may incur an estimated cost of US$162,000.

RESPONSIBILITY

According to the Lilly hierarchy, a DM was the direct manager of medical representatives. DMs were expected to recruit MRs, develop them, and to build their business. RMs, the bosses of DMs, were responsible for coaching DMs, being a role model within the region and strategic management of the business.

TALENTS PROFILE

Currently, Lilly's recruiting advertisements (see CS Exhibit 2.8) in all types of media heavily illustrate the company's ranking, and reputation. However, there were only several lines for the job description. A typical job posting for a medical representative position on an advertisement would read as follows:

> *One to two years of work experience in pharmaceutical sales. [The] candidate must*
> *be hard working, show integrity, and be a team player. Must have a bachelor's degree*
> *related to medicine or having [sic] a relevant medical background.*

CS EXHIBIT 2.8: A TYPICAL RECRUITMENT AD

Translation

Eli Lilly provides you with:
• an ideal career
• real life.

Eli Lilly is one of the top 10 leading pharmaceutical companies committed to providing answers that matter for some of the world's most urgent medial needs. Its products treat depression, schizophrenia, attention-deficit hyperactivity disorder, diabetes, osteoporosis, and many other conditions. With its three key values, "respecting employees, being honest and upright, pursuing excellence," Eli Lilly has been frequently ranked among the 100 best employers by *Fortune* Magazine. In 2000, Eli Lilly has again won many awards and was highly appraised:

One of the top 100 best companies by the *Industry Weekly* (US); sixth of the top 15 most respected pharmaceutical companies by *Fortune* Magazine; 55th of the leading 1,000 companies by *Business Week* (US).

In order to meet the rapid development of the company, we look for candidates to be:
• Pharmacy Representatives / Senior Pharmacy Representatives
• In Shanghai, Ningbo, Wenzhou
  * responsible for product promotion in hospitals
  * bachelor or above, preference with a major in pharmacy / medical science / biology / chemistry / business / marketing
  * willing to take challenges, ambitious, able to work under pressure
  * with good communication skills and high team spirit

www. Lilly.com/careers

The candidates should be healthy, speak fluent mandarin, have good communication skills and work hard.

Our company will provide systematic technical training and a competitive package, while offering personal career planning and development.

Interested candidates please mail within 10 days your detailed CVs, copies of the education certificates and ID card, a picture, together with your contact information, to the following address.

CASE STUDY: ELI LILLY AND COMPANY, CHINA AFFILIATE, WAR FOR TALENT

Although Lilly measured each medical representative by a matrix designed from the sales representative competency model, seven leadership behaviors and three values, none of these variables were mentioned in the advertisement. Also ignored were the differentiating requirements for the different product lines that medical representatives would have to be responsible for.

SOURCING

As soon as these advertisements were publicly posted, there were numerous responses and résumés sent to Lilly. However, very few of the applicants were qualified. According to one HR manager:

> In the recruitment hot seasons, we usually get more than 1,000 résumés after one advertisement. It is really exhausting to read them through. However, high quantity doesn't mean high quality. Usually only 10 to 20 résumés are attractive enough for an interview.

In other months, advertisements did not seem to be a cost-efficient way to recruit only one or two representatives. In such cases, district and regional managers had to rely on their personal channels to search for candidates externally, or to look for internal transfers. Some of the senior DMs were really good at establishing a potential talent pool for their region. This demonstrated the effectiveness of such a channel for obtaining talent.

There was a tendency in Lilly to recruit experienced medical representatives rather than fresh graduates, as experienced talent delivered results faster. However, both Xi'an Janseen and Pfizer had 20% of their employees hired directly from the university campus. Some people at Lilly argued that products of these companies were OTC (over-the-counter) and required little specialization. Therefore they said that campus recruiting was thus appropriate for them but not necessarily for Lilly. On the other hand, no data were available to demonstrate the stability of these fresh graduates with their employer.

SELECTION PRACTICES

Whenever there was an opening, DM, RM, and field HR were mutually responsible for recruitment, but each played a different role. Only RMs and HR held the authority of making offer decisions.

CASE STUDY: ELI LILLY AND COMPANY, CHINA AFFILIATE, WAR FOR TALENT

Usually, HR advertised in the leading or specialized recruitment newspapers once it was established that an advertisement was required. HR was also responsible for résumé screening and recommending candidates to the DM for the first round of interviews.

Although psychometric or IQ tests were very popular everywhere, Lilly did not use them to test candidates before the interview. Once entering into the interview process, a candidate had to go through three interviews, first by the HR, next by the DM, and last by the RM. In so doing, Lilly wanted to capture a full-lens picture of the candidate and ensure that the right target talents were there. Reference checks were the last step to safeguard judgment.

INTERVIEW

Before the interview, Lilly asked the candidates to do certain IQ tests to double-check their education level.

Lilly had a well-defined list of requirements for a medical representative. For example, the competency model (see CS Exhibit 2.9) defined requirements from the technical view; seven leadership behaviors focused on career potentials in Lilly; while Lilly's values evaluated candidates from the cultural perspective. Some DMs relied on one set of the above requirements as the criteria to design their own interview questions.

After the interviews the DM, RM, and HR would review the candidate to

CS EXHIBIT 2.9: COMPETENCY MODEL

Strategic target
To find out the selling potential of Lilly's products by providing the best medical
treatment solution to the customers and then meeting their satisfaction.

1. Sales	2. Regional management
1.1 Technical knowledge	2.1 Regional analysis
1.2 Customer relation and customer knowledge	2.2 Plan and implementation
1.3 Company visit	

discuss and decide whether or not to make an offer. A consensus had to be reached between the three before one was made. However, managers often found themselves trapped in long arguments over the criteria before reaching a consensus.

EVALUATE AND ACT

In order to ensure the company hired qualified talents, Lilly trained all new DMs in professional skill selection. It designed an interview guide that highlighted the key dimensions for judging qualifications and a list of key questions to ask during interviews. In addition, the guide covered how to pre-read a résumé, how to open an interview, and how to deliver the closing speech. There were also blank areas on the sheets for managers to record comments and examples made by the interviewee. The critical part of this guide was the questions under each requirement.

For new DMs, some practiced their interview skills right after their training if there were openings in their region, while others did not have the opportunity unless vacancies were available.

In order to ensure timely and high recruitment quality, Lilly held RM accountable for "annual turnover rates" by region as one of their performance evaluation criteria. The target turnover was 18%. Both RM and HR emphasized an estimated time frame in which they needed the position to be filled. Each month, the management committee reviewed recruitment results and the key matrix.

URGENT NEEDS OR NEEDS FROM DIFFICULT CITIES

Whereas the whole recruitment process worked well in normal cases, it could not effectively satisfy urgent needs or needs from certain difficult cities. Under both cases, the recruitment period usually extended well beyond the company's expectation and resulted in considerable business loss.

One DM from certain difficult cities in East China said:

> We feel that we lose control in such situations. There is always limited supply of good candidates. We have to pray on good luck to catch one, but such luck is very rare. Sometimes we are forced to sacrifice quality in order to refill the opening earlier.

CASE COMMENTARIES

COMMENTARY 1
WILLIAM H. MOBLEY, PHD
PROFESSOR OF MANAGEMENT,
CHINA EUROPE INTERNATIONAL BUSINESS SCHOOL (CEIBS)
FOUNDER OF MOBLEY GROUP PACIFIC LIMITED

Eli Lilly and Company, like many other major firms in China, is facing an increasingly competitive labor market. Lilly appears to be experiencing lower turnover than the industry average, due no doubt to its clear values and leadership behaviors, and sound basic HR processes. However, the turnover rate is still high in terms of the Lilly growth and cost-effectiveness strategy. Of particular concern is the high turnover during the first one and a half years with the firm.

Lilly will need to assure implementation of systematic employee engagement and retention processes, and not seek the simplistic solutions proffered by some consultants and vendors. Multiple studies have shown that key factors in attracting and retaining professional talent in China are:

- opportunity to learn, grow, and develop
- strength of the relationship with the boss
- compensation factors.

At a minimum, Lilly management will want to ensure that these three factors are well addressed. The first factor requires individualized development plans that are not simply an end-of-the-year discussion, but rather a continuing process of valid strengths and gaps assessment. This requires:

- dialogue, action planning, and follow-up among the employee, their boss, and HR champion regarding the individual's development needs in terms of both current role and future roles

- effective and very visible development actions, including project and task force assignments
- active mentoring
- professional knowledge and skill development
- shadowing of next-level executives, opportunities to interact with senior executives, targeted training and development experiences, and so on.

The second factor, strength of relationship with the boss, requires not only relationship-skilled bosses, but bosses who are highly effective coaches. To some extent, Lilly can create a coaching culture which includes effective coaching mindset and skill training for all managers. This will help address the top two issues in talent recruitment and retention.

The third factor, compensation, requires constant benchmarking of external and internal equity factors, something Lilly surely does. In the highly competitive professional labor market of China, Lilly like other major firms will continue to experience upward salary pressure. I am reminded of a quote years ago from Fred Herzberg at a conference: "Money is like food. Feed me a great breakfast and I say thanks; but by mid-morning, I am asking what's for lunch. Give me a good pay increase and bonus at the end of the year and I say thanks; and several months later I am asking; when and how much is the next one?" Ensuring that the top performers are well rewarded is essential.

In my own research, writing, and consulting on employee turnover, I have suggested seeking to build multiple attachments between the employee and the company. These multiple attachments include the three key factors listed above: opportunity to learn, develop, and grow; relationship with the boss; and competitive and equitable compensation and benefits. Other important sources of attachment include being part of a winning team; interesting job content; being listened to and treated with respect; having a line of sight to the company's vision and strategy; future with the firm.

Organizationally, Lilly will want to ensure that it is building its brand in the China professional labor market as well as in the customer market. It will want to ensure that it is creating a very positive selection ratio and that it is using valid selection assessment tools that tap knowledge, skills, attitudes, and motivations, so as to get the top talent. It will want to ensure that its on-boarding process is well designed and executed, so as to help build an understanding of the Lilly culture and values; the clarity of expectations; coaching and mentoring; and the bonding needed for retention. Lilly already is doing many things well.

A "cost of turnover" study may suggest what else they can invest in to enhance retention and still reduce net costs. A regular organizational culture survey has been shown to help diagnose organizational effectiveness (including turnover) – note this is not the same as an employee satisfaction or attitude survey. Finally, Lilly will want to ensure that relevant talent development and retention metrics are included in the Dashboard and Balanced Scorecard, and weighted appropriately in the bonus.

COMMENTARY 2
ANGELI KWAUK
AREA DIRECTOR OF HUMAN RESOURCES,
CHINA GRAND HYATT SHANGHAI

What are the CEOs' expectations on their HR professionals? What is the focus of the HR team these days? Talent acquisition, talent retention, talent development? All of the above.

The challenge that Eli Lilly is facing is not unique for HR specialists working in China these days, despite the fact that we are working in the world's most populous country. The rapid growth of the China economy, the surge of foreign firms into China or the expansion of their China operations, and the time lag for the country's education system to catch up with market demands are just a few of the many factors that are accentuating the current talent shortage. Similar to Eli Lilly, CEOs and presidents of multinational firms see the business potential of China and expect significant growth of their companies in this country. However, with the escalating payroll costs in China, HR specialists are constantly skating on thin ice, seeking to maintain a healthy balance between growth of the company's business and growth of labor.

Other than the above, HR professionals are also encountering a new challenge: learning how to deal with and manage a rather different generation of workers – those born in the 1980s, commonly known globally as the "millennials." This generation of workers is arriving in the workplace with higher expectations and this is no different in China. With their expectations, the millennials are expecting to be fast tracked with career advancement every one to two years, and not having to pay their dues. They are also more open and expressive, wanting to know about compensation, benefits, and career advancement prior to taking up a job. Having grown up in the digital age, and familiar with the Internet and all kinds of digital devices, they are definitely more knowledgeable, informed, and technology savvy than the previous generation. This is especially so in China, with those born after 1979 coming from one-child families and raised by their grandparents and parents, where they are naturally the center of attention.

HR professionals, along with the other management in the company, have to take into consideration the characteristics of the millennials and learn how to adopt and cope with this generation. They must be aware that millennials frequently involve their families in major decisions like finding a job.

In the case of Lilly's HR issues in 2003, one of the primary challenges was to recruit enough qualified employees, especially MRs who were front-line sales staff with direct impact on the company's financial growth. These MRs also had to stay in Lilly long enough to maintain and/or improve productivity. While it was mentioned that the MRs play a critical role in the link between the company and the customer with respect to delivering medical information and building brand image, the position of MRs is not highly regarded in the organization. Competition for MRs is very stiff with a turnover rate of as high as 30% in the industry.

The MRs report directly to the DMs, who together with their direct superior, the RMs, are responsible for recruitment. Selection interviews are conducted by all three parties separately: HR, DMs and RMs. However, the DMs do not make the final decision about the hiring of the MRs, nor are they accountable for employee turnover.

As the DMs are the ones working closely with the MRs, training and developing them, Lilly should consider amending the selection decision and performance evaluation of staff turnover to include the DMs. In this way, the DMs would then take ownership of mentoring the MRs through their careers. With proper coaching and counseling skills, DMs could "nip in the bud" any problems that the MRs encounter and stop the leaking bucket of the talent pool.

The job specification for these MRs required a Bachelor or higher academic qualification, thus they are well educated and most of them are likely to fall into the millennials category. They require attention, motivation, recognition, and a clear vision of their career path. Lilly might want to explore different ways to motivate the MRs and give them the due recognition for the important role they play as MRs. A systematic and more "transparent" career planning process should be set up to help retain and develop the existing talent.

Lilly's tendency is to recruit experienced MRs rather than fresh graduates. They believe that experienced MRs could deliver faster results. Putting out recruitment advertisements or going to job fairs in China nowadays can indeed be like trying to "find a needle in a haystack." Much effort will be exhausted on responding to non-qualified candidates. However, experienced talent in a limited supply pool could mean higher salary expectation from the recruits and paying a premium for poaching from other pharmaceutical companies. Though depending on the senior DM network for recruitment is a proven effective channel for recruiting potential talent for Lilly, it also exposes Lilly to the risk that if a DM leaves, the pool of talented MRs could also follow suit.

Talents recruited from Lilly's rivals, while experienced, can have their own set ideas of how things should be done, thus they might not be as enthusiastic or open as fresh graduates in embracing the "Lilly Way" on the three values and seven leadership behaviors. Without a strong inculcation of the culture and commitment to Lilly, talents could perhaps be easily "bought," as is evident of SOEs going into the foreign firms to "buy" mature representatives during these recent years.

The recruitment advertisement shown in CS Exhibit 2.8 mentions the awards received by Lilly from *Fortune Magazine*, *Industry Weekly*, and *Business Week*. However, the focus of the youngsters in China may be more on things that matter to them and are closer to home like Lilly's reputation in China, company growth and vision in China, career opportunities, and so on. In the advertisement, one of the job requirements listed first is, "willing to take challenges, ambitious, able to work under pressure," all of which are virtues that the millennials, together with their family, might not value as much as the previous generation. While these competencies are certainly important, perhaps the company values and culture, along with a realistic and systematic career plan, should be explained during the interview recruitment process, rather than put upfront on the advertisement since the applicants are more concerned about tangible growth, development, and a career path.

Recruitment through the Internet is one of the major tools millennials use in their job search. Thus a Chinese website dedicated to job vacancies with more comprehensive information about the company, including the job specification, company's values, and so on, could therefore be a very important recruitment vehicle. Campus recruitment of focused groups is important, even if it is not Lilly's current strategy to recruit fresh from school. However, the positive brand image can pay off in the future. In years to come, these efforts will bear fruit that Eli Lilly could reap.

No doubt, like Eli Lilly, many companies are facing challenges in acquiring, retaining, and developing their talent pool. Human resource issues are constantly under the spotlight, especially in China. Without the right HR strategy in place, the growth of any company will slow down, if not come to a complete stop.

COMMENTARY 3
XIAOTONG LI
HR DIRECTOR, SHARED SERVICE ORGANIZATION
HENKEL (CHINA) INVESTMENT CO. LTD

To improve the current situation at Lilly, Mary Liu needs to look into two major areas: recruitment and retention.

In recruitment several things can be done:

1   Recruiting all year round. Currently, Lilly recruits when there are vacant positions. Due to the fast development of the company, it is advisable for Lilly to set up a national talent pool in China. HR managers discuss with business managers and work out a staffing plan for the future years. Based on this plan, HR can look for high potentials and take them on, even if there are no immediate vacant positions. The advantage of having a talent pool is that Lilly will create a reserve of good candidates when there is a vacancy. The company will not be in a hurry to look for candidates.

2   Broadening the sourcing channel. It seems that Lilly heavily depends on recruiting through newspaper advertisements. The advantage of newspaper ads is that they convey the message clearly to those who have read the ad. The disadvantage is that many potential and good candidates will not see it. Due to the high cost, companies usually put up the advertisement only for a few days. The reader coverage therefore is limited. Looking for working opportunities through websites is now more and more popular, and it proves to be both effective and cost efficient. Lilly can use its own website or some public recruiting website to source candidates all year round.

3   Campus recruitment should be considered by Lilly to build up its talent pool. The advantages are that the company can select high-potential young people, and that it can imbue the students with its own values and competency model. It is important that

young graduates are trained to the company's expectations from day one. These high-potential candidates can have a strong loyalty to the company. The challenges are: since they are top students in college, they normally have high career expectations. Companies need to provide them with a clear career path and development opportunities to attract them. Another challenge is the mindset of current business managers. Lilly prefers to have experienced staff that can generate results in a short time. There is a conflict in short-term and long-term interest. HR needs to work with company business managers on a young graduate recruitment plan to guarantee that the company has high potential talents to support its fast development.

In order to ensure the effectiveness of campus recruitment, HR needs to select top universities and establish relationships with them and their graduates. Lilly can offer opportunities to attract young graduates to get to know Lilly and join the company. Among the possible practices, internship has proved to be an effective way for both parties. During their university studies, students need to acquire working experience. Lilly can offer such an opportunity, even at a very early stage – say, at grade 2. During the internship, Lilly can observe the performance and identify future candidates. HR can keep close track of the high-potential candidates and attract them to join Lilly. Through such communications, both the candidate and Lilly can make good decisions regarding employment, and it will help the candidate to adapt to Lilly's working environment in a shorter period of time.

4   A shared recruitment platform should be set up. It seems that at this moment recruitment for different regions is done locally. Field HR managers help their DM and RM to recruit candidates. Company internal information sharing is not sufficient in China. HR needs to set up a recruitment platform where the information about candidates and vacancies can be publicized, and joint efforts

in recruitment activities, like campus recruitment, can be implemented. This platform can also help business managers by sharing their experience in recruiting, their talent pool, and sourcing channel.

5   Encourage referrals. Almost all MRs have a medical background, and probably come from the same medical schools. This means that MRs can be potential "headhunters" for Lilly. All vacant positions should be communicated openly to the organization. A mechanism should be set up to encourage company employees to recommend candidates for the company.

With all the actions, HR will diversify and increase channels to source candidates for the company. This is only one possible way to solve the talent problem. On the other hand, which is also very important, the company needs to retain its talents. The industry's turnover rate is 30%, although Lilly has a lower rate. Considering that 50% of the people who left in 2003 only stayed with the company for 1.5 years, and the company has invested a lot in its staff, the retention issue is as crucial as recruitment.

Several things can be done:

- Enhance the MR position status in the company – MR directly links with the customer and brings business to the company. It is critical that each MR knows and feels proud of it. HR should help MRs to understand their value to the company and be proud of the value of what they do.
- Career orientation – HR should help MRs to work on their career development plan. For high-potential people, apart from internal promotion, they should get more chances to build up their personal competencies and be more competitive in the market. The company should encourage MRs with high potentials to take positions in different functions to strengthen their capabilities and experience.

- Apart from job rotation and promotion, Lilly can also offer opportunities for international assignments. This is another effective way to keep good people in the organization. Apart from getting wider exposure, the transferee can also bring back new know-how and management practices to China after they finish their assignments. At the same time the host countries can also benefit from the transferee's knowledge and experience.

In one word, to cope with increasing demand for talent and to compete in the talent war, the HR department needs to work innovatively to find new talents and to keep them.

NOTES

1 *Runaway Bride* is a movie in which a woman (Julia Roberts) kept abandoning husbands-to-be at the altar.

2 C. Barlett and S. Goshal, 1992, "What is a global manager?", *Harvard Business Review*, September–October, Vol. 70, No. 5, pp. 124–132.

3 The 3S model appeared in *Leadership Talent in Asia* by Mick Bennet and Andrew Bell, John Wiley & Sons, Singapore, 2004.

4 Business Forum Asia, April 2004.

5 This case study was prepared by Jacqueline Zheng, HR Manager of Eli Lilly China, and Juan A. Fernandez, professor at CEIBS. It was prepared for class discussion, rather than to illustrate effective or ineffective handling of an administrative situation. Certain names and other identifying information may have been disguised to protect confidentiality. The case was originally published by CEIBS in 2005. Published with permission.

6 Intercontinental Marketing Services (IMS) is the leading provider of business intelligence and strategic consulting services for the pharmaceutical and healthcare industries.

7 Sidney Taurel to all Lilly employees in his Leadership White Paper of 2000.

Chapter 3
Joint ventures: Dancing the Chinese tango

INTRODUCTION

A joint venture is like a marriage in many ways. As the famous Russian writer Leo Tolstoy put it, "Happy families are all alike; each unhappy family is unhappy in its own way." Even large MNCs will sometimes suffer from an arranged marriage in China. *Financial Times*, in 2002, reported about the painful joint venture (JV) of Pepsi Cola in Sichuan, the most populous province of China.[1] In 1994 Sichuan Pepsi was established as one of the 14 bottling JVs of Pepsico in China. Pepsico took a 27% stake in the JV, and three of the seven seats on the Board. Hu Fengxian, the boss of Sichuan Pepsi, held three important positions: chairman, managing director, and chief legal representative. Thanks to Hu and his team's connections and business acumen, the JV was a financial success and beat Coca-Cola in Sichuan. However, the partners of Sichuan Pepsi seemed to have different objectives from the beginning. Sichuan Pepsi wanted to launch its own branded beverages, something Pepsico did not approve. Another problem emerged when Sichuan Pepsi was selling to areas covered by other bottlers. Pepsico fined it. Moreover, the ownership of the Chinese partner changed without consulting Pepsico. When Pepsico demanded entry to the factory to inspect the accounts, the security guards refused to let them in. The episode ended in a propaganda war against each other in the Chinese media. Pepsico accused its partner of mismanagement, financial irregularities, and lavish spending by executives. The local partner countered with charges of unfair pricing policies, illegal fines, and even corporate espionage. In the end, Pepsico filed to international arbitration to terminate the JV. The story seems perfect for a soap opera.

Pepsico's experience in Sichuan might be an extreme case of JV, in China, but it also provides a rare window into the complex and dynamic institutional environment in China. Foreign investors have frequently struggled to find the right formula for business success in China. In the initial years of the economic opening, having a Chinese partner was considered part of that formula. In many ways, foreign investors had no choice as a Chinese partner was most of the time imposed by the government. This initial situation has fundamentally changed in recent years as a result of China's entry into the WTO (World Trade Organization) in December 2001. Changes in the legislation allowing more choices and past experience with JVs have significantly reduced the appeal of joint ventures.

Around 71% of the total foreign-invested enterprises established in China in 2004 took the form of WFOEs, which shows a growing preference of foreign investors to go alone.

Regulatory changes and foreigners' increasing familiarity with the Chinese business environment make it easier to fully own their local operations. Most of the advantages a Chinese partner brought to the JV – connection with the government, distribution networks, and brand recognition among others – can now be obtained by simply acquiring the Chinese company.

Historically, we can identify a number of phases during the 25 years plus of the opening process of the country. In the 1980s, most multinationals had no choice but to enter the market in the form of JVs with a partner selected by the government, usually ailing SOEs. At that time, there were a large number of regulatory restrictions that impeded WFOEs. The situation changed in the 1990s, when regulations became more open and allowed MNCs to operate as WFOEs in a wider number of industries. In this period, most MNCs moved to a second-generation investment in large-scale projects, world-class operations, and usually in the legal form of WFOEs. Finally, after China entered the WTO in December of 2001, the regulations granted even more freedom to foreign companies. In more recent years, foreign investors have added local company acquisitions to their menu of options for achieving their growth objectives in China.

In general, the experience of MNCs with JVs has been mixed. Basically, JVs have gained a certain bad reputation for being difficult to manage. Reasons for this include differing expectations, overestimation of the partner's market position, and conflicting management styles. The risk of failure is further complicated in China by the changing relationship between the government and enterprises. The *guanxi*-dominated institutional environment and the economic reform characterized by "Crossing the River by Feeling Each Stone"[2] increased the level of uncertainty and risk to the business environment.

In order to succeed in such an environment, one must be prepared to face what the Chinese with one colorful expression denominate as "crouching tiger, hidden dragon."[3] Foreign investors not only have to deal with the local partner, but also with myriad invisible vested interests. The local partner is in some instances just an instrument of those with higher interests. Those hidden partners can change their priorities, affecting the initial agreements and expectations of the JV, therefore completely changing the dynamics of the partnership. One type of hidden partner comprises officials from the local government, which are usually the real bosses behind the Chinese partner. In such a situation, the local government can use their power to protect the JV by providing cheap land, tax benefits, or guaranteeing large orders. On the other hand, it can control the appointment of key executives, impose unreasonable requirements for local tax collection and job creation, and even secretly intervene on the management of the JV.

Exhibit 3.1 depicts the complicated interaction between the different parties in the JV. The nominal counterpart for the foreign investors is the local partner. However, the Chinese management usually has strong *guanxi* with local authorities, and is thus able to control the partnership using that power in case of disagreement. In this sense, the Chinese management and the local government officials are like "crouching tigers and hidden dragons." Due to the powerful *guanxi*, they are usually in a position to change the rules of the game in their favor. If both the local officials and the management feel neglected, they will become a major source of problems for the foreign partner. Foreign investors, in order to protect themselves from such an imbroglio, must deal not only with the local partner and the Chinese management of the JV, but also with local officials. It is a balancing act of various interests. As the title of this chapter indicates, managing a JV is like dancing the tango. Both parties try to dominate the other;

EXHIBIT 3.1: WEB OF RELATIONSHIPS

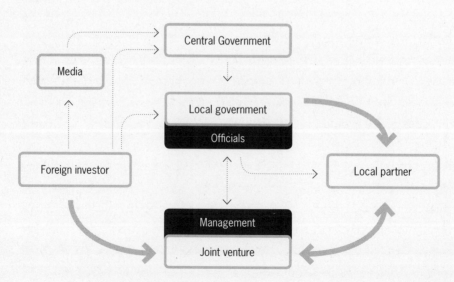

it is like a continuous struggle. However, when both dancers are able to follow the music, a beautiful dance is produced.

MNCs enjoy relatively more power than SMEs. When conditions change, MNCs can leverage their resources to influence the situation in their favor. However, SMEs can easily be the victims of these volatile situations as they have fewer resources to defend themselves. Even the judiciary route does not offer enough guarantees. The Chinese judicial system is still too immature to represent a viable system for protection. Although its effectiveness is improving, there is still a long way to go before China reaches the level of legal protection prevalent in developed countries where the rule of law is well established. Furthermore, legal ownership of enterprises is often vaguely defined and thus disputable. As an example, even today, people are still trying to guess the real ownership of Haier, the most famous home appliance maker in China.

Another interesting aspect is the dynamic gaming between central and local governments. While central governments pretend to be blind to many irregular actions by local governments, it can become extremely harsh when they cross certain lines. The smart strategy for a JV is to keep a close relationship with local government, while not irritating the Central Government – not an easy balance to maintain.

Foreign companies should establish an effective means of self-protection from the beginning when entering into a partnership with a local company. Such means include majority position in the joint venture; a legal agreement as airtight as possible; reliable *guanxi* with high-ranking local officials; and management control of the JV, especially in the area of finance and HR. It is important to clarify who the real owner of the Chinese partner is. Other advisable measures are to resort to international arbitration in case of disputes and the establishment of sound *guanxi* with Central Government officials. As it is easy to imagine, most of these issues can be avoided by establishing a WFOE or by acquiring the Chinese operation.

In case of a dispute, leveraging the influence of the media can also be a very effective defense. In China, the government and courts are strongly influenced by media reports and public opinion. It is a smart strategy to show oneself as a victim. Unfortunately, MNCs run the danger of being depicted as global giants bullying humble local enterprises, which may result in the public opinion supporting and defending the local enterprise even if they are the offenders.

As a general rule, the most efficient way to deal with conflict of interest in China is to do it informally by establishing and maintaining good relationships with the relevant parties. The legal route is time consuming, unreliable, and may damage the company's public image. In China, courts are greatly influenced by government officials and they usually protected "national interests." Thus, MNCs might have little chance of winning a dispute, especially if they are unable to provide hard evidence.

The danger is that foreign investors are often misled by the potential partner's good connections. *Guanxi* can help the joint venture to take off, but it may turn against the foreign partner if things don't go as expected. The ideal situation is to choose an honest and reliable partner, but that is not an easy task. The only reliable method is to start with someone you know who is honest, and has a proven record dealing with you or people you know.

Taking into consideration the dynamic nature of the business, MNCs must exercise control through careful structuring of the JV operation. The terms of the agreement must allow the MNC control over decisions related to key issues, such as transfer pricing, technology protection, investment and expenses, appointment of senior executives, and so on. Joint ventures should have a clear chain of command, and sufficient degree of autonomy from parent companies. MNCs must also constantly reevaluate their policies toward their local partners in accordance with the changes in the business environment. If there is any suspicion of wrongdoing, the MNC must take quick action before the partner gains enough power to put them into a difficult situation.

However, it would be unjust to characterize all Chinese partners as totally unreliable. We could certainly say the same of some foreign investors. As one consultant shared with us, some foreign investors may have had the same type of problems with a partner of any other nationality, even with partners from their own country. Finding the right partner is not an easy task in China as with anywhere else.

As the following case study shows, foreign enterprises are not always the victims and the Chinese the villains. Sometimes, JVs don't succeed due to the myopia of the foreign partners. In the following case, Peugeot had a good start but the situation began to go wrong, until Peugeot lost a golden opportunity to gain a strong position in China's automobile market. In 1985, Peugeot established a joint venture in South China. They introduced their management system, controlled key decisions, and promoted their own company culture. They even taught French to the Chinese employees. Before 1992 the JV enjoyed positive results. However, with the increase of competition, many problems emerged. The French automaker was accused of producing outdated car models at too high a price and of low quality, besides providing poor service. By 1996 its production had dropped so much that it almost ceased to operate. The situation was aggravated by serious cultural conflicts and internal fights, until the JV finally ended in divorce.

Following the case study, you will find two commentaries: the first by Per Jenster, Professor of Management, CEIBS; and the second by Wei Joo Chai, Factory Manager, Shanghai Kerry Oils and Grains Industries Ltd. The first commentary provides insightful analysis of the reasons why Guangzhou Peugeot didn't succeed, while the second analyses from the perspective of entry strategy and ways to achieve partnership strategy.

CASE STUDY
GUANGZHOU PEUGEOT AUTOMOBILE CO., LTD[4]

In 1985, the seventh year of China's opening and reform, Peugeot Citroën of France (PSA) entered China, a market believed to have huge potential. The Guangzhou Peugeot Automobile Company Ltd (GPA) was established as a JV between Peugeot and a local SOE in Guangdong Province, China's first "window" to the outside. The performance of GPA turned out to be a real disappointment. It produced only 100,000 cars during 1985–1996, and the accumulated losses amounted to 2.9 billion yuan. By 1996, GPA almost stopped production. Ironically, Shanghai Volkswagen Co., Ltd, one of Volkswagen AG's JVs, was achieving amazing success. The local partner of GPA lost its patience and threatened to exit. It seems that the distance between dreams and reality can be enormous. What should Peugeot do next?

Peugeot

Peugeot is one of the largest automobile manufacturers in Europe, dating back to the nineteenth century. Peugeot Elder Brothers Company was established in 1810, specializing in small metal accessories. The first Peugeot car was produced in 1889. Then Peugeot merged with Citroën to form PSA. Peugeot produced more than 40 million cars in more than 100 years, making it a leading car maker in the world.

China's auto industry

Shortly after the establishment of the People's Republic of China, the government decided to develop the automobile industry. In 1951, China First Auto Works (FAW) was set up. Despite the monotonous car model at that time, the output increased rapidly from 1,654 in 1956 to 40,000 in 1965, and 135,000 in 1975.

After China's opening and reform from 1978, the development of the automobile industry accelerated. After reaching an output of 200,000 in 1980, China

CASE STUDY: GUANGZHOU PEUGEOT AUTOMOBILE CO., LTD

began to introduce advanced technologies and allow joint ventures with foreign car manufacturers. In 1983, Beijing Jeep Co., Ltd was established by the Beijing Automobile Manufacturing Factory and the American Motor Company to produce Cherokee Jeeps. In 1984, Chang'An Machinery Factory and Suzuki Motor Corporation entered an agreement to produce mini cars. In the same year, Shanghai Automobile Corporation and Volkswagen AG jointly established Shanghai Volkswagen to produce Santana cars. Meanwhile, Nanjing Automobile Corporation got approval from Fiat to produce light vehicles (see CS Exhibit 3.1). Peugeot decided to follow its international peers.

China's auto industry administration system was rather complex and the power was shared by the China Automobile Corporation, provincial governments, ministries, and the automobile groups. In addition, all automobile groups reported to the State Planning Commission. In 1993, the Automobile Bureau of

CS EXHIBIT 3.1: HISTORY OF CHINA'S AUTO INDUSTRY AT A GLANCE (1949–1996)

- In **March 1951** China First Auto Works was established in Changchun.
- In **July 1956** the first made-in-China truck rolled off the lines.
- In **1967** China Second Auto Works was established.
- In **April 1983** the first Santana rolled off the lines in Shanghai.
- In **January 1984** Beijing Jeep Co., Ltd was set up as a joint venture between the American Motor Company and Beijing Auto Works.
- In **May 1984** Chang'an Machinery Factory declared the introduction of the mini cars from the Suzuki Motor Corporation.
- In **March 1985** Shanghai Volkswagen was established.
- In **March 1985** Nanjing Auto Corporation announced the introduction of Iveco from Italy.
- In **March 1985** the State approved the establishment of GPA.
- In **March 1986** Tianjin Auto Corporation announced the introduction of Xianli from the Daihatsu Motor Co., Ltd.
- In **August 1987** the State Council specified three car production bases – FAW, Second Auto Works, and Shanghai.
- In **May 1988** the Golden Cup Auto Co., Ltd was established in Shenyang.
- In **September 1988** the China North Industry (Group) Co., Ltd reached an agreement with Daimler Benz about introducing heavy cars to China.
- In **August 1989** the first batch of Audi cars rolled off the line in FAW.
- In **November 1990** Volkswagen and FAW announced the setting up of a joint venture whose target annual output was 150,000 cars, the largest auto joint venture in China so far.
- In **December 1990** the China Second Auto Works signed an agreement with Citroën to form an auto joint venture in China.
- In **April 1993** the Jiangxi Isuzu Auto Co., Ltd was established in Nanchang.

CASE STUDY: GUANGZHOU PEUGEOT AUTOMOBILE CO., LTD

Ministry of Machinery Industry was established as the regulatory body for the automobile industry.

Guangzhou Peugeot

Peugeot considered Guangdong Province an ideal place because of its neighboring location to Hong Kong, and its living standard was the highest in China. In addition, there were already many joint ventures in this province. Guangdong's long distance from Beijing was also considered an advantage that would give it more independence compared with other provinces. Most important, the local government was eager to develop its automobile industry.

Peugeot was among the first to negotiate with Guangzhou Municipal, which started from 1980. After a long and tough negotiation, GPA was finally established in September 1985. Peugeot and BNP Paribas respectively held 22% and 8% of GPA's equity. Peugeot invested its technologies. Guangzhou Auto Factory and the China International Trust and Investment Corporation (CITIC) respectively held 46% and 20% of shares. The rest of the 4% was taken by the International Finance Corporation (IFC) (see CS Exhibit 3.2). Guangzhou Auto Factory was a state-owned small factory that specialized in making passenger cars and had no experience in making sedans. GPA was supposed to produce Peugeot 504 and 505 models with a target output of 50,000. According to their 20-year agreement, GPA would be jointly managed by the Guangzhou Automobile Group and Peugeot. Especially, the GM would be appointed by Peugeot before 1994. Moreover, it was stipulated that at least one of the two managers in each department should be appointed by Peugeot and he/she would have the right to veto.[5] The agreement foresaw an investment of US$150 million and a target output of 15,000 vehicles annually in the first stage, and an investment of US$300 million and a target output of 45,000 vehicles in the second stage. Taking into consideration the strong position of Guangdong, they decided to act first and report afterwards.[6] As a

CS EXHIBIT 3.2: EQUITY STRUCTURE OF GUANGZHOU PEUGEOT

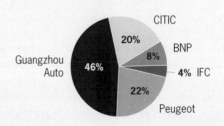

CASE STUDY: GUANGZHOU PEUGEOT AUTOMOBILE CO., LTD

result, GPA didn't get approval from the Central Government at first. Only after the establishment of GPA did Guangdong inform the Central Government.

Initial success

GPA did a lot in improving internal management and tried to standardize working procedures through a management system. They clarified responsibilities, rights, and compensations for each position. Many colloquia and parties were held to enhance the communication between foreign and Chinese employees. The company also tried to improve employee satisfaction by setting up a staff arts and sports association, building staff houses that cost 45.3 million yuan,[7] and perfecting the medical insurance, social security arrangements, and so on. In order to improve the language skills of employees, GPA sent Chinese employees to learn French at a local university, and held courses on French culture and Peugeot culture from time to time. In addition, some of the key staff would be sent to Peugeot for training.

GPA mainly produced the 504 and 505 models of Peugeot and was one of the eight car bases in China. GPA began to sell cars in 1989, targeting government officials and taxi companies. The Peugeot 505 model sold well and its sales volume jumped from 2,715 in 1987 to 20,404 in 1992, accounting for 16% of the domestic market. At the 1992 peak, Peugeot cars were so popular that buyers even had to purchase the car through *guanxi*.[8]

Problems emerged

JVs are like marriages, so conflicts are unavoidable. Even at the very beginning, Peugeot found that local employees lacked necessary skills due to the fact that most of them came from the state-owned Guangzhou Automobile Factory. GPA had to send Chinese employees to France or send expatriates to China to train Chinese staff.

The requirement of the local content ratio seemed to be an obstacle for GPA. According to the agreement, GPA should raise this ratio to 90% within five years. However, Peugeot found that there were few qualified parts suppliers and the Guangdong government prohibited procurement from other provinces to protect its interests. On the other hand, Chinese partners blamed Peugeot for intentionally delaying localization to sell more parts to GPA. Peugeot's total investment in GPA was no more than 400 million yuan, but the revenue through selling parts was as high as 4 billion yuan. In 1992, a serious dispute broke out. Peugeot planned to import engine cylinders from France while the Chinese side insisted on international bidding. After a 24-hour quarrel, they finally decided to buy the products from a German company. This event destroyed mutual trust. A survey of GPA staff said that:

> *All surveyed think that Peugeot's main objective is to make huge profits quickly. … French managers' decisions are myopic and their focus is to sell technologies, equipments and parts to GPA. … What Chinese managers care about is to develop a local auto industry, thus they focus on raising local content ratio. …*[9]

Volkswagen set up JV parts suppliers rather early, but Peugeot acted slowly and GPA had to rely on imports for a long time. Another unfavorable factor was that the French Franc appreciated about 110% against the Renminbi in the late 1980s, significantly increasing the import cost. At the beginning of the 1990s, Peugeot cars sold at 200,000 yuan per vehicle, higher than the 180,000 of Santana, its main rival. By 1992, the local content ratio of Santana had increased to 75%, while GPA only achieved that ratio by 1994. By 1997, the cheapest Peugeot car sold at 170,000 yuan, while a Santana only cost 135,000 yuan. Partly due to the restriction on procurements outside Guangdong, the quality of Peugeot cars was bad. As analyzed by some financial media:

> *What's wrong with GPA? First, Peugeot controlled the joint venture though it only holds 22 percent of shares. Before 1994, Peugeot not only appointed general managers, but also controlled such key departments as finance and procurement. As a result, the localization process of GPA has been slow, and its local content ratio only reached 65 percent in 1994, which means high import cost. It is amazing that the total compensation for about 20 expatriates from France is around 50 million yuan, which nearly equals to that of all the 3,000 Chinese staff. Moreover, Peugeot did so for its own self-interest rather than the interest of the joint venture.*[10]

CASE STUDY: GUANGZHOU PEUGEOT AUTOMOBILE CO., LTD

In those good old days, most of GPA's profits were distributed in the form of dividends. However, Shanghai Volkswagen reinvested its profits into upgrading production facilities and technologies, and successfully designed a new model Santana 2000 in the mid-1990s, when GPA still held on to the old model. The Peugeot 505 was first produced in 1978 as a new-generation product of the Peugeot 504, and became obviously uncompetitive and outdated in China by the mid-1990s. The Peugeot looked less distinguished than FAW's Audi 100, which was more attractive to government officials who were identity-sensitive (see CS Exhibit 3.3). Moreover, the Peugeot was not ideal for taxi purposes due to its high oil consumption.[11] Wu Yingqiao, an industry expert, said:

CS EXHIBIT 3.3: PEUGEOT 505, SANTANA 2000 AND AUDI 100

CASE STUDY: GUANGZHOU PEUGEOT AUTOMOBILE CO., LTD

> *When GPA was established, Peugeot was experiencing a difficult time in new model design. It is natural that the Peugeot 505 looks unattractive.*[12]

GPA obtained less support from local government than Shanghai Volkswagen. The Shanghai government invested as much as 5–6 billion yuan in supporting Shanghai Volkswagen, while the corresponding support for GPA was no more than 1 billion yuan. In Guangzhou, which was relatively open and free, the government was not willing to push officials and enterprises to buy Peugeot cars, while almost all taxi cars were Santana. In order to prevent Tianjin Xianli entering the Shanghai market, the Shanghai government made a strict requirement for taxi engineer standards in 1996. The seeming advantage of staying far away from Beijing was now a disadvantage because the Central Government gave little support to GPA. In March 1994, the State Planning Commission issued the Auto Industry Policy, which declared the support of eight major car makers; that is, the "Big Three," "Small Three," and "Mini Two."[13] Though the Guangzhou Automobile Group appeared in the list, GPA was absent from the project list that was supported by the Central Government. An employee of GPA complained:

> *GPA has been an "orphan". At the beginning of the 1980s, Guangzhou was positioned as a Separate Planning City, which was under the charge of the State Planning Commission rather than Guangdong Province. In the negotiation process, the Chinese side described Guangzhou as "The heaven is high and the emperor is far away", which became an embarrassment rather than freedom. At that time, the State Planning Commission decided quotas of imported parts and car output. Guangzhou's position as a Separate Planning City made it difficult to obtain enough quotas from the Central Government. GPA also seemed to have few useful partners.*[14]

GPA's marketing model was also problematic. Due to the government policy and system at that time, GPA's sales were outsourced to an independent local company. Thus, it was hardly possible to adopt the dealership model that is common in international auto markets. Inconceivably, people in North China had to travel to Beijing to buy Peugeot cars. Jia Xinguang, an auto expert, gave a sound analysis:

GPA produced cars by assembling pre-made completely knocked-down (CKD) kits and had no long-term plan in China … The performance of the Peugeot car is poor but the price is higher than that of Santana. Peugeot sold well before 1992, when the market was a sellers' market, and it couldn't make its way through any more when the market became a buyers' market in 1994. In addition, GPA was relatively conservative in marketing operations, and was reluctant to make enough investment in production, management, and marketing. We can say that it is doomed to fail.[15]

Zeng Qinghong, vice-general manager of the former Guangzhou Passenger Car Group, added:

GPA's products are okay and it was even once difficult to buy Peugeot cars. However, the after-sale service, quality, cost control, and product upgrades are poor. How can such a product be a bestseller?

An article introduced the Peugeot 505 and it pointed out some design problems:[16]

Though Peugeot 505's engine performance was average, its underpan was good, making it one of the few car models that could reach a speed of more than 100 miles per hour in China at that time. However, there were no highways in China; bad road conditions made its advantage useless. In addition, the design of Peugeot 505 was quite European in style. Its air-conditioner system was too weak, in that Guangdong was much hotter than France. Moreover, its circuit system broke down easily in such a moist environment as Guangdong's. The inexperienced Chinese partner failed to find these problems.

Since the Chinese partner had no experience in making sedans and Guangdong's manufacturing industry was still weak, the rise of the local content ratio resulted in a deterioration of the Peugeot cars' quality. Chinese consumers discarded Peugeot 505 even two years earlier than French consumers, which was an exception in the car history of developing countries.

With the acquiescence of local government, some illegal car markers destroyed the auto market order in Guangdong. These car makers assembled cars with imported, mostly illegal, parts. In the mid-1990s, there were more than 70 il-legal car makers with an annual output of less than 100 cars each. Although local government announced they had closed many of them, some car makers continued to produce and sell the newest foreign car models and seized about 10% of the Guangdong market.

Cultural conflicts

Potential cultural and interest conflicts should also be held responsible for the decline of GPA. One former GPA employee who later got a PhD in strategy management from the University of Illinois described vividly his feeling for GPA:[17]

> *Most Chinese staff study hard to learn French, but foreigners don't learn Chinese ... Foreigners' pride not only exists in language, but also in every aspect in management. ... French managers tend to ignore Chinese managers because they lack modern management skills and experience, say nothing of learning from the Chinese. However, Chinese managers, many of whom were powerful and respected people before joining GPA, are angry with the French managers' manners. Unavoidably, they will do something unfavorable to the company secretly. ... Neither does the company learn from customers ... As far as Peugeot 504 and 505 are concerned, taxi companies consider it too oil-consuming, and government officials consider it not distinguished enough. Regrettably, GPA has been blind to these complaints.*

A survey among GPA managers and employees disclosed the rooted cultural division:[18]

> *French people are strict in working and brave enough to express ... opinions. ... Chinese employees are relatively implicative and seldom make straightforward speeches. As a result, the French dominated management of the joint venture, and Chinese managers felt left aside. ...*
>
> *GPA transplanted the line functional structure of Peugeot and emphasized hierarchy and divisions. The Peugeot system was based on extensive experience in more than 20 countries and required employees to obey rules and standards without any discount. But in fact most Chinese employees had been working in a no-competition*

environment, and many of them were lazy and ignored rules from time to time. …
Thus, some jobs failed to reach the Peugeot standards. As an illustration, some car
parts should be localized to satisfy the local content requirement. However, domestic
parts couldn't meet the requirements of Peugeot drawings and this led to some
operational errors and inferior quality. French employees were angry with this, while
Chinese employees had difficulties which were hard to explain. …

GPA's system was basically that of Peugeot, and it didn't fit the Chinese situa-
tion well. Moreover, they didn't discuss rules and standards before implementing and
Chinese employees were resistant to them. The enforcement of French managers only
incurred more resistance from Chinese employees. As a result, Chinese employees
tried to use Chinese ways whenever possible and were reluctant to help French
managers perfect the system.

The tough method of the French side finally led to a strike because Chinese
employees couldn't tolerate the insults by French managers.[19]

As showed by the survey, two-thirds of questionnaires and all interviewees thought that Chinese and French partners failed to align investment objectives. Twenty-seven percent of interviewees mentioned the huge value difference in the JV, 67% of interviewees thought that GPA had no clear corporate values. In terms of decisions, 55% of interviewees pointed out that Chinese decision styles were different from those of the French. Although it was stipulated that major decisions should be agreed to by both sides, French managers were reluctant to negotiate with Chinese managers.

Decline

The honeymoon period was short. From the second half of 1993, stockpiles appeared in China's auto market. The problems with Peugeot cars (like an outdated model, bad quality, high oil consumption, expensive accessories, and poor service) made Peugeot a bad choice. In 1993, only 16,763 Peugeot cars were sold. However, total sales in China's auto market soared. In 1994, GPA only produced 4,485 cars and 1,241 trucks, and its loss amounted to 100–200 million yuan. Meanwhile, the output of Shanghai Volkswagen reached the new high of 100,000. Though GPA's output bounced to 7,000 in 1995, its loss

CASE STUDY: GUANGZHOU PEUGEOT AUTOMOBILE CO., LTD

enlarged to 320 million yuan. In contrast, Shanghai Volkswagen enjoyed an exciting profit of 2 billion yuan in 1995. In 1996, GPA's output was reduced to 2,544, while Shanghai Volkswagen's output rose to 146,000, which accounted for 50% of China's auto market. Due to the sharp deterioration of the financial status (see CS Exhibit 3.4), GPA's assets and liabilities were respectively 3.05 billion and 3.04 billion yuan by the end of 1996, meaning that the company was nearly bankrupt. Ironically, GPA invested 1.47 billion yuan in car production facilities and 1.8 billion yuan in 25 auto parts enterprises during its 10-year history, but its maximum output was only 20,000 and accumulated output was as small as 100,000.

CS EXHIBIT 3.4: FINANCIAL DATA OF GPA (1992–1995)

Items	1992	1993	1994	1995
Gross output (RMB '0,000)	196,153	256,540	69,998	101,266
Fixed assets (RMB '0,000)	427,670	52,612	87,205	107,145
Sales revenue (RMB '0,000)	244,438	255,832	85,351	109,776
Profit before tax (RMB 100 million)	2.97	3.03	0.98	n/a
Profit after tax (RMB 100 million)	1.87	1.90	0.05	-3.21

Source: Vanhonacker, Wilfried R., "Guangzhou Peugeot Automobile Company Ltd: Partnership Breakdown," INSEAD/CEIBS, 1999.

Time to make a decision

It was not the first failure that Guangdong province experienced in developing its auto industry. In 1989, Panda Motors planned to invest US$1 billion in Guangdong to build an export-oriented factory. Due to its lack of experience in auto-making, Panda Motors was only a tool of the Unification Church to test the China market, and closed in 1996 without a single car produced. In 1995, Mercedes-Benz decided to establish a mini-car factory in Guangdong and an auto engine factory in Hainan, which neighbors Guangdong. The total investment amounted to US$591 million, but the plan was finally laid aside due to a dispute between the Chinese and German investors.

In 1992, the Chinese side began to negotiate with the French side about the third phase of GPA, which was expected to reach an output of 150,000, costing 900 million yuan. Peugeot hoped to invest its technology, but the Chinese side thought it was worth little. The negotiation came to a dead end. After the bad

CASE STUDY: GUANGZHOU PEUGEOT AUTOMOBILE CO., LTD

situation with GPA, the Chinese side doubted whether Guangzhou should even develop an auto industry. But what was to be done with these huge costs and more than 2,000 employees? The Guangzhou government finally decided to change its French partner.

Citroën, another brand of PSA, also found its plan in China filled with frustration. In 1987 Citroën began its contact with China Second Auto Works, later known as Dongfeng Auto Co., Ltd, and gained approval to establish a JV in 1989. However, the JV, Dongfeng Peugeot Citroën Automobile Co., Ltd., did not produce cars until 1996.

Peugeot obviously held different opinions about the difficulties of GPA. An executive of GPA complained:

Peugeot only held 22% of all shares, and couldn't control sales.[20] At that time, both the amount of imported parts and [level of] car production were controlled by the State Planning Commission. Chinese concepts of consumption were also different from those in France.[21]

In other countries, specialty stores can combine the functions of sales, after-sale services, car maintenance, customer survey, and so on, which cannot be implemented in China. Actually, marketing is absent in GPA. We even had no idea of what customers like, need and complain about, and their affordability. GPA's decline seemed to be inevitable.[22]

Seeing the admirable achievements of Shanghai Volkswagen, Peugeot had a quite bitter feeling. Japanese car makers didn't enter China due to a concern over the small scale of China's auto markets. By the mid-1990s their worries disappeared. As soon as the Guangzhou government hinted that new partners would be welcome, many leading car manufacturers, including GM, Ford, BMW, and Honda, rushed in. How should Peugeot handle this miserable marriage?

CASE COMMENTARIES

COMMENTARY 1
PER V. JENSTER, PHD
PROFESSOR OF MANAGEMENT
CHINA EUROPE INTERNATIONAL BUSINESS SCHOOL (CEIBS)

Peugeot's entry into China in the mid-1980s was visionary and aggressive, and its decision to set up the Guangzhou Peugeot Automobile joint venture was intended to give the company an early entrant's advantage. In contrast, Japanese car makers exhibited a more pessimistic view about China's auto market and the opportunity to achieve economies of scale without being able to develop a sound distribution infrastructure. It turned out that the Peugeot choice of Guangzhou Auto Factory, controlled by Guangzhou government, was less than an ideal candidate for several reasons:

- First, the Guangzhou Auto Factory had little experience in sedan production and marketing, thus adding limited value to the joint venture.
- Second, at that time, the Central Government had significant control and its policies had a decisive influence on the success of auto projects.
- Third, despite its strong will in developing the local auto industry, Guangdong province lacked the necessary industry infrastructures and local government was reluctant to support the auto industry through administrative interventions. Actually, taking into consideration Peugeot's bad relations with local government caused by its perceived arrogance and toughness in the JV, local government naturally had no incentive to provide extra support.

The decline of Guangzhou Peugeot can be attributed to many reasons, including poor market knowledge and inferior product design, quality, pricing, service, and marketing. However, all these problems were rooted in poor management of the JV.

Although JVs had some advantage over local companies, these initial advantages concealed the subsequent problems of dual parenthood. With the increase in competition, these problems were destined to surface sooner or later. Therefore, it is reasonable to attribute the failure of Guangzhou Peugeot to the following reasons:

- Peugeot was reluctant to localize, as manifested by expatriates only emphasizing learning French, transplanting the Peugeot system without making necessary adaptations, and ignoring Chinese managers even though the Chinese side held more shares in the JV.
- The joint venture did not establish its own mission, vision, and shared values and culture, thus intensifying the internal hostile atmosphere.
- Peugeot had no long-term commitment to the joint venture, which led to myopic behaviors such as outdated car models, a high dividend payout ratio, and short-term profits from selling parts to the JV.
- Peugeot didn't respect its local partner and destroyed mutual trust. Without support from Chinese managers and employees, systems could not be appropriately implemented. The hostile atmosphere from the Chinese workers resulted in a serious strike where the Chinese Central Government and French Consulate had to intervene; this greatly damaged the image of Peugeot.

In retrospect, Saint-Geours, president of Peugeot, summarized three lessons to succeed in China. He believed in choosing a large company as a partner, in providing [the] newest and [most] modern car models, and in a well-organized sales network.

However, there are lessons far beyond these, including respecting the local partner, respecting local staff, having long-term commitment and patience, establishing values and a vision for the JV, maintaining a sound relationship with the Central Government, and most importantly, knowing the local market and consumers. In the process of trust building, effective communication and mutual benefits are very important. In order to know your future partner well, you should obtain as much information as possible, including business license, brochure, legal representative, industry competition, and awards the company received. Especially, a site visit is imperative in order to get reliable information. You should try to observe employee attitudes and talk to managers, from the lowest to the highest ranks.

The Chinese side also had a lot to learn. First, leave enough equity to the foreign partner to make the venture sufficiently interesting and to avoid potential conflicts of interest. Second, insist on equal power, or at least the necessary power, to protect yourself. Third, build a vision, trust, and commitment. Last, but most important, choose a qualified partner with the strength, motivation, commitment, and willingness to invest.

Research to identify cultural-, information- and networking-related factors: key success factors with the following details.

Cultural-related factors:

- developing interpersonal relationships
- familiarity with the Chinese negotiation process
- understanding the Chinese thinking process
- learning traditional Chinese management styles
- becoming acquainted with Chinese criteria for employee evaluation and work assessment.

Information- and networking-related factors:

- effective communication with Chinese firms from overseas
- effective communication within China
- efficiently and legally collecting business and industry information in China
- recruiting technical personnel locally

- developing regular contacts with Chinese government agencies
- understanding Chinese governmental policies
- understanding the relationships between Chinese partners and corresponding government agencies
- recognizing the real authority (or decision-makers) within Chinese organizations and local governmental agencies.

In April 1996 the Guangzhou government decided to change the partner in Guangzhou Peugeot Automobile Co., Ltd. The Guangzhou government had become more cautious in choosing a new partner and listed 19 conditions. Competitors for the opportunity included BMW, Benz, Fiat, Opel, Hyundai, and Honda. In May 1998 the Guangzhou government and Honda established a JV, Guangzhou Honda, which turned out to be a surprising success.

Guangzhou Honda was very efficient and only five months after its establishment, the first car rolled off line. In addition, Guangzhou Honda spent only less than US$200 million to establish a facility with an output of 30,000 vehicles per year. The first car model of Guangzhou Honda was the Accord, which had been a bestseller for the previous six years in the United States. Despite the big failure in Guangzhou Peugeot, the Guangzhou government finally turned its auto dream into reality through its cooperation with Honda.

COMMENTARY 2

WEI JOO CHAI

FACTORY MANAGER

SHANGHAI KERRY OILS AND GRAINS INDUSTRIES LTD

Peugeot was one of the first foreign car manufacturers to enter the China automobile industry in a time when automobile output in the country was increasing rapidly. However, it did not achieve the same success as its competitor Volkswagen AG, which entered China more or less at the same time. It missed the opportunity to establish a strong foothold in the Chinese market despite its early entry. Before deciding its next move, Peugeot has to examine what went wrong between 1985 and 1996.

On the surface, causes of the JV failure with Guangzhou local government seem to be too obvious: car models that did not meet market demand, poor quality, lack of strong local parts suppliers, and poor marketing. But these are just symptoms of the problems. Two fundamental issues that should have been addressed were an entry strategy and a partnership synergy.

Entry strategy

Strategic goal: First, Peugeot had to be clear about its strategic goal for entering the Chinese automobile market. Was it a short-term goal to reap profit from technology investment and sale of parts? Or was the company really serious in regarding China as a strategically important market with a huge potential for growth? From the case study we could not tell what the intention of the company was. But from its actions and behavior it is perceived to be more of the former. Peugeot invested 22% in the JV in the form of technology, but the GM and at least one or two managers in each department were appointed by Peugeot. Progress in the localization of the management team was slow. Peugeot's commitment in terms of investment, localization of the team, introduction of new models and technology, and developing a local components partner did not substantiate the seriousness in establishing a long-term foothold in the Chinese market.

Entry mode: There is a spectrum of options to enter into a new market. On one side the involvement could be a minimal investment commitment as a business partner in the form of supplier, consultant, and so on. On the other side there is full commitment in terms of equity investment. Between the two are various forms, including contractual arrangement, partnership, or JV equity investment. In this case a JV arrangement seems to be appropriate to acquire a certain equity stake for a production base in China. It is not possible in the regulatory context for such investment to occur without a local government partner.

Selection of partner: It is easy to comment in retrospect that maybe Peugeot should have gone to Shanghai where the government was more supportive and committed in developing a local car industry. Or maybe Peugeot should have waited for approval from the Central Government before completing the deal, as it is important in the complicated administration system of China's automobile industry to get support from all the parties concerned. The second concern is valid. But for the first concern, nobody could have known in the beginning how committed local government would be. Peugeot had its valid reason to select Guangzhou as its entry base in view of its booming economy and eagerness of local government to develop the industry. The key issue is management of a partnership relationship, which will be discussed below.

Partnership synergy

Mutual goals: There seemed to be a lack of consensus in terms of the mutual goals of the JV. Guangzhou local government hoped that through partnership with a strong foreign player they could expedite development of the local automobile industry. If it were the strategic intention of Peugeot to establish a long-term and strong presence in China, both parties could have identified mutual goals that resulted in a win–win situation, as follows:

- The introduction of improved technology to gain a competitive advantage in the market. This would include manufacturing technology to improve efficiency and quality, or technology for improved functionality of the cars.
- Fast growth in market share with the right products, complementary marketing and distribution channels, appropriate support from a local partner, and so on.

- The development of strong local parts supply partners.
- The localization of a management team.

The above goals were not manifested in the actions of both partners. Car models introduced were not attractive to the buyers. Fuel consumption was high, air-conditioning was weak, and the appearance was not distinguished enough for government officials. The quality of the car was also lower than expected. Due to slow localization progress, the JV had developed few strong local part suppliers. This resulted in high costs and also affected car quality. Local partners did not provide sufficient support to the venture in terms of marketing and sales. There was no requirement for government bureaus and taxi companies to give priority to cars produced by the venture. The marketing company appointed by the local partner was ineffective, and Peugeot had no control over sales. There was a lack of integration in the management team between foreign and local managers.

Trust: During the years of the JV, the partners failed to build trust. The French managers tended to ignore the Chinese managers because they lacked modern management skills and experience, and they did not take initiatives to learn the local culture. This did not help with trust building. The company spent a lot of effort in improving staff welfare and employee satisfaction, and encouraging local employees to learn the French language and culture. Improving staff satisfaction is different from building trust, which requires open communication, and team effort toward common goals. The French managers were perceived as arrogant and aloof by the Chinese managers. The company's system was basically that of Peugeot, and was implemented without discussion and consultation with local staff. There was also conflict in *management style*. The French are more open and direct in their communication style, whereas the Chinese prefer a more implied way to express opinion. All these contributed to sub-optimal decisions where local managers were unwilling to highlight certain decisions not appropriate in the local context. In some cases, the local managers even secretly did something detrimental to the company. The consequence was a vicious cycle of suspicion and distrust within the company.

From the above discussion it is not difficult to see that the seeds of failure had been planted in the JV from inception. Insufficient commitment, no alignment of goals, and inappropriate handling of mutual relationship not only did not bring out the intended synergy between the two partners, they actually caused damage to the JV, as evidenced by a series of mistakes and sub-optimized decisions.

Moving ahead

Over 10 years the mistrust and unhappy relationship between the two partners was too difficult to be reversed. Peugeot needed to learn from past mistakes for future endeavors with other local partners. They need to note the following:

- Commitment should be compatible with its long-term strategic goal, in terms of technology transfer, developing new models, re-investment of profits, and so on.
- Proper approval should be sought from all relevant parties in the earliest stage.
- Both parties should seriously talk about the goals of the venture and ensure that they are acceptable to both sides.
- The next step is a more detailed discussion on how to achieve the above goals, and a timetable should be set.
- Peugeot needs to be more sensitive to local culture and make an effort in nurturing trust from the beginning.
- Open discussion and the integration of the management team should be emphasized. Everyone in the management team should be given the opportunity to be involved in discussions and management decision-making.
- The localization process, in terms of the management team and

local parts suppliers, should be placed high on the agenda and demonstrated by actions.

Just like for any other company, to be successful the JV must function as one team, one integrated organization. Simply put, two teams in a venture to serve respective self-interests just won't work. In this case, the outcome is a lose–lose situation, a far cry from the intended synergy effect.

NOTES

1 Richard McGregor, "Bad Blood in Beverage Land," *FT.com*, London, October 1, 2002, p. 1.

2 "Crossing the River by Feeling Each Stone" refers to Deng Xiaoping's policy of moving ahead with economic reforms slowly and pragmatically.

3 "Crouching tiger, hidden dragon" is a term used by the Chinese to describe people who look ordinary but actually have excellent Kongfu. This term is also the title of an Oscar-winning film directed by Ang Lee.

4 This case was prepared by Dr. Shengjun Liu under the supervision of Professor Juan A. Fernandez at CEIBS. The case was prepared on the basis of class discussion, rather than to illustrate the effective or ineffective handling of an administrative situation. Certain names and other identifying information may have been disguised to protect confidentiality. The case was originally published by CEIBS in 2004. Published with permission.

5 As far as Shanghai Volkswagen was concerned, each side appointed five Board members and the Chinese side appointed a chairman of the Board.

6 In China, the Central Government paid attention to the overall planning of the country but local government only cared how to ensure the growth of local economy. Thus, local government often eluded the intervention from the Central Government by means of act first and report afterwards.

7 Renminbi (RMB), literally "the people's money," is China's official currency. The basic unit of the currency is yuan. In 2004, US$1 = 8.26 yuan approx.

8 Literally translated, *guanxi* means "relationship," but its meaning is much deeper than that. It's a semi-formal system of cultivating and maintaining profitable relationships (particularly in business) by giving and receiving favors. *Guanxi* leads to more *guanxi* in the same way that business networks are formed in the United States, except that it is almost impossible for strangers to develop *guanxi* on their own. Instead, some type of relationship must exist before "formal" *guanxi* (the exchanging of favors, even if that favor is simply to return a phone call) can be established. (Source: Eloise Kendy, "China Communiqué: 'Guanxi' and groundwater," *Queen City News*, December 11, 2002).

9 Li Ye, et al., "A Survey on the Cross-culture Management in Guangzhou Peugeot," *Journal of South China Polytechnic University*, 1998.

10 Ma Henghai, "A View on the Crisis and Future of China's Auto Industry: Lessons from the Exit of Peugeot," *Auto and Parts*, p. 15, 1997.

11 Governments and enterprises respectively accounted for 58% and 24% of the Chinese auto market, and families only had limited purchasing ability.

12 Zhou Guangjun, "Peugeot, the Once Failure, Come Back Again," *Beijing Entertainment Newspaper*, April 2004.

13 The "Big Three" refers to First Auto Works, Second Auto Works, and Shanghai Volkswagen; the "Small Three" refers to Tianjin Auto, Beijing Auto, and the Guangzhou Automobile Group; the "Mini Two" refers to Guizhou Yunque and Chang'an Auto.

14 Ge Xiao, "My Days at Guangzhou Peugeot," *Bund Pictorial*, May 1, 2003.

15 Yang Mingwei, "Will Guangzhou Honda Become Another Guangzhou Peugeot?" *China Economy Times*, May 14, 2001.

16 Ye Hong, "A Strange Evergreen Tree: The History of Peugeot 505," *Auto Fans*, April 3, 2004.

17 Ge Xiao, "My Days at Guangzhou Peugeot," *Bund Pictorial*, May 1, 2003.

18 The survey interviewed 10 middle-level managers, sent out 40 questionnaires, and reclaimed 33 of them.

19 Li Ye, et al., "A Survey on the Cross-Culture Management in Guangzhou Peugeot," *Journal of South China Polytechnic University*, 1998.

20 Volkswagen had a 50% stake in Shanghai Volkswagen.

21 Wang Danni, "Interview With President of Peugeot China: Come Back After Six Years, Make History Experience," *GD-HK Information Daily*, December 14, 2003.

22 Wang Zheng, "Peugeot Come Back With Priority on Marketing," *People's Daily*, August 4, 2003.

Chapter 4
Dealing with headquarters: The art of juggling

INTRODUCTION

It would be a mission impossible to propose a general model on how to organize international operations valid for every type of company. Each has its own characteristics, depending on the nature of their business, their global strategy, their history, culture, size and geographical span, and, last but not least, the type of leadership they have. On top of all these, organizations have to adapt in a dynamic way to the changing business environment. This requires a sporadic modification to their structures.

The organization design can never be perfect; even if it works well under certain conditions, the dynamic nature of the environment and internal growth makes it less efficient with time. Multiple business units, in combination with different geographical zones, make the design of organizations a constant challenge. Besides, the smooth and efficient working among the different parts of the organization depends not only on its systems and design but also on the quality of its leadership.

In a multi-business global organization, there are often four protagonists interacting with each other, as depicted in Exhibit 4.1.

The main task of business managers is to coordinate the activities of their businesses across the different geographical areas in which they operate. This implies identifying business opportunities and achieving global-scale efficiency and competitiveness. The functional manager must achieve economies of scale by centralizing certain functions, such as finance and human resources, while leaving some degree of autonomy to the different country and business units to adapt to the different legal and market conditions of their locations. Country managers focus on the needs of their local markets, relationship with the host government, and coordination of activities of the different businesses in their

EXHIBIT 4.1: THE FOUR PROTAGONISTS

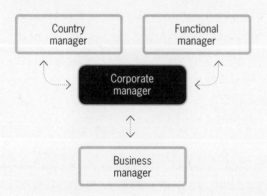

area of influence. Finally, the corporate manager must balance the needs of the above-mentioned three protagonists, allocate resources, and identify opportunities and risks across borders and across businesses.

It is beyond the purpose of this introduction to analyze the complexity of this network of relationships. Instead, we will focus on two of the protagonists: the corporate and the country managers.

The corporate manager

The main responsibility of the corporate manager is to add value to the different business units and regions. People at headquarters (HQ) may be busy with visiting operations in different countries and preparing strategic plans, but in the end all activity is useless if it doesn't add value to such operations. To add value HQ should be doing something that the various units cannot do by themselves.

Kenichi Ohmae[1] declared, "For many companies, even – perhaps especially – those with decades of international experience, it has been difficult to move beyond the headquarters-dominated form of multinational organization. Habit dies hard. Headquarters, after all, were where the critical decisions got made; headquarters were the center of the universe. Local subsidiaries might have been closer to customers, but they were distinctly second-class citizens." And he concludes, "No one imagines the headquarters should serve them."

It is sometimes difficult for headquarters to materialize this mentality change, which implies a shift from masters to partners, or even servants that assist and help their different country units. One danger Ohmae indicates is the impulse by people at headquarters to manage by averages; that is, to neglect the differences between regions in the world and apply standard solutions to all. No doubt HQ play an important role in coordinating and establishing the general direction of the corporation, but it is also critical that they listen to and support their country units.

To avoid this problem, corporate managers must develop a deep understanding of the critical success factors (CSFs) of each business unit in their organization.

A parent that does not understand the CSFs in a business is likely to destroy value instead of creating it.

Corporate managers should identify those CSFs and consequently the opportunities for adding value to their country operations. One way of doing this is by:

- listing major challenges faced by a business
- examining each challenge to see whether it contains a parenting opportunity
- documenting what influences the parent has on the business and whether those influences are addressing parenting opportunities.

Corporate managers must intervene in order to create the conditions for sharing and cooperation among the business units (BUs). Often BU managers compete with one another for resources, recognition, and ultimately for a job promotion. They respond to that pressure by engaging in self-interested behavior, acting like barons seeking favor from the king. Corporate managers, therefore, must encourage interaction among the senior executive group. Better communication and teamwork lubricate the tension, forcing senior executives to deal with one another, face to face, enhancing the opportunities for executives to talk and to learn from one another.

Corporate executives must also manage the political conflicts among BUs. They must use their authority to provide superior solutions in ways that no other BU or regional executives can. Corporate executives must also be able to link the activities of the different parts of the company so they follow the overall strategy.

What actions can be initiated at head office? Here are some ideas:

- recruit and promote people across countries
- promote international rotation and career paths
- develop international management skills by facilitating training programs with people from different regions
- use cross-divisional and cross-geographical teams
- create competence centers at international level
- establish communication systems not only toward the center, but also laterally among the different parts of the organization

- increase the diversity of top management by including different nationalities
- increase the diversity of the Board of Directors by incorporating international members
- send the most capable people where the critical action is. After their assignment, these people can return to head office with the experience they have gained.

Some companies have established country Boards of Directors to appraise local management, help units to respond faster to local conditions, assist in strategic planning in the region, and supervise the ethical conduct of the unit. They can also appoint a chairman from the host country that can help to integrate with the local community and the local political system.

The country manager

The role of the country manager, especially in a country as big as China, resembles very closely the role of the corporate CEO. China is a country of continental size in area and in population.

The following diagram is a representation of the web of relationships, of which the country manager shares a part. The type of relationship is different, depending on the company. In more complex matrix organizations, the number of lines can be exponentially proliferate, making any decision a slow and convoluted process.

EXHIBIT 4.2: COUNTRY MANAGER LINKS

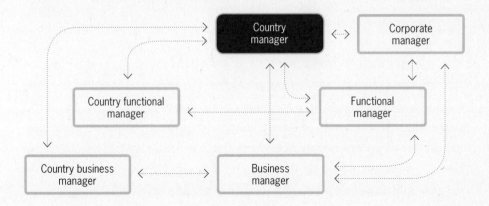

Generally, the country manager needs to interpret local information and communicate it to HQ. Another important condition is that they should be imbued by the corporate culture and be able to transmit it to the units under their supervision. They must also have enough influence and assertiveness to defend the country unit at HQ so that they can make the necessary adaptations to the corporate strategy when executed in their areas of responsibility.

John A. Quelch and Helen Bloom[2] identified a number of roles for the country manager:

1 Government relations: as MNCs extend their activities to more and more countries, they must deal with many different types of government.
2 Local customers: the country manager must respond to the increasing local customer desire for personal attention.
3 Local competitors: country managers need decision power at the local level, not only to compete successfully with other MNCs, but also to avoid being outflanked by nimble local rivals.
4 Acquisitions and JV: MNCs are responding to global competition by expanding their operations through local acquisitions and JVs. Country managers have an important business development role: looking for local companies to acquire and identifying promising partners.
5 Ideas: new products and best practices are usually generated in the field by people who observe and listen attentively to customers, not by HQ executives. Good country managers create the conditions that invite employees to put forward ideas.
6 Organizational efficiency: country managers must often balance product, function, and geography to realize the smooth running and efficiency of the company in their regions of influence.

In very general terms, we can say that the role of the country manager can vary, depending on the development stage of the company operations. In the early stage the country manager acts as an entrepreneur and has to be able to understand local markets, generate ideas, and take advantage of opportunities. At this stage the country manager usually operates autonomously within general guidelines from headquarters. In the growth stage, country managers must combine the entrepreneurial spirit of the initial stage with the skills of an administrator. They must be able to implement the systems and the structure for the organization to grow. Finally, once the company operations are well established their role changes again. Their role becomes that of a strategic partner of the head office with a say in the strategy executed in the region under their responsibility. The three stages can be performed by the same person if that person has the necessary flexibility to grow with the operations of their company. However, the central office can decide to send executives with the management strengths that fit a particular stage of development of their Chinese operations.

As we have discussed, flexibility and adaptation are important for a sound HQ-subsidiary relationship. In China, flexibility is of special importance due to its significant difference from Western culture, the rapidly changing institutional environment, as well as the huge size of its market. As a Chinese saying goes, "A general could disregard orders from the emperor when he is fighting in the battlefield." The underlying logic lies in the asymmetrical information between HQ and subsidiary.

In the following Picanol case study, you will have the opportunity to understand the painful situation for many expatriate managers. Picanol was founded as a family business in 1936. It manufactures weaving machines for the textile industry and is headquartered in Belgium. Following the changes in corporate strategy initiated by the new CEO, Picanol China is facing great challenges to redesign its organization structure. The case traces the development of the new organization and new HR system, together with the problems that ensued. It also discusses how an expatriate manager works with HQ and local employees. The case describes the history of Picanol and the company under the new CEO, who introduced a new business unit structure. Picanol China, under the leadership of expatriate manager Hans, is in a dilemma – whether to implement the new structure rigidly or be flexible.

Following the case, you will find three commentaries: the first by Willem Burgers, Professor of Marketing and Strategy, CEIBS; the second by Hans-Peter Bouvard, Director Business Dev. Northern Asia, Reichle + De-Massari Far East (Pte) Ltd; and the third by Gary An, General Manager, Amphenol East Asia Electronic Technology (Shenzhen) Co., Ltd, and Amphenol Commercial Products (Chengdu) Co., Ltd. The commentaries make sound analysis of the dilemma the protagonist is facing, the pros and cons of different solutions, as well as the strategy for handling the challenge.

CASE STUDY
PICANOL CHINA[3]

"This is going to be big challenge!" Hans de Gusseme, General Manger, Picanol Sales & Services, China, closed the door of his corner office. Past the glass walls, people could tell that he was having serious thoughts. De Gusseme had just finished reading a big package sent from the company's new CEO, Jan Coene. In the package, Coene detailed his strategy for Picanol and introduced a radically different organization structure. De Gusseme had expected some big changes from Coene, but he had never imagined such an innovative organization design. He was a little excited, but most of all he was worried. He wondered whether the new design would work in the Chinese market. Would the new design cause big disruptions to his business?

Picanol N.V.[4]

Picanol is a leading designer and manufacturer of high-performance weaving machines for the textile industry, headquartered in Ieper, Belgium. Picanol had branches in the United States, Asia, and Europe. Since 1968 the company had been listed on the Brussels Stock Exchange, and later Euronext. In 2000 it made about 6,000 machines a year and had some 80,000 Picanol weaving machines used in 2,600 mills around the world (see CS Exhibit 4.1 for Picanol's weaving machines). More than 2,100 employees worked for Picanol globally in 2002.

Picanol was founded by the Steverlynck family in 1936, and had always remained in the control of the family. The company went through significant technology development and fast market expansion under the 40-year management of Emmanuel Steverlynck. Emmanuel was a man of strong character and managed Picanol single-handed. In 1986 his son Patrick Steverlynck became the president and CEO of the company (see Appendix for a detailed history of Picanol management). The textile industry was maturing. Weaving machine manufacturers faced a very challenging environment to stay in business. Many players went through mergers and acquisitions to survive. Despite the adverse environment, Patrick had the vision of "developing Picanol into the best textile group."

At the time Patrick took control, Picanol was still a family-run firm in essence.

CS EXHIBIT 4.1: THE WEAVING MACHINES OF PICANOL

CASE STUDY: PICANOL CHINA

The Steverlynck family, as the major shareholder, made most of the operation decisions. Initially, Patrick brought in two GMs, intending to install professional management at Picanol. The company used a typical functional design of many SMEs for its organization (see CS Exhibit 4.2 for the organization chart). One GM was responsible for "Technical"-related businesses such as R&D and production, while another GM took control of "Economics." As Picanol grew, each functional group became bigger. This affected Picanol's agility, resulting in slower response to business requests and changes. The function-based organization structure made it inefficient when dealing with increasingly complicated market needs.

In 2000 Patrick communicated to shareholders that he wanted to broaden Picanol's business range in order to break the cyclical nature of machine business. This caused significant concerns among shareholders. They questioned whether diversification was a viable strategy and whether the organization leadership was ready for such a daunting task. Meanwhile, Picanol remained a traditional company in terms of management. The top management was composed mostly of Flemish nationals, who had been with the company a long time. Patrick realized that the incumbent management lacked the capability to achieve his vision,

CS EXHIBIT 4.2: PICANOL N.V. ORGANIZATION CHART BEFORE JAN COENE

and he decided to bring in someone who had a successful track record managing a diversified, global organization. In March 2001 Coene became the new president and CEO, while Patrick remained as the chairman of Board of Directors.

Picanol N.V. under the new CEO[5]

Coene had served as the president and CEO of ABB Service Worldwide for nearly a decade before he took the post at Picanol. Together with Patrick Steverlynck, he set Picanol to adopt a three-theme strategy: "Corporate Governance," "Customer Success," and "Profitable Growth." Coene introduced a new BU structure to make the company flatter (see CS Exhibit 4.3). The BUs were customer-oriented and built-up around the various textile markets. Coene wanted Picanol to "operate closer to its customers so that it can understand their business needs even better and use this knowledge as a basis for generating new products, systems, and total solutions. These total solutions should help smooth out the typically cyclical nature of the sector."

CS EXHIBIT 4.3: JAN COENE'S NEW ORGANIZATION STRUCTURE FOR PICANOL N.V.

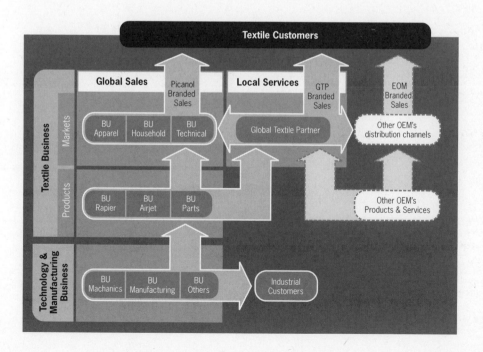

Under the new structure, each BU operated independently and was responsible for its own profit and loss account. "Volume for volume's sake is no longer an objective. We're aiming primarily for profit before growth," said Coene. "Picanol would develop market-focused technologies and services that capitalize on specific customer needs, such as the upgrading of existing machines at customers' premises, weaving mill control, consultancy, and similar activities." The high level of autonomy ensured that BUs could stay agile in the fast-changing market. The small scale of operation made costs more transparent and accounted for. In areas with significant synergy potentials, "Champion" roles were created to facilitate cooperation between BUs.

BU Apparel, BU Household, and BU Technical were mainly for marketing and sales. In the sales of weaving machines, good understanding of technical details and industry-specific knowledge were critical. Therefore the marketing part was organized on the basis of the three customer segments, which had different requirements of machines and technology. The Apparel segment concentrated mostly on clothing textiles, while the Household segment operated in the household and interior textiles. The Technical segment covered a lot of industrial usage, such as glass fiber, tire cord, automotive fabrics, airbag, protection wear, gauze, parachutes, and so on. Each of the three BUs had a marketing manager and technology expert working together at Ieper to provide individual, segment-focused support such as technical consulting, quotation making, and manufacturing arrangement. The three BUs operated globally to meet the diverse needs of customers.

The Global Textile Partner (GTP) BU was the only BU that operated locally and aimed to provide full service solutions to customers. This could include providing other original equipment manufacturers' (OEM's) products and services. The other three BUs – Rapier, Airjet, and Parts – were product development and manufacturing units operating globally. They were the internal suppliers to the three marketing BUs and GTP. Each BU was specialized in one particular technology, and was responsible in making machines that fitted customer needs. Last, Mechantronics, Manufacturing, and Proferro BUs served as suppliers to the three production BUs and other clients.

Coene considered that human resources were the most critical to his success. The BU structure, aside from its commercial rationale, was also intended to create an entrepreneurship environment. It was meant to stimulate employ-ees to be results-oriented and to have a sense of responsibility. Coene hired a chief resources officer (CRO) to make HR a fully functional group. The HR created a set of sophisticated procedures to guide employee selection, training and development, and performance evaluation and promotion. Coene also rec-ognized that his management team was not diversified. The traditional Picanol profile was that of the male Belgian engineer. Coene commented that he needed to add more women and international people. For that reason Picanol created a "Reverse Mentor" program. The program actively searched for employees who did not fit the typical profile to work closely with a member of the management team. These employees were encouraged to question engrained Picanol patterns and to bring in new ways of thinking. In this effort, Picanol aimed to become "a worldwide multicultural entity in all the various disciplines and at all the various echelons."

In terms of financial control, Coene appointed a new chief financial officer (CFO). The Financial Department developed a couple of tools to help BUs monitor their performance monthly. The Financial Dashboard measured purely financial performance, such as revenue and net profits. The Balanced Scorecard contained about 20 measurements to assess performance that could not be directly measured in Euro terms. All the measurements were objective and fact-based. Examples included the hit rate of quotations, or whether each employee generated a new idea. The Financial Department also gradually introduced International Account-ing Standards (IAS), aiming to use them for external reporting in 2004. As part of the "Corporate governance" strategy, a lot of attention was put on external finan-cial reporting to provide timely and qualitative information to shareholders.

Coene also established Picanol's "Code of Ethics." "Ethics is really the most important thing in doing business. It's a matter of how you treat other people." According to Coene, good corporate ethics drove high quality. "Quality doesn't mean just obtaining all sorts of certificates, it also extends to the way in which you answer the phone or welcome someone." In addition, Coene also formal-ized a series of policies guiding R&D activities, quality, suppliers management, environment, and health and safety issues. All of these policies were published in the company's *Policy Manual*, providing clear guidelines for managers and employees to follow.

CASE STUDY: PICANOL CHINA

Despite all the changes and interruptions caused by the reorganization, Picanol performed well financially. In 2001, the first year that Coene was in office for the most part, Picanol N.V. recorded a consolidated turnover of EUR 402.6 million and a net profit of EUR 11.6 million. The turnover and profit were increased by 21.6% and 51.7% over year 2000 respectively.

Picanol N.V. in China

Like most foreign businesses, Picanol did not establish operations in China until the early 1980s when China opened its doors to the world. Initially, all deals were made through "China Textile Machine Trade Corporation" in Beijing, a government agency that controlled purchasing quantity and price centrally. (Most industries were still under the centrally planned economy system at the time.) Initially, Picanol sent only a couple of people to sell to the government agency. But the business conditions soon changed in late 1980s. China opened its doors to foreign businesses and took away many central agencies. Picanol found it had to face the weaving mills directly, which amounted to tens of thousands in the Chinese textile industry.

The textile industry had always been a key industry in the Chinese economy. According to public and Picanol internal data, there were about 20,800 companies employing 7.6 million people in China's textile sector in 2001. The sector recorded US$67 billion in revenue in 2001, of which US$53 billion was exported, making China the world's largest manufacturer and exporter of textiles and garments. Textile exports alone represented 15% of China's total export trade volume in dollars in 2001. China's accession into the WTO was expected to give China's textile industry another boost. In 2005 members of the WTO relieved all quotas of textile goods from China. The industry was expected to grow by 375% after China's accession to the WTO. Picanol was aware of the great potential of the Chinese market, and decided to invest heavily in the country.

Late in the 1980s, Picanol started using distributors based in Hong Kong to sell to the China market. It also set up a Technical Service Station (TSS) in Shanghai that offered technical backup, training, and spare parts for users in China. But the business volume soon grew enough to justify opening representative offices. In 1992 Picanol established sales offices in Beijing and Guangzhou. It opened up

CS EXHIBIT 4.4:

PICANOL CHINA SALES (1999–2002)

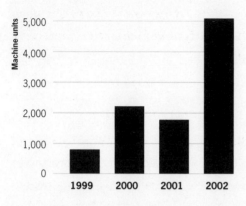

the third sales office in Shanghai in 1996. The three offices formed Picanol China and maintained a headcount of around 15 people over the years. Picanol assigned a country GM to supervise the sales and services activities. Since 1999 Hans de Gusseme has been the GM. Machine sales in China experienced cyclicality just like in the rest of the world, but overall sales had followed a fast-growing trend. The compounded annual growth rate from 1999 to 2002 was 173% (see CS Exhibit 4.4).

Picanol Suzhou Textile Works (PST) was the first overseas manufacturing plant Picanol opened in 1994. It was located in Suzhou, a city 130 kilometers north of Shanghai. Many foreign companies set up manufacturing plants in Suzhou due to its highly educated workforce, proximity to Shanghai, and local government incentives. PST was built to anticipate changes in China's duty-free policy on imported textile machines. The plant also lowered the production cost for Picanol models so that they could compete with low-price domestic products. For that reason, PST produced only lower end models to serve the lower segments. High-tech models were still produced in Belgium. PST employed about 200 people and was headed by Wang Jicheng, who had spent eight years in R&D at Picanol's headquarters in Belgium.

Hans de Gusseme

Hans de Gusseme graduated from the University of Ghent, Belgium, in 1991 with a degree in Electronic Engineering. After graduation, he worked as the global sales manager for an electronics company for four years. During that period de Gusseme traveled to 46 countries. He joined Picanol in 1996 and became the managing director of the firm's unit in Turkey. In 1999 he was transferred to China to serve as the GM of Sales and Services.

Having been in a management position in various countries, de Gusseme commented on his experience of managing people from different countries. As a European, de Gusseme gave lots of emphasis on teamwork. "You need to get along well with the team members and create a good team spirit if you want to get something done in Europe. People enjoy having autonomy and flexibility. When you assign them a certain task, they are usually reliable and meet their deadlines. You need to trust people and give them plenty of room to run the show. People will put you off if you boss around."

De Gusseme spent more than three years in Turkey. There he gained his first international experience in a management position. The management style was quite different. "The culture in Turkey is more hierarchical than in Europe; people expect you to give orders. You have to be more authoritarian to be effective, and you need to exercise a lot of close supervision. For instance, I had to control salesman's travel schedules. Otherwise there was always the possibility that they made the trip for personal affairs rather than for Picanol business. Having a job was necessary for them, but not the number one priority in their life. Sometimes I even had to teach the salespeople how to behave in front of customers. My experience from Turkey is that face-to-face communication with the employees is critical. You have to be around to let them feel the pressure and the urgency to get the job done." "But," de Gusseme cautioned, "you have to be absolutely correct and know your limits. Being bossy does not mean you do not respect them."

Before coming to China, de Gusseme expected to meet "obedient and submissive" employees. Like many Westerners, Hans had certain stereotypes of Orientals in his mind. What he found was a surprise. The Chinese employees cared about the company performance and were not hesitant to give constructive suggestions to management. They were self-motivated and enjoyed being given autonomy. They commanded valuable knowledge about the peculiarities in the China market. And they were proud of and wanted to be appreciated for their knowledge. "They are invaluable resources and can help you in many ways. But you have to gain their trust and respect first." De Gusseme made a big effort to understand the Chinese workers. When he first started in China, he took sales rides, and followed Chinese salespeople around to learn from them. "*Guanxi*[6] is very important in China. Not only do you need good *guanxi* with your customers, you also need to build *guanxi* with your employees."

De Gusseme was also concerned with communication. His Chinese language skills, in his own words, were at the "survival level." Although Chinese employees working in Western companies generally commanded decent English skills, communicating accurately and effectively in a non-native language was still a challenge to many. Due to cultural differences, their communication style could also be different. For example, a Belgian in Ieper was offended by the brief email message sent by a Chinese employee. The recipient was expecting some detailed response and saw the brief message as irresponsible. But the Chinese simply did not understand the problem. "The Chinese are not used to asking many questions even when they don't understand; you need to actively probe them and clarify ambiguities up front." Once he took a hold of the Chinese style, and established trust among the employees, de Gusseme found himself able to communicate with his employees in English effectively. "After you have worked closely with the same group of people for a while, sometimes you get to understand each other without saying the words."

Another big challenge de Gusseme had was to understand the local markets, and how business was done there. Gaining customers' trust was as critical as in any other region. But the problem was that too many brands existed for each product category, and very few had succeeded in becoming well-known and well-trusted brands nationwide. In addition, there was no price transparency, and multiple distributors and agents could be involved in the selling process. Due to the lack of clarity in the market, customers turned to personal relationships when seeking trust. The business community was formed around several closely knit "loops" that were made of people from the same geography or industry. A salesman had to spend a long time to build up such networks. De Gusseme found that the relevance of personal relationships was unusually strong in China's business environment.

Chinese employees at Picanol China

The Chinese employees came from various backgrounds. For instance, one of the sales engineers was once an assistant professor of mechanics in a textile college, and had been with the company since the Shanghai office was established. Another sales engineer studied trade and economics, worked as an agent for the

Hong Kong distributor company Picanol used in the late 1980s and early 1990s, and was invited to join Picanol China. The majority of the salesmen in Picanol China had been with the company for a long time, usually for more than six years. The average age of the salespeople was 40.

Generally, people enjoyed the stability of the company, and the simplicity of a relatively small operation in China. Employees were happily "stuck" in their positions. It took a long time for a salesman to build up his technical knowledge about the specific weaving machines and it took an even longer time to build up his network to sell the machines. The salespeople had invested a lot of time and effort to be in the play. If they would switch to other companies, they were very likely to start over again unless they were selling comparative weaving machines. But that option did not come in handy. There were only six major players with world-class weaving machines: Tsudakoma and Toyoda of Japan, the Radici Group and Panther from Italy, Dornier from Germany, and Picanol N.V. Although the competitors had established representative offices in China, pay from these companies was not much better than Picanol's. The local machine manufacturers were of lower technology and could not match Picanol's salaries. For people in their late forties and fifties, many would not want to move and spend much effort in starting over. For them, their roots were already deep in the regional markets they served.

Picanol's salespeople were very proud of the company and its pioneering role in weaving machine designs. They knew the local markets and their territories well and had extended networks to feed them with business leads. What they found most helpful was a manager who could communicate with the HQ effectively on their behalf. Sales engineer Zhao Yue Sun commented: "Communicating to headquarters effectively is very important to us. The customers in China have different needs from those in Europe, and we need to make the HQ staff understand the difference. Sometimes there is a conflict with Ieper on pricing or manufacturing. And I feel like I'm working between a rock and a hard place. Customers are like the rock, they always want the best product and service at the lowest price. And Ieper can be a hard place if you don't explain your situation well. I know how to face the rock, but I need someone to stand back to back with me to deal with the hard place. A foreign GM who is capable of convincing HQ can help us a lot. A Chinese GM would be less likely to serve as a bridge between us, even though he may have more experience and local market knowledge."

They also mentioned some managers who said yes to everything that came from Ieper, without taking into account local conditions. The Chinese felt quite frustrated working with them.

The Picanol China organization before Coene's arrival

At the time, the Picanol China organization had three representative offices managed by de Gusseme (see CS Exhibit 4.5 for the organization chart). He also influenced the service station a lot. Often sales would ask service to give out parts free of charge to facilitate sales. This reflected the emphasis on sales in the old organization.

Sales territories were divided by geography among the nine salespeople. A sales engineer was responsible for all machine sales in a defined region. This would allow a salesperson to establish strong *guanxi* with customers and to fully exploit the network. It also helped to save time and budget spent on travel as the salespeople served customers clustered in a region. Employees were used to

CS EXHIBIT 4.5: PICANOL CHINA OLD ORGANIZATION CHART

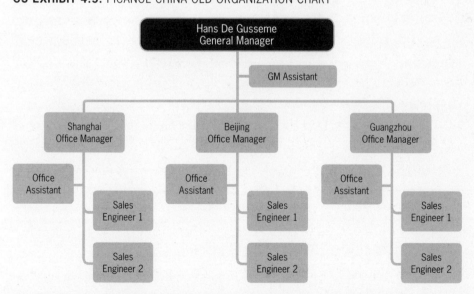

Note: The office managers supervised each office's activities, but were also actively engaged in sales activities.

the geographical structure, as it was clear and straightforward. Picanol's biggest competitors were also using this geographical design in China.

Picanol, as a whole, had used such a geographical design for 20 years. The salespeople were compensated by a fixed salary, which was subject to an annual raise based on the years of service. No bonus system was tied to individual or office performance. The rationale was to protect employees from the cyclical nature of the machine business in the textile industry. But some employees felt a bonus system would be more motivational.

Under this old structure, de Gusseme enjoyed a high degree of autonomy in managing the China operation. His major responsibilities were to facilitate all businesses between Picanol and China customers, which included setting contracts, pricing, and reporting to Sales VP at HQ. There was a budget but de Gusseme was not bound to it. So long as he sold enough machines, his performance was great. Due to the overlap between sales and service, profits were hard to allocate to each department. Consequently, profits could not be used for performance evaluation. In addition, de Gusseme handled all HR matters, such as recruiting and salary setting. There was no corporate guidance on HR practices. De Gusseme mostly used his intuition to make decisions. For instance, it took him about two hours to make a hiring decision after reading the résumé and interviewing the applicant.

Regarding performance management and personnel development, de Gusseme set sales targets and gave salespeople evaluations annually. The evaluation, like their boss's, was purely based on volume of machines sold. Picanol provided materials for sales support, but offered no formal training. Salesmen learned their trade on the job. Cai Zhi Jie, a sales engineer in the Shanghai office, commented: "You have to learn to swim when you are thrown in a pool. Otherwise you drown." As these people realized that their worth was tied to assigned territories, they were not expecting any big promotions other than an annual salary raise. "I would be useless if I got moved," Zhao Yue Sun reflected.

The expected new China organization

When de Gusseme was informed about Coene's new design, he knew what he had to do. But he wondered whether the new design would be the most effective in the

China market. In accordance with the new design received from HQ, Hans drew a
new organization chart for Picanol China (see CS Exhibit 4.6). His operation would
be split into three BUs: Apparel, Household, and Technical. De Gusseme had to
decide which BU he wanted to be in, and how he could find two regional managers
for the other BUs. De Gusseme felt the three office managers currently in the position lacked sufficient management skills to be promoted. It would also be politically
challenging to pick two managers out of the three. But if the office managers were
not selected, they would be "demoted" to regular sales engineers. Although their
salaries would not be touched, people would still feel that they would lose "face."

CS EXHIBIT 4.6: EXPECTED NEW PICANOL CHINA DESIGN

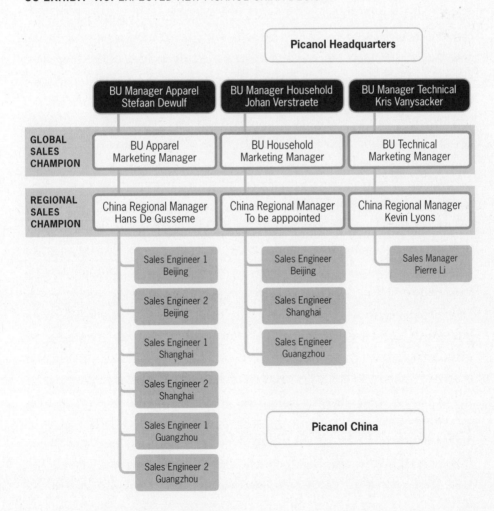

Moreover, the three sales engineers would be each assigned to three customer segments: Apparel, Household, and Technical. This would create a significant imbalance in workload. Apparel accounted for 80% of the business, while Household and Technical represented only 18% and 2% of the business respectively. Besides, there was no clear distinction between the apparel and household segments in China. About 20% of weaving mills made both kinds of fabrics, and could shift from being apparel-focused to household-focused quickly, depending on market demand.

Another big problem would be customer relationships. Many customers had befriended their particular sales engineer, and would be upset in dealing with a strange face instead of their usual contact. China's textile industry was relatively old-fashion in terms of management practice. Most companies were either state-owned or small private enterprises. These customers still followed the traditional way of doing business based on personal relationships. It would be extremely difficult to explain Coene's "customer success" strategy and what benefits the focused attention on specific segments could bring.

Then there was the challenge to educate his people. These salespeople were comfortably stuck in their geographical territories. They had established their roots. Now they would have to cut lots of their connections and build new ones. And they had to waste more time on traveling. Although Coene provided a nicely written letter explaining the changes, de Gusseme doubted that his people would be convinced. After all, Coene was far away and had a limited knowledge about China's business conditions.

De Gusseme also had to understand the changes to his responsibilities. The foremost change would be the new reporting structure. Instead of a single Sales VP, de Gusseme would have to report to three BU managers in Ieper (at least temporarily before he could find two other managers). Suddenly he wondered whether he could work among three bosses simultaneously. The financial control system would be tighter. De Gusseme would need to do an accurate forecast for all three BUs. It was quite a challenge to get accurate data in China, as the market was rather fragmented and it lacked reliable sources of statistics. On top of it, de Gusseme would face more pressure for profits. Besides volume of machines sold, he would also be measured on profit margins, and total profits of the entire BUs. All service-related work would be marked to GTP, an independent BU.

De Gusseme could no longer ask "favors" for free parts or services. Operationally, he would have less freedom to make decisions.

The new Picanol HR system

Coene's reform also brought in a thick policy manual. In particular, de Gusseme felt the HR system would have a big impact on his operation. Soon after the appointment of the CRO at HQ, the HR department established a sophisticated selection process. Various tests were designed to measure a candidate's fit with the company and with a specific position. These tests included career orientation, IQ tests, quantitative tests, English skill tests, and psychological profiles. Specific HR consultants worked with hiring managers to prescribe pertinent tests. Every candidate had to pass those tests to be qualified. To take into account different cultures, some tests were adjusted or localized. In China, psychology tests were provided by a local branch of an international test agency.

De Gusseme was not sure it was worth going through so much fuss to hire a sales engineer. It was already difficult to find the right people. He needed someone who had solid experience and knowledge about the textile industry. Furthermore, the candidates must have good English skills and sales personality. The textile industry, being a low-tech and mature industry, was not particularly attractive to the latter group. Most of his salespeople graduated from textile colleges. But even when he found someone who satisfied the above criteria, there was no guarantee that the person would perform well in the real world. What could de Gusseme do if an ideal candidate (in his judgment) did not pass the tests?

Coene wanted his management staff to be professional and equipped with sophisticated skills. De Gusseme thought it ideal to hire top business school graduates with textile industry experience to head the two BUs. But he found this wish challenging. Although Picanol was a great company and had been doing well in China, top B-school graduates would not consider it attractive to work in a relatively small operation in a mature industry. They preferred to join brand names such as GE and Microsoft. Picanol was just a neglected name among the thousands of foreign SMEs that operated in China. Competition for talent was a key issue for many of these foreign companies.

In terms of hiring new people, it turned out to be difficult as de Gusseme had expected. At a cocktail party, he met Pierre Li, who was enrolled in a full-time MBA program. The two men talked briefly, and exchanged business cards. De Gusseme had a good impression of Li. He looked like a typical MBA student, enthusiastic and outspoken. He spoke English fluently and had a good understanding of Western culture. More importantly, Li had worked for a Hong Kong-based textile group for eight years before coming to Shanghai. When Li expressed his interest in Picanol later, de Gusseme invited Pierre to a formal interview immediately. De Gusseme wished he had the authority to extend an offer to Li right on the spot, just like in the old days. But he had to follow the company procedure and send Li those tests. De Gusseme was worried: "If the results of Li's tests do not match with Picanol's requirement, I will not be able to hire him. The company consulted with experts to set up those tests. Maybe there is something that I can't tell through résumés and interviews."

Another part of the new HR system was the training programs design by head office. The salespeople welcomed them; however, they found those programs not well tailored to their specific needs. Cai Zhi Jie said: "I found the commercial training eye-opening, but it was not related to my work directly. The classes were taught by European professors and the topics were interesting to me. But the tactics may not be applicable here. Most of my clients were farmers around 10 years ago. Although they are buying the most advanced equipment, their education level and views on business cooperation remain elementary. Besides, bargaining can be brutal at times. We don't always follow rational negotiations. I don't think that such a situation could be expected by a European, who is not familiar with the China market." In addition, the salespeople also found it difficult to attend long training programs. Zhao Yue Sun once had a schedule conflict between a large contract and a company-wide sales meeting. He was directed by de Gusseme to stay and finish the contract.

Chinese staff's first reaction to the changes

The Chinese employees had read about Coene and his initiatives in the company's quarterly magazine *Picanol News*. Initially people did not feel the change would have significant impact on them. Cai Zhi Jie confessed: "I did not feel the change strongly at the beginning. Maybe it was because we are too far away. If there should be changes, they would come gradually. So long as people around us like de Gusseme stay here, I am not worried."

But when de Gusseme handed out the new structure, people brought up various concerns just as he expected. De Gusseme started to explain Coene's strategy and new structure in detail. "Jan Coene is a very capable CEO, and he designed this structure for the entire company with a global perspective. You have never seen anything like this, I haven't either. I have the same concerns as you do, but we don't know if it will work or not. We're all learning. We've got to give the new thing a try."

The salespeople agreed to try the new operation. But problems soon surfaced. A sales engineer from Household went to a weaving mill in Wuxi, Jiangsu, a city heavily involved in the textile industry. After the visit, the purchasing department mentioned that the weaving mill next door was looking for some machines. "I told them that I had to send someone from Apparel to visit," the salesman said. "Those people in Wuxi thought I was nuts." In Shandong province, where personal relationships were of particular importance to business, a sales engineer was angered to see some of his clients taken away. And some customers were complaining too. Because most customers were labeled "Apparel", Apparel sales engineers at times found the workload overwhelming. They also felt embarrassed to take their colleagues' clients.

De Gusseme was almost immediately hit with the dilemma of either sticking to the new system or losing contract opportunities. He was concerned that there was no way of achieving both. His gut feeling was not to lose any sales, but would Ieper understand and accept the compromise?

Meeting with Coene

In June 2003 Coene asked de Gusseme to visit Belgium HQ to discuss the China situation. Coene was not happy that the implementation of the new organization structure was taking so long. He expected de Gusseme to give him good reasons. De Gusseme wished someone could help him sort out the questions in his mind. Given the small size of Picanol China, should he implement the new structure rigidly or be flexible? Will the new design cause more disadvantages than advantages? How he could convince his CEO of the special conditions in China?

Appendix: History of Picanol management

1973: Bernard Steverlynck became CEO of Picanol. Bernard was an academic professor of Chemical Science, and obviously was more interested in academic activities. He managed Picanol's internal operation but left any external affairs to his brother Emmanuel Steverlynck.

1976: Emmanuel Steverlynck took the number one spot. He had a paternalistic style and made decisions on his own. Despite his seemingly autocratic style, Emmanuel was very wise to consult all parties before making a decision. Emmanuel also believed that a strong organization depends on dynamic and dedicated employees. He established "collective employee selection days" where a group of current employees interview candidates. Emmanuel often presided over these sessions.

1980–1986: Patrick Steverlynck served as Assistant to the CEO. He had started his career within Picanol in the Customer Service Department.

1986: Patrick Steverlynck became Chairman. In reality he served as the CEO of the company and supervised daily business activities.

1989: Herwig Bamelis, who had been the number one person in Finance, was appointed GM of IT/Finance – the "Economical GM". At the same time, Eckhard Thometscheck was appointed as GM for R&D and Production – the "Technical GM."

1992: Patrick brought in Walter De Reuse to energize Sales and Services.

1995: Herwig Bamelis became a Board member and Walter De Reuse became the "Economical" GM. Walter De Reuse and Eckhard Thometscheck comprised the "dual management" structure from 1995 to 2001.

1996: Patrick initiated the concept of a "service firm" for Picanol when Jan Coene joined the Picanol Board.

2001: Jan Coene impressed Patrick Steverlynck with a detailed proposal to carry the "service firm" forward. Patrick decided to ask Jan Coene to take the CEO post.

CASE COMMENTARIES

COMMENTARY 1

WILLEM P. BURGERS

PROFESSOR OF MARKETING AND STRATEGY

BAYER HEALTHCARE CHAIR IN STRATEGY AND MARKETING

CHINA EUROPE INTERNATIONAL BUSINESS SCHOOL (CEIBS)

This case study reads like a Greek tragedy. You can see the disaster coming, but the players have no idea, and there is no way you can tell them. You are in the audience, shouting, but the players do not hear you.

Jan Coene is a bit of a caricature. He is the personification of the textbook approach gone out of control. He is an ideologue, a man who finds good ideas and then makes those ideas of paramount importance. In a presumably inflexible, traditional company, he becomes the most inflexible, traditional of all. It is just a different tradition he follows: the mantras of the most recent management fad. He imagines himself the cosmopolitan leader assigned to bring the Flemish countryside into the new century. He thinks Picanol's management is not diverse because the managers are all Flemish. In other words, he thinks all Flemish are the same. He must think all Chinese are the same too and therefore rearranging geographical territories is non-problematic.

There are many Chinas: all are different in culture, economic development, history, language, cuisine, and people. The diversity is at least as great as we find in Europe. Would Coene assign a Flemish sales engineer to Wallonian customers? Perhaps he would, but I imagine that, all else being equal, it is easier for a Walloon to sell to a Walloon.

A reorganization by customer needs rather than according to customer geography or a customer *guanxi* network makes a lot of sense. But it is advisable not to run too far ahead of history and to remind ourselves that we run our current system with people who fit the assumptions and methods of the current system. Can they flourish in the new system? Can they be replaced? These are good questions that are not being asked. Coene will discover what every ideologue discovers sooner or later: people are a major obstacle to ideology.

Hans de Gusseme is a torn man. Is he a representative of Picanol headquarters in the China operation, or is he the representative of the China operation in Picanol HQ? Naturally, his daily environment pressures him to function as the defender of the local interest. His career interest reminds him, though, that he works for Picanol.

Aside from being torn between Picanol HQ and Picanol China, he must also weigh the immediate damage from implementing Coene's ideas against presumed future benefits. The short-term damage will be blamed on him while his successor may receive the praise for the long-term benefits. How much longer is de Gusseme expected to stay in China? If he stays only for one or two more years, the wiser approach for him personally will be to only minimally implement Coene's reforms.

Local opposition to global reform initiatives is natural. Local organizations naturally try to optimize their own operation and are not so interested in arguments that optimization by all the different local operations of a global organization will lead to sub-optimization for the organization overall. The complaints about the sales training are typical in this regard. While the salespeople in China complain that it does not really fit Chinese reality (the many Chinese realities), probably our salespeople in Brazil worry about the Brazilian reality, and Mexicans worry about the Mexican reality. If Picanol tried to adapt its sales training to all the different realities worldwide, there could be no sales training.

The challenge for de Gusseme is to convince Coene that his slow implementation is not motivated by a knee-jerk reaction to change, not by personal career considerations, and not by an inclination to sacrifice Picanol interests to local interests, but that it is driven by a desire to make the reforms succeed rather than fail. Before de Gusseme tries to convince Coene, he needs to examine his own motivations though, and he needs to decide which reforms and ideas:

- deserve speedy implementation
- need delay

- need modification
- make no sense.

Both the "customer success" strategy and the concept of the "service firm" probably make sense in Belgium, where technology provides less of a competitive edge and low-cost competitors abound, and for the same reason it should make sense in China too. Implementation might be more difficult in China, or it might be easier.

The HR tests may be useful. But what evidence of their usefulness exists? Have these tests been tested in Belgium? Have these tests been tested in China? De Gusseme should note to HQ that Picanol is a big name in Belgium, but not in China, and that experienced international management talent is not so rare in Belgium, but is definitely hard to come by in China. If Pierre Li is willing to undergo the humiliation of taking all these tests in order to land a job with Picanol, then maybe that shows there is something wrong with Li.

Separation of service-related work in a separate BU is a classic prescription for disaster. How will GTP set prices? When GTP raises prices this will be very good for its profits, but not so good for equipment sales. GTP prices will be set to maximize GTP profit and thereby reduce Picanol sales and profit. For their part, equipment salespeople naturally will downplay the need for any service whatsoever. Here is an example of a reform that is designed to make life easier for HQ, to make the company more manageable, to make PowerPoint presentations more impressive, and to chase customers out the door.

It is easy in this case to fall into the trap of thinking that Coene is an insensitive ideologue, a bull in a China shop so to speak, and that therefore all his reforms make no sense. Yet, some of his initiatives appear reasonable and overdue, be they in Europe or in China. Some of the reforms – the HR reforms perhaps – are dubious. The separation of service-related work into an independent BU definitely makes no sense. In all cases, implementation cannot ignore the fabric of relationships among people, inside and outside the company, that serves to sustain this company and any company, be it in Europe or in China.

COMMENTARY 2

HANS-PETER BOUVARD

DIRECTOR BUSINESS DEV. NORTHERN ASIA

REICHLE + DE-MASSARI FAR EAST (PTE) LTD

The situation within the Picanol N.V. China organization is not an un-known case to many of us. Several companies investing in new markets and surpassing the critical size are facing similar organizational challenges – functional organizations against a sort of matrix organization.

The long-term target of Picanol is to break the cyclical nature of the machine business by broadening the business range. Without leaving the core competencies of a company, this can be easiest achieved with adding value, like service and maintenance, into the product portfolio, creating a full solution for end-users. Service and maintenance is also a way to create long-term relationships with customers. Service is known too for higher margins that are spread over the year and which do not have any cycles.

Patrick Steverlynck's decision to bring Jan Coene in as new CEO supports this need very strongly and is a good move. Coene's work experience for nearly a decade within ABB Service Worldwide gives him the best background someone could have. ABB, for many years a product-oriented company, changed during the last decade into a service-oriented company, selling solutions rather than products. Coene must have experienced within these years what this means for a multinational corporation and what resistance this might cause in the field.

This brings us to Hans de Gusseme, so far a product-oriented person with an engineering degree, with product sales experience from around the world. Due to his background and working experience I would expect him to have good cultural sensitivity; that is, in countries like China, an idea of the "everyday survival kit." Within the years that he's been lead-ing Picanol in China, he's been able to build up trust in his team. In 2000, approximately one-third of the newly produced weaving machines were sold in China. This shows the importance of the local market for Picanol, and I am sure that Coene must have realized this very quickly after enter-ing Picanol N.V.

On the other hand, many new setups tend to perform the easiest sales with the slimmest organization able to act as fast and as flexibly as possible. Many newcomers in China first open representative offices in Beijing, Shanghai, or Guangzhou, and then after a few years of experience they increase their exposure by changing the legal structure into a branch or legal entity. Offices in other cities are added to extend the coverage in the country and to support local customers. Many SME companies have a similar setup and are quite successful in doing so.

However, success can be a way of losing flexibility. More employees need better ways of communication, more control, and better steering systems to succeed in the long term. Picanol China has reached this phase and needs to rework and rethink its mid-/long-term strategy in the local market.

Many heads of Chinese organizations face this situation. They feel misunderstood by HQ – sometimes I hear voices complaining that the biggest challenge is not the never-ending fight in the market, but the never-ending fight with HQ.

De Gusseme has three choices:

1 RESISTANCE (ALSO CALLED THE "NO-ERS")

De Gusseme could resist HQ's wishes, and try to explain why the new organization will not work in China. He could use historical facts to support his position. First, the good sales figures of sold weaving machines in the past were all done with the old organization. The *guanxi* that has been built up over the last few years would be in danger with the new customer-focused organization, as other persons would take over responsibility for this account. Many customers in China are used to getting "service" for free; a separation of this within Picanol China would make these free services difficult, if not impossible, and this will have a great impact on sales results. There are many other reasons for this, such as additional headcount and cost, and additional travel costs due to less coverage.

2 FULL INTEGRATION (ALSO CALLED THE "YES-BUTTERS")

Full integration would be the easiest way for de Gusseme in this meeting.

There are obvious advantages, like the clearer profitability calculations that can be done for each customer and product segment. This visibility can help to identify high-profit products and markets in the Chinese weaving machine industry and can ensure that the long-term investments are done in the right place.

The danger is that specific market needs for China, like personal long-term relations, would not be taken enough into account and that de Gusseme would identify them as "Yes, this might work, but ..." Every local structure of a company needs to adapt to the local customs of the market, and this might be the missing point of a full integration.

3 COMPROMISE (ALSO CALLED THE "WHY-NOTTERS")

Why-notters move the world and create new things. De Gusseme should take on this new organization as a chance to build up something more consistent and strong for the future in China. Overall, Picanol China is still small in size and has the potential to grow into something more important.

De Gusseme can therefore show Coene that he has understood the main message from the company – he would change as much as possible but leave some room for possible local adaptations in China.

First, he should see the BU organization as a chance of strengthening and increasing the push into the market. More dedicated and more specialized people can better identify customer and product needs. They can create mid- and long-term sales and marketing strategies. To maintain existing *guanxi* in China, he should also recommend the creation of a matrix organization. Office managers need to be kept in place to take the regional responsibility for the overall regional market, and to measure operation expenses and net sales in total. This would help to avoid confusion in the sales organization and among relationship-based customers. As well, this would keep them motivated, as they would not lose their position. In a way the three office managers would be responsible together for the more holistic BU of GTP, seeking full service solutions to customers.

On the other hand de Gusseme should build up the "BU organization," adding one responsible BU Manager for Apparel, one for Household, and one for Technical, taking the responsibility for net sales and net profit. One has already been put on board. Pierre Li would fit in well with the new organization. He would lead technology and strategy by the Global Sales Champion, but report to de Gusseme for the day-to-day activities. The advantage of this matrix would allow Picanol China to take the best out of both – on the one hand, global strategy and technology, and on the other the local market and customer knowledge. Free services could then be added to the marketing budget of the office managers and this would still be available where needed. Steering tools for the sales engineers, like the Balanced Scorecard, could be decided by office managers, together with the BU managers. Training and evaluation processes could be adapted to the different levels.

However, there is never a perfect organization, just humans that can make every organization live or die. The new challenge that de Gusseme can propose might have the right to live, as it could combine best of West and East, at least till Picanol China has reached the next level of size.

COMMENTARY 3

GARY AN

GENERAL MANAGER

AMPHENOL EAST ASIA ELECTRONIC TECHNOLOGY (SHENZHEN) CO., LTD

AMPHENOL COMMERCIAL PRODUCTS (CHENGDU) CO., LTD

The challenge that Hans de Gusseme, GM of Picanol's Sales and Service, faced is quite common in a lot of multinationals' subsidiaries in China. The organizational changes in HQ require the same approach. Is it going to be the correct one for China? Do we need to consider any different approach? Which one is better for the company's long-term development: centralization or decentralization?

Picanol is a traditional family-owned European company, in which managers are not only measured by their financial performance. The company does have a budget, but most subsidiary heads are not bound to it as in the case of de Gusseme.

Jan Coene, President and CEO of Picanol, made a big change. He implemented a BU structure in the company with the aim of long-term revenue and profit growth. Each business operated independently and was responsible for its own profit and loss (P&L). Each business focused on specific markets and products. The high level of autonomy ensured that business could stay agile in the fast-changing market. This typical decentralized organization allows clear accountability for individuals and organizations. Performance measurement becomes more straightforward, top line and bottom line, which creates an entrepreneurship environment and can bring higher growth and higher return.

This profound structural change will benefit the company in the long run, but it will bring a lot of pain in the beginning. Clear accountability is the key to the company's profit growth and higher return on equity. Result-oriented and clear responsibilities can be a tremendous motivation for business development.

It is easy to understand de Gusseme's concerns, due to the impact of the changes on the Chinese business. In China competition is very fierce. *Guanxi* plays a major role in customer relationships. Many customers have multiple demands and require multiple product lines crossing different markets. They need to show flexibility to serve those customers.

De Gusseme can still implement the strategy coming from HQ, despite the difficulties. But he needs to implement it in a flexible way. He could distribute his resources according to business volume and according to the different regions in China. As Apparel accounts for 80% of total revenue, he needs to put the most resources in this market: 10 people out of the total of 15 employees reporting to him. For Household, this is a segment that could grow rapidly with quick economic development. De Gusseme needs to be ready for that. He could place one person in this market in each sales office reporting to the marketing manager. Meanwhile, due to the limited market size of Technical business in China, one person could take care of this market for the whole country. Once the business grows, de Gusseme can add more resources into this segment. In each sales office, one sales coordinator as administration manager should report to him. For those customers with multiple product demands, he can appoint a key account manager.

Another important factor is the absence of a bonus system in Picanol, which is a big disadvantage in the business world. A commission plan could be put in place to motivate salespeople. The plan needs to reflect the requirements of both top line and bottom line.

De Gusseme needs to train his team to understand fully why the company is implementing this new structure, how individual performance will be recognized, and how important it is to maintain a reasonable bottom line to allow the company to grow further. The pain will be short term. If the team executes well, the company could develop much faster in China and in the world.

NOTES

1 Ohmae, Kenichi 1991, *The Borderless World*, Harper Business: New York.
2 "The Return of the Country Manager," *McKinsey Quarterly*, No. 2, 1996.
3 This revision was prepared by Professor Juan A. Fernandez from CEIBS. The original case was written by Wei (Wendy) Liu (Darden MBA 2003) under the supervision of Professor Fernandez and Professor James G. Clawson of Darden. The case was prepared on the basis of class discussion rather than to illustrate either effective or ineffective handling of an administrative situation. Certain names and other identifying information may have been disguised to protect confidentiality. The case was originally published by CEIBS in 2004 and revised in 2006. Published with permission.
4 Some data in this section were from the Picanol N.V. 2001 annual report and the company website, www.picanol.be.
5 From the Picanol N.V. 2001 annual report and the company website, www.picanol.be.
6 *Guanxi*: Chinese for personal networks. *Guanxi* played a big role in everyone's daily life. Most Chinese had the mindset to build and use *guanxi*. *Guanxi* was built either through friendship or favor-granting. People leveraged their *guanxi* to achieve more than what they could on their own.

Chapter 5
Counterfeiters in China: Catch me if you can[1]

INTRODUCTION

"If you don't have a counterfeiting problem, you don't have successful products." This phrase describes a paradoxical situation for many companies operating in China. If you fail to offer good products, you have to close down your company for lack of business, but if your products are great, they will be copied. The worst consequence is that you will be out of business anyway. One cannot deny that IPR is an extremely important issue for most companies operating in this market, whether Chinese or non-Chinese, as both are equally its victims.

As an underground activity, it is difficult to accurately estimate the scale of counterfeiting in China. What we can certainly say is that IPR infringement affects nearly all industries, especially software, media, consumer electronics, and luxury goods. Other industries affected include food and drinks, textile, clothes, leather, pharmaceuticals, chemical products, machinery, cosmetics, cleaning products, and many more. Highly taxed products like tobacco and alcohol are also ideal counterfeiting targets. Counterfeiters usually focus on industries with low capital investment and a relatively simple production process. Most counterfeiters are individuals and SMEs. Direct sale is their traditional distribution channel, but other channels have also been used such as trade fairs and the Internet.

Counterfeiting is a rapidly developing business and is increasingly becoming more sophisticated. Counterfeiters use villages in remote areas in inland China as their production base, which makes them more difficult to detect. Besides, they can rapidly move from one locality to another when the authorities close down their operations. Their activities are also expanding internationally with a growing number of exports, especially to Africa and the Middle East. In summary, counterfeiting is becoming better organized and growing on an international scale.

After China joined the WTO in December 2001 there were hopes that counterfeiters would be cracked down on quickly. These hopes did not materialize, despite the serious efforts made by the Chinese Central Government. Why is counterfeiting so hard to curb? Among the most important reasons are the relatively weak Chinese legal system, protectionism from local authorities, and some historical and cultural factors.

The Chinese legal system

Although China has aggressively adopted new laws and regulations to protect IPR, the enforcement of those laws still remains questionable. Cases often experience prolonged judicial procedures before a sentence is issued. This situation is aggravated by the lack of professional judges, especially in the less-developed areas of the country.

Improvements have been made in efforts to punish the infringers. For instance, the threshold for criminal prosecution of individual counterfeiters has been lowered from $12,000 worth of goods to $6,000 with one brand, and $3,600 with two or more brands. However, economic sanctions are still too weak to deter counterfeiters. On average, penalties are less than RMB10,000. Besides, only around 1.1% of victims were compensated in judicial judgments and only 2.3 people out of 100 defendants were sentenced (DRC[2] 2004). Surprisingly, the equipment used to counterfeit was sometimes returned by the authorities to counterfeiters.

Protection from local authorities

Although the Central Government is strongly committed to fighting counterfeiting, local governments sometimes work in the opposite direction. Companies usually find it difficult to get support from local governments in persecuting IPR infringers. The reason is simple: counterfeiters are sometimes the main source of employment and economic resources in those villages. Local government officials turn a blind eye to counterfeiting, or even actively cooperate with them. It is not rare that local officials receive bribes, but on occasion they are simply afraid of retaliation by criminal organizations if they conduct in-depth investigations on their illegal activities.

Cultural and historical factors

Another factor contributing to the situation is the general permissive social attitudes with regard to IPR. The public in China in general lacks the consciousness of property rights. Even today, many Chinese, especially in rural areas, have no idea of what IPR is. This situation has some historical and cultural roots. Under the Communist regime, private property was totally banned. At that time companies were encouraged to openly share their technologies. In 2004 China for the first time included the protection of private property in its Constitution. Besides, Chinese education has historically emphasized learning by imitating the best.

* * *

What can companies do under these circumstances? First of all they should start by conducting an IP audit to identify their vulnerable areas. Once those areas are identified, multiple measures should be implemented. Following the well-known 4Ps of marketing (product, price, place, and promotion), we have developed the 4Ps of IPR: product, process, people, and prevention.

EXHIBIT 5.1: PROTECTING IPR

By *product* we mean taking the necessary measures to protect the product by applying mechanisms that prevent competitors from gaining access to your technology. *Process* refers to protecting the production process know-how. In that sense, it is important to establish long-term relationships with suppliers and distributors so as to create trust in the supply chain. A frequently heard piece of advice is to avoid bringing core technologies to China. In case you have to, break down the technology into several elements so that your employees do not have access to the whole picture. By *people* we mostly refer to employees. Make ethical behavior one element to consider in the selection process of new employees, create a code of ethics, and provide ethical and IPR training to your organization. Finally, *prevention* refers to having the legal mechanisms in place. Those include patents, trademark registration, non-competing clauses in contracts, and so on. Make sure your own house is in order by ensuring that all your patents, trademarks, and copyright documents have been applied for and registered in China.

It is not infrequent that some of your former suppliers or partners become your "best" counterfeiters. New Balance, a Boston-based athletic footwear company, found that its Chinese supplier secretly made tens of thousands of extra running shoes. Unilever found one of its suppliers had sold excess inventory of soap directly to its retailers without informing it. An expert explained, "There are two positions within a Chinese commercial relationship. There's the front door, then there's the back door." Some Chinese enterprises use the back door for doing business without your knowledge. Therefore, you should check the background and records of business partners, of your key employees, and of your most important suppliers. Make sure they are honest. Not an easy task, but worthwhile trying.

Other measures to protect your IPR are educating customers about special methods for identifying fake goods, setting up a hotline to encourage reports on counterfeit activities, and working closely with police and tax officials. Make your employees, suppliers, and distributors your eyes and ears in identifying counterfeit goods.

Participating in company associations is also a recommended practice. The creation of the Quality Brand Protection Committee (QBPC) is a good move in this respect. QBPC was founded in March 2000, starting with 12 members. Now it has more than 100 foreign company members. In the past years, QBPC has worked very efficiently promoting IPR protection. They have organized frequent meetings with Central Government officials, such as Vice-Premier Madam Wu Yi; organized conferences; carried out advertisement campaigns; communicated best practices among member enterprises; lobbied the government to revise laws and regulations; and trained Chinese officials and judges. It is important to avoid confrontation with Central Government officials; if you criticize them they will be uncooperative.

Be prepared to dedicate enough resources to fight counterfeiting and protect your IP. Louis Vuitton spent more than $16 million in 2004 on investigations and legal fees.[3] Also, in order to beat Budweiser beers, Anheuser-Busch began to use expensive imported foil on the bottle that was difficult to find in China and thus prevented counterfeits. In addition, you should hire professionals to keep an eye on any clue or hint on possible infringements. Though this kind of investment will push up your costs, it will save you more eventually. While total victory is unattainable, multinationals will have to fight for their IP rights.

Although IPR infringement is prevalent in China, the situation of the auto industry is somewhat special for several reasons. First, independent Chinese automakers are too young to obtain the necessary technologies for car making using their own resources. Second, automakers usually make huge investments and are considered strategic companies in the province in which they are located and even at the country level. Thus, they enjoy special attention and protection if necessary from all levels of government. Finally, the government still exercises strict controls on foreign car makers, and therefore has great influence on them. IPR disputes are common in China's automotive industry; several multinational car makers have also brought infringement cases forward.

In the following case, GM China versus Chery, General Motors was trapped in a difficult IPR dispute. Chery, a Chinese domestic car maker, launched a new mini car model, the QQ, in July 2003. This was several months earlier than the planned launch date for General Motors' new mini car, the Chevrolet Spark. The QQ looked very similar to the Chevrolet Spark and was priced much cheaper. General Motors claimed that the Chery QQ was a knockoff of the Matiz, a model owned by GM Daewoo. The QQ turned out to be a real hit with consumers while sales of the Chevrolet Spark were much lower than expected. To make matters worse for General Motors, Chery was aggressively expanding into other countries where General Motors had a presence.

General Motors had its hands full: it had to compete with Chery head to head in the market while deciding what actions to take in regards to their IPR infringement claim. They considered: (1) asking for the mediation of the Chinese government; (2) private negotiations; (3) suing Chery in China; and (4) going to trial in other countries.

Following the case studies, you will find two commentaries: the first by Gerald Fryxell, Professor of Management, CEIBS; and the second by Doug Ho Song, Managing Director, Doosan Leadership Institute, Doosan Group. Both commentators give a comprehensive analysis of the disputes, and then provide solutions from the perspective of General Motors. They also point out the lessons to be learned from this case for multinationals eager to win in China.

CASE STUDY
GM CHINA VERSUS CHERY, DISPUTES OVER INTELLECTUAL PROPERTY RIGHTS[4]

Piracy is such a way of life in China that people are surprised when a movie, software package or handbag bought there is not ripped off. Now you can add passenger cars to the list of counterfeit goods. – Forbes[5]

In July 2003, SAIC-GM-Wuling Automobile Co. Ltd (SAIC[6]-GM-Wuling) held a special conference in Shanghai together with GM China. The conference, "Insights on the R&D of the Chevrolet Spark," aimed to promote the Chevrolet Spark model, which was planned to be launched in December 2003. Unexpectedly, GM China warned the audience of the hidden dangers of designing and manufacturing cars simply by copying. The warning was aimed directly at SAIC Chery Automotive Co. (SAIC Chery), a competitor who had successfully captured the market segment Chevrolet Spark was targeting, with its introduction of the QQ two months earlier. The QQ was more than just a little bit similar to the Chevrolet Spark. In fact, both the Chery QQ and the Chevrolet Spark were based on the Matiz model owned by GM Daewoo Auto & Technology Company (GM-Daewoo). To compound matters for Chevrolet, the QQ was priced at US$6,000, much lower than the planned US$7,500 retail price for the Spark. Some puzzled journalists at the conference asked Phil Murtaugh, the CEO of GM China, "Which is the original, the Chevrolet Spark or the Chery QQ?" Faced with this situation, GM China believed it was imperative they took action. However, they were unsure what would be the best method to present their evidence and what actions they should take.

History of GM in China

General Motors Corp., founded in 1908, was the largest vehicle manufacturer in the world. The company employed approximately 325,000 people and had a presence in more than 200 countries and regions worldwide. In 2003 GM sold 8.6 million vehicles, accounting for 15% of the global market.

General Motors entered the China market in the early 1990s. After outbidding its US rival Ford, it established the largest JV in China with the SAIC in 1997, and subsequently it began to manufacture Buicks in 1999. By the end of 2003, General Motors had introduced the Cadillac, Buick, Chevrolet, SAAB, Opel, and AcDelco brands to the Chinese market. The company employed a total of 11,000 staff in China. General Motors was involved in five automotive JVs, and one JV technical center and had two wholly owned subsidiaries in China. General Motors planned to cover different segments of the automotive market with these five joint ventures. More specifically, Shanghai General Motors Co. would focus on medium to high-end vehicles, Shanghai GM Dongyue Motors Co. would concentrate on economical cars, Jinbei General Motors Automotive Co. would primarily make multi-purpose and business-purpose vehicles, and SAIC-GM-Wuling would target the mini-vehicle market. CS Exhibit 5.1 contains a complete list of GM China's subsidiaries.

General Motors increasingly recognized the importance of the China market to their global strategy and long-term prospects. In June 2004, Rick Wagoner, the CEO, announced an additional US$3 billion investment in its JVs with

CS EXHIBIT 5.1: SUBSIDIARIES OF GM CHINA

Source: www.gmchina.com.

SAIC to expand its business in China, and moved General Motors' Asia Pacific HQ from Singapore to Shanghai, China.[7] By April 2004 General Motors had captured 11% of China's automobile market, second only to the 26% market share owned by Volkswagen, another important partner of SAIC. The Chinese automotive business was much more profitable than that in North America, as shown by General Motors' profits of US$437 million on sales of 386,000 autos in China, compared to profits of US$811 million on sales of 5.6 million autos in North America.[8]

Chery

Chery was based in Wuhu city in Anhui province in east China, an inland province around four hours from Shanghai by car. The company's predecessor was the Anhui Automotive Parts Co. Founded in 1997 Chery was a pillar of the local economy, accounting for nearly 44% of Wuhu's GDP. Zhan Xialai, Chairman of Chery, was also the secretary of the Wuhu Committee of the Communist Party of China (CPC). Chery started manufacturing automobiles in May 2000 and had an annual capacity for 300,000 automobiles. The company obtained ISO 9001 certification in February 2001 and was the first local automobile maker to achieve TS16949 certification, which was considered the strictest certification system in the world.

Though established in 1997, Chery did not obtain permission for manufacturing passenger cars until January 2001. In that year, the company sold 30,000 cars, and increased that number to 50,000 the following year. Unlike most Chinese car makers, who manufactured cars through JVs with foreign car makers, Chery was determined to go at it alone. The company's strategy was to be an independent automobile manufacturer by integrating worldwide resources and serving both domestic and international markets.

A forced marriage between SAIC and Chery

When Chery was established in 1997, it was done so without formal approval from China's Central Government. By the end of 2000, more than RMB1.7 billion had been invested in the company; however, Chery still found it difficult to get a formal legal qualification. Following mediation by the Central Government, the Anhui government, and the Shanghai government, the Wuhu government decided to transfer 20% of Chery's equity to SAIC at no charge, on the condition that SAIC would be excluded from dividend payouts and management. It was through this arrangement that Chery's autos were included on the National Auto List and allowed to be sold in the Chinese market.

The resulting rise of SAIC Chery has since become somewhat legendary. Despite its short history, SAIC Chery sold 90,000 cars domestically in 2003 and exported 1,200 cars, accounting for 50% of all Chinese-branded automobiles exported that year. The speed at which SAIC Chery entered the international markets surprised its domestic competitors. In May 2003, SAIC Chery announced the establishment of a JV in Iran to make 50,000 autos per year. With its low prices and eye-catching models, SAIC Chery had emerged as a representative of China's national brands. Following the initial 20% stake in Chery in 2000, SAIC had continually tried to increase its equity investment in SAIC Chery, but had been met with reluctance by the Wuhu government. SAIC and SAIC Chery continued to have a relationship in name only. Though SAIC helped SAIC Chery in products and technologies, SAIC Chery maintained a separate sales and production system. Moreover, SAIC was not even informed about SAIC Chery's Board meetings. The marriage between SAIC and Chery was doomed to be expedient.

China's automotive industry

The automotive industry was a fast-emerging one in China and was continuing to attract new entrants. During 1992–2002, the average production growth was 15% annually (see CS Exhibit 5.2). Decreasing import tariffs, increased car model options, and the boom in auto loans saw a surge in the demand for cars. In 2003 China manufactured 4.44 million vehicles, with an additional 35% increase in production over the prior year, making it the fourth-largest automobile-manufacturing nation in the world. Passenger cars accounted for 45% of all vehicles manufactured, about 2.02 million in quantity. As estimated by J. D. Power & Associates, there are only eight vehicles for every 1,000 residents in China versus 940 vehicles in the United States, and 584 vehicles in Western

CS EXHIBIT 5.2: THE RAPID GROWTH OF CHINA'S AUTOMOTIVE INDUSTRY

Source: Xu Xiaofeng, "Research Report on the Automotive Industry," Tequ Securities Research Institute, 17 June 2002.

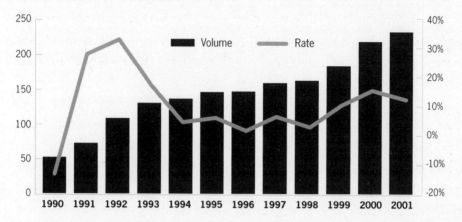

Europe. It was no wonder that so many automotive giants saw China as the battleground for global industry leadership.[9]

China set strict restrictions for foreign enterprises to invest in its automotive industry, the most notable being a maximum 50% equity stake in JVs. In the late 1980s, Volkswagen AG became the first foreign company to enter the China market. By the late 1990s many more automotive giants were rushing into China. Today, nearly all the major players in the world's auto market have established a presence. See CS Exhibit 5.3 for the opening process of China's auto industry. Most of the leading car manufacturers in China were JVs (see CS Exhibit 5.4 for the top 10 car manufacturers in China in 2003).

The Chevrolet Spark and the Chery QQ were both classified as mini cars. Mini cars refer to cars less than four meters in length and with an engine displacement of less than 1.3L. For a long time, the Tianjin Xiali Automobile Co. and the Chongqing ChangAn Auto Co. dominated the mini car market in China, each with an output of 100,000 cars per year. However, both companies have recently been plagued by stale designs and an out-of-date appearance. In 2001, Geely, a new domestic car maker, successfully entered this segment and hence ignited the interests of other competitors. According to the *China Automotive Industry News*, 227,340 mini cars were sold from January to July in 2003, an increase of 141.5% over the same period last year. This growth rate was much higher than that of both the medium and high-end car segments.

CASE STUDY: GM CHINA VERSUS CHERY

CS EXHIBIT 5.3: EVOLUTION OF CHINA'S AUTOMOTIVE INDUSTRY

Source: McKinsey, New Horizon: MNCs' Investment in Developing
Countries – An Overview of China's Automotive Industry, www.mckinsey.com.

Completely closed (before 1985)	Limited foreign participation (1985–1997)	More foreign participation (1998–2001)	Accession into WTO (since 2001)
External factors			
• No imports or foreign investors	• Limited joint ventures, approved by government • High import tariffs and quotas • Low entry barriers for local company due to protectionism	• Encourage foreign investment • Conditions of equity percentage and local production ratio • Distribution controlled by government	• Tariff reduced to 25% and quotas removed • Remove restrictions for foreign investment in lower stream (such as distribution and auto finance)
Industry dynamic			
• Big three automotive SOEs • Planned economy	• Volkswagen became the first foreign investor and dominated for nearly 10 years	• More car models • Four JVs dominated market • Vertical integration	• Fiercer competition, lower price, and higher quality • More auto parts export
Performance			
• Outdated technology, few models, USSR technology • Produce for government purchase	• High price, extremely profitable • Under-developed related industries resulting in high costs	• Enhanced productivity • High profits	• Price war eroding profits, but economies of scale help to alleviate the profit decline • Continuous investment resulting in overcapacity

CS EXHIBIT 5.4: TOP 10 CAR MANUFACTURERS IN CHINA

Source: China Association of Automobile Manufacturers.

Ranking	Company	2003 output	2002 output	Increase (%)
1	Shanghai Volkswagen	405,252	278,890	45.31
2	FAW Volkswagen	302,346	191,695	57.72
3	Shanghai GM	168,991	111,623	51.39
4	FAW Xiali	166,721	89,920	85.41
5	Guangzhou Honda	117,178	59,080	98.34
6	Dongfeng	105,475	84,378	25.00
7	ChangAn Automobile	102,083	67,846	50.46
8	SAIC Chery	101,141	50,398	100.68
9	Guangzhou Aeolus	66,134	39,047	69.37
10	Beijing Hyundai	55,113	0	–

CASE STUDY: GM CHINA VERSUS CHERY

Disputes over the Chery QQ

Both the Chery QQ and the Chevrolet Spark looked quite similar to the GM Daewoo Matiz (see CS Exhibit 5.5). The Matiz was a very popular mini car that rewrote the rulebook of city cars after its introduction in 1998. It achieved a single model sales record during its first year of sales in South Korea. The car was manufactured in Daewoo's factories in India, Romania, and Poland. In addition to its sales success, the Matiz won many awards including the World's Most Beautiful Automobile of 1998, the Best Mini Car Model at the U.K. international auto exhibit in 1998 and the World's Most Beautiful Mini Car of 2002.

CS EXHIBIT 5.5: THE MATIZ MODEL OF GM DAEWOO
Source: SINA Auto.

The Chevrolet Spark was the Chinese version of the GM Daewoo Matiz, except with the addition of a luggage rack. Besides the similarity in appearance (see CS Exhibit 5.6), the Chery QQ and the Chevrolet Spark also had several common technical parameters. See CS Exhibit 5.7 for a comparison between the Chery QQ and the Chevrolet Spark. In terms of physical size, the Chery QQ was slightly larger than the Chevrolet Spark, but this was hard to discern.

CS EXHIBIT 5.6:
QQ AND CHEVROLET SPARK
Source: www.qianlong.com.

QQ

Spark

The immediate success of the QQ could have been attributed to its fresh looks and the company's innovative marketing tactics. With a low retail price of US$6,000 per car, Chery made it nearly impossible for its competitors to compete on price. In addition, Chery was able to capture many young fans and establish the QQ as a symbol of coolness and style through a series of marketing efforts named "QQ Love," which included online quizzes, promotions, and writing competitions.

CASE STUDY: GM CHINA VERSUS CHERY

CS EXHIBIT 5.7: PARAMETER COMPARISON BETWEEN QQ AND CHEVROLET SPARK

Source: Chengdu Qiche Web, www.auto028.com.

Vehicle dimension	QQ	Chevrolet Spark
Length	3,550 mm	3,495 mm
Width	1,508 mm	1,495 mm
Height	1,491 mm	1,485 mm
Wheelbase	2,348 mm	2,340 mm
Track/front	N/A	1,315 mm
Track/rear	N/A	1,280 mm
Min. turning diameter	9.5 m	9.2 m
Ground clearance	125 mm	130 mm
Approach angle	21 degrees	21 degrees
Departure angle	33 degrees	33 degrees
Base curb mass	880 kg	840 kg
Full-loaded weight	N/A	1,215 kg
Fuel tank capacity	N/A	35L
Luggage capacity	190–1308L	180–1300L
Engine		
Model	N/A	Daewoo M-Tec
Type	L4, OHC	L3, SOHC 6-valve SOHC6
Displacement	1051 mL	769 mL
Max power	38.5kw/5,200 rpm	37.5kw/6,000 rpm
Max torque	83Nm/3,000 rpm	68.6Nm/4,600 rpm
Compression	9.1	9.3
Bore × stroke	65.5mm×78mm	N/A
Driveline	FF	N/A
Transmission		
Type	5-speed manual	5-speed auto/manual
Suspension		
Front	Mcpherson strut	Mcpherson strut
Rear	Dependent	Trailing arm
Steering		
Type	N/A	Rack-and-pinion, power steering
Brake system		
Front/rear	Disk/drum	Ventilated disc/drum
Wheels and tires		
Wheels	13in aluminum	4.5J × 13 aluminum
Tires	175/60 R3	155/65 R13
Performance		
Max. speed	140 km/h	140 km/h
Economical parameters		
Fuel consumption	4.4L/100 km, constant 60 km/h	4L/100 km, constant 90 km/h
Emission	Euro II	Euro II

Bitter quarrels

According to General Motors, GM Daewoo had only formally authorized SAIC-GM-Wuling to manufacture and sell Chevrolet Spark. It had never authorized any other company to use any of the Matiz patents or technologies in China. General Motors questioned Chery's R&D processes. In general, the R&D process of a new car was a complicated process with 15 steps that took 40 months to complete. However, SAIC Chery spent only two years on the R&D for their QQ model. Li Zhenfan, the executive responsible for the development of Matiz 150 at GM Daewoo, commented:

> It took us 51 months and US$200 million to upgrade the Matiz from the first to the second generation. The development of the Matiz's engine cost an additional several hundred million dollars.[10]

Zhang Jie, the interior furnishing director at the Pan Asia Automotive Technical Center, warned:

> Non-standard manufacturing processes might result in seven dangers: difficulty in driving, easy color fading due to sunlight, automotive parts failure, material vulnerability under extreme temperatures, bad vehicular performance, poor vehicular and parts anti-erosion performance, and decreased safety.[11]

Despite these queries, SAIC Chery was very confident about its R&D process. The company had invested RMB700 million, including RMB500 million in the institute building. It had recruited several industry experts, including Xu Min, who served as the director of Chery's Automotive Engineering Institute and had previous experience at Delphi and Visteon as an engine expert, and as a vice-president who was named the Best Auto Designer of 2003 in China. There were a total of about 600 people who worked at the institute, including 35 foreign experts from Ford, General Motors, and other automotive companies. In 2004 SAIC Chery was named the only automobile company among the 153 national bases for transformation in China's "863 Plan."[12] Xu Min was obviously proud of these achievements; he commented:

> *Toyota, as a late mover in the world auto industry, could catch up with its unique model. So, why can't the Chinese find a new mode of development characterized by better efficiency, quality, and technology?*[13]

An article written to state leaders vividly described the details of Chery's R&D:

> *Some automobile companies decided to rely solely on their joint ventures and planned to dismiss the people in their technical center. Therefore, these people (around 20) hoped to join other auto companies and SAIC Chery sent invitations to them … In order to demonstrate their abilities, they worked day and night and were able to design the Oriental Son and the QQ within eight months.*[14]

Sun Yong, Sales Director, SAIC Chery, added:

> *The QQ has obtained 25 national patents in appearances, interior furnish and structure. Thus, it is ridiculous to say that we violated the Intellectual Property Rights (IPR) of others.*[15]

Chen Jiangang, a professor at Shanghai Jiaotong University, held different views:

> *Even though the Matiz didn't apply patents for its design, its appearance should automatically be protected according to Copyright Law.*[16]

Though SAIC Chery firmly denied these accusations, an interesting sentence appeared on its website:

> *At a stage of growth, we absorbed some product advantages from rivals.*[17]

A newspaper in Beijing depicted the IPR disputes as a plot of MNCs:

> *After the Chery Flagcloud was brought to market, Volkswagen bought one vehicle and took it back to its headquarters in Germany for further study. To their surprise … it*

was a great car that was selling at a low price ... Then, in May 2002, Volkswagen asked SAIC to forward its suggestion of acquiring SAIC Chery ... SAIC Chery turned down the offer without hesitation ... In July 2002 Volkswagen asserted that SAIC Chery had violated its IPRs ... Admittedly, the QQ and the Oriental Son may have imitated some aspects of the Matiz and the Magnus, or were inspired by the concepts of other car models, but there was nothing done against the law.

GM was angry with Chery for two reasons. First, GM simply didn't believe that such a young company could develop two new models on its own in such a short period ... Chery had developed the two models by means of reverse engineering ... Reverse engineering is a common practice in the automotive industry and is legal. Second, the QQ destroyed the dream of Chevrolet for its Spark ... Facing huge financial losses, it was no wonder that MNCs bitterly disliked Chinese companies with their own IPRs.[18]

In April 2003 General Motors entrusted an agent to investigate the Chery QQ in further detail. It turned out that the vehicular structure, exterior appearance, interior design, and core parts of both the Chery QQ and the Chevrolet Spark were nearly the same. Surprisingly, most parts were exchangeable between the two models.[19]

A common headache for foreign automobile companies

General Motors was not the first foreign automobile enterprise troubled by IPR issues in China. Daimler Chrysler had previously accused the Geely Automobile Co. of copying its vehicle railings. However, Geely won the case in November 2003 because it owned the relevant patents. In February 2003, Toyota accused Geely of copying its trademark and misleading consumers. Geely used the TOYOTA trademark and the phase "Meiri[20] Automobile, Toyota Engine" in its advertisements. Toyota's suit was turned down by the courts in November 2003. Volkswagen threatened to take SAIC Chery to court. Since some suppliers of Shanghai Volkswagen[21] serviced SAIC Chery, some parts of Chery's automobiles were the same as those in the Santana, the flagship model of Shanghai Volkswagen. After the mediation of their mutual partner SAIC, SAIC Chery agreed to compensate Volkswagen approximately US$18 million.[22] Nissan sued the Great Wall Automobile Holding Co. for copying a Nissan SUV model sold in the US market. Honda also entered into several suits. It won the case against the Chongqing Lifan Group, which sold motors in the brand HONGDA. The Lifan Group was ordered to compensate approximately US$180,000 to Honda. Additionally, Honda also sued Shuanghuan Automobile for copying its CR-V model.

SAIC Chery's ambition to go abroad

The IPR disputes at home did not dampen SAIC Chery's ambitions of expanding into international markets. SAIC Chery made a very strategic move in deciding to first penetrate into markets deemed less important for MNCs. In October 2001 SAIC Chery began exporting cars to the Middle East. It negotiated with companies in Pakistan, Egypt, Syria, and in other countries about establishing JVs. By October 2004, SAIC Chery's factory in Iran had started manufacturing cars. In addition, the company set up 21 dealerships in Syria, which sold 3,000 Chery automobiles. It was said that SAIC Chery even planned to transfer some technologies to foreign companies. A European car manufacturer approached SAIC Chery to discuss the possibility of an OEM. Even with these groundbreaking moves and its initial success, SAIC Chery still had a difficult time in the international markets due to its relatively unknown brand, lack of talented personnel, as well as other key factors.

GM's choices

On November 8, 2003, the first Chevrolet Spark rolled off the production line. Sales numbers were far less than expected. By August 2004 only 365 Spark cars had been sold. On September 22, 2004, SAIC Chery declared that the new QQ EZDrive would be available soon. The very next day, SAIC-GM-Wuling announced a price reduction of the 0.8L manual transmission Spark by US$1,932 to US$5,531. Accordingly, the price of the automatic transmission Spark was lowered by 13.7% to US$7,584. This 26% price cut set a new record for domestic mini cars. On October 10, SAIC Chery began selling the new QQ EZDrive at a price just 1 RMB higher than that of the Spark. In 2004, the sales quantities of the

QQ and the Spark were estimated to be 6 to 1 (see CS Exhibit 5.8). The price cut was a painful decision for SAIC-GM-Wuling, as described in a report:

> The price cut meant huge losses for SAIC-GM-Wuling ... It seemed that SAIC-GM-Wuling had few alternatives. It had to dispose of inventories and, more importantly, compete head-to-head with the Chery QQ ... SAIC-GM-Wuling only realized profits of US$16.7 million last year ... After such a significant price cut, SAIC-GM-Wuling still had to maintain a sound after-sales service system, which would be a challenging task ... The only possible reason for such an action is to dispose of inventories of the 0.8L Spark to pave the way for the 1.0L Spark, which will be launched on the market in November. 1.0L Spark will be the new hope for SAIC-GM-Wuling.[23]

According to Rick Wagoner, CEO of General Motors: "There is always risk when you're investing in an emerging market. But the bigger risk is not being there."[24]

Even before the disputes over the Chery QQ and the Chevrolet Spark were resolved, another SAIC Chery model ran into IPR trouble. In early December 2003 GM China accused the SAIC Chery Oriental Son, which was introduced to the market in July 2003, of being a copy of GM Daewoo's Magnus. Again, SAIC Chery defended itself, saying that the Oriental Son was developed independently by SAIC

CS EXHIBIT 5.8: SALES VOLUME OF QQ AND CHEVROLET SPARK (JAN.–JULY 2004)
Source: Accuracy Automotive, CAND Weekly Digest, September 6–10, 2004.

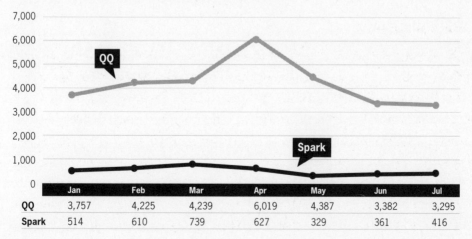

	Jan	Feb	Mar	Apr	May	Jun	Jul
QQ	3,757	4,225	4,239	6,019	4,387	3,382	3,295
Spark	514	610	739	627	329	361	416

Chery, was protected by many of its own patents, and did not violate any IPRs. On December 3, 2003, a vice minister of foreign affairs said in a press conference that China's Ministry of Commerce had held meetings with GM China in order to find solutions to the disputes between General Motors and SAIC Chery.

Faced with the aggressive actions of SAIC Chery, both in China and abroad, General Motors needed to do more than just cut prices. First, the company needed to figure out how to protect its interests in China. Second, General Motors needed to decide how to best deal with the Chinese government. Should General Motors attack the government, attempt a private settlement without government interference, or use the government as a mediator? General Motors questioned its chances of winning the case should it be taken to court. How should General Motors react if the Central Government supported SAIC Chery? It was very important for General Motors to not jeopardize its relationship with the government. Lastly, General Motors wondered if it was better to simply take action against Chery outside China.

CASE COMMENTARIES

COMMENTARY 1

GERALD E. FRYXELL

PROFESSOR OF MANAGEMENT

CHINA EUROPE INTERNATIONAL BUSINESS SCHOOL (CEIBS)

The case poses the following question: what should GM China do about Chery's alleged and flagrant reengineering of its GM-Daewoo "Matiz" model?

GM China should consider the following actions:

- It seems advisable for General Motors to attempt some form of litigation against Chery … albeit it is most likely to lose. It should be remembered that the legal system in China is not very mature and it would appear that there are sufficient differences between the QQ and Spark to make it less than obvious that the QQ was a blatant violation of GM's IPR. Consequently, it would be naive of General Motors to expect the "rule of law," as it knows from its operations in the "developed" world, to be firmly and consistently applied. For one thing, the whole notion of IPR is relatively new to China, and Chinese society remains very accepting of the notion of "copying" in all its forms. The legal system is also just developing, and in China, in line with its cultural traditions, judges tend to be more flexible and generally impose rather lenient penalties. Moreover, General Motors should expect Chinese judges to be somewhat biased toward the small local company that is being pressed by a global giant. Another consideration is that such a lawsuit may be negatively received by the public for the same reason. Regardless, General Motors is still the player with the deepest pockets and needs to send a signal to Chery to think twice before flagrantly copying its products. The reader should also recall that Chery seems intent on leading Chinese automobile manufacturers in export markets and it would be in some of these places that General Motors might have more luck with litigation.

- General Motors should also do what it can to try to impede the possible flow of information to competitor(s). This can be accomplished mostly via tighter security over its information and by making sure that details about models are sufficiently dispersed such that locals would have difficulty in "stealing" plans and designs. On the other hand, there is little that General Motors can do to protect against the practice of "reengineering" (the disassembly and copying of specific parts once a product is available in the marketplace). It should be remembered that Chery was formed from a company that previously made automobile parts and was probably quite skilled at this. In addition, the fact that SAIC is a JV partner for both competitors is also troublesome. While the case seems to imply that SAIC has little direct influence on Chery, some individuals at SAIC undoubtedly possess a great deal of information and this must surely lead to a conflict of interest for them. Thus, General Motors should force SAIC out of this alliance with Chery. This is something that both Chery and the city of Wuhu would appear to have little resistance towards.

- Most fundamentally, however, General Motors should arguably *not* be in the mini-car market in the first place and should divest its interests in the SAIC-GM-Wuling JV as a product line where it is not well positioned in the marketplace. It must face the reality that it is going to be very hard to compete with a local – and apparently very nimble – competitor for a market segment where customers are very price conscious, where General Motors has little preexisting brand identity, and where product development speed and government connections are crucial. Indeed, regarding the latter points, it is remarkable how Chery beat General Motors to market by some eight months (presumably after a much later start if they stole the designs). This, along with local marketing savvy, literally preempted the Spark's sales, leading ultimately to drastic price cuts for the Spark just to get rid of unwanted inventory. The JV structure, in itself, probably slowed down product design/launch cycle times and, globally, General Motors has a reputation for being slow to market. Consequently, it should not, indeed cannot, compete on price with a local manufacturer like Chery. Its best hope lies in manufacturing a good quality car with advanced technology at the higher end – less price-elastic market segments.

This case study is informative in reminding foreign companies that it is important to protect their IPRs, but also that it will be challenging to do so in China. MNCs must do everything they can to protect their IPRs. This includes such basic items as registering IPRs and filing for patents (something General Motors unfortunately overlooked until it was too late), while maintaining good government relations so as to gain the cooperation of the authorities in enforcing their IPRs. Companies in China also need to be more innovative in many other ways; this can include special packaging, establishing "hotlines" in an attempt to find out where counterfeit operations may be, or hiring special agents who work in this area. Fundamentally, companies must position their products and brands strategically, so as not to be vulnerable to competition from counterfeiters.

COMMENTARY 2
DOUG HO SONG
MANAGING DIRECTOR
DOOSAN LEADERSHIP INSTITUTE
DOOSAN GROUP

It is obvious that there is counterfeiting. Chery sold 90,000 cars in 2003 and exported 1,200 cars, accounting for 50% of all Chinese-branded automobiles exported that year. This result can be addressed as somewhat legendary. Unlike other Chinese car makers, Chery has the strategy to be an independent automobile manufacturer.

How can Chery achieve this tremendous growth? How did Chery, a late-comer, win in China's car market, which is characterized by fierce competition? Being independent may be rewarding in the long run but it cannot explain their success. In my opinion, they have used some creative ways.

The Chery QQ is very similar in appearance to the Matiz, the original model for the Chevrolet Spark. According to the General Motors' study, parts are exchangeable between the Chevrolet Spark and Chery QQ. Allegedly, the QQ was developed in an extremely short time and at a very low cost. Chery spent only two years on R&D for their QQ model, while other average car manufacturers need 40 months to complete the whole process of any new car model. GM Daewoo spent US$200 million to upgrade the Matiz from the first to the second generation. But Chery spent only RMB200 million (US$25 million) to develop a new model from scratch.

Another critical fact is that Chery's Oriental Son is the supposed copy of GM Daewoo's Magnus. Both the Chery QQ and Oriental Son were designed after the Matiz and Magnus, and both are produced by the same company. This cannot be a coincidence. In my opinion, this is the secret of SAIC QQ's success. This explains how an independent company without prior experience and with limited capital is doing so well in such a difficult market.

How should GM China act with regard to IPR disputes?

The Chinese market is very attractive to all car makers in the world. GM China should protect its interest in this market and it cannot be silent regarding Chery's behavior. However, it is not easy to determine how far GM China should go into the dispute. There could be a backlash if GM China tries to have Chery stop selling the QQ and Oriental Son entirely.

Most probably, Chery must have considered all the related rules and regulations before launching QQ. They may even have elaborated a strategy to counterattack General Motors on IPR disputes. Although GM China could be successful in forcing Chery to stop selling the QQ, the cost would be huge in terms of money and public image.

So at the beginning of proceedings it would be very important for GM China to define their goal carefully. Establishing this goal definition is the most important decision for GM China. On one side, General Motors can create some noise by using the media to place pressure on Chery. On the extreme, General Motors can follow the litigation path by trying to force Chery to stop selling the QQ and to pay damages to GM China. GM China should decide which appropriate path to follow after careful consideration of the risks and costs.

What should GM China's real concern be?

It seems obvious that Chery copied General Motors' car. However, Chery's success in the Chinese market cannot be explained only by this. Chery certainly has some strengths. GM China should study Chery closely and learn from it. Chery sells the QQ at a very low price, but with good profit. This means Chery can utilize resources more effectively than GM China. Also, Chery's marketing is successful – they understand Chinese customers very well. This is another lesson for General Motors.

It may take time for Chery to catch up in technology, but once they do, they will become a very serious competitor, not only in China, but also in the global market. This may be the real challenge for GM China.

NOTES

1   This is the title of a movie in which Leonardo di Caprio plays the role of a money and cheque counterfeiter who always manages to escape the FBI.

2   DRC refers to Development Research Center under the State Council of China.

3   Frederik Balfour et. al. 2005, "Fakes!" *BusinessWeek*, February 7, pp. 46–53.

4   This case was prepared by Dr. Shengjun Liu under the supervision of Professor Juan A. Fernandez at CEIBS using public sources. The case was prepared on the basis of class discussion rather than to illustrate either effective or ineffective handling of an administrative situation. Certain names and other identifying information may have been disguised to protect confidentiality. The case was originally published by CEIBS in 2005. Published with permission.

5   John Muller, "Stolen Cars," *Forbes*, February 16, 2004.

6   SAIC refers to Shanghai Automotive Industry Corporation.

7   Its Asia Pacific region consisted of 14 countries, including India and New Zealand. It grew most rapidly in GM worldwide.

8   In 2002, the business in China accounted for 80% of Volkswagen's profits.

9   David Welch, Dexter Roberts, and Gail Edmondson, "GM: Gunning It in China," *BusinessWeek*, June 21, 2004.

10 "QQ and Spark: Chevrolet and Chery Compete in Mini Car Market," *Sichuan Online*, October 1, 2003.

11 Ibid.

12 Also known as the National High-Tech Research and Development Program.

13 Zhu Hong, "What Does the Going Abroad of National Brands Mean?" *Auto Weekly*, *Xinhua Daily News*, November 11, 2004.

14 Jin Lvzhong, "Chery Uncovered Two Legends of China's Automotive Industry," *China Engineering Science*, September 2004.

15 Zhou Guangjun, "A Face-to-face Competition between QQ and Spark," *Beijing Entertainment Newspaper*, May 30, 2003.

16 "Inside Story of GM-Chery IPR Disputes," *21st Century Business Herald*, September 17, 2004.

17 Wang Ning, "QQ Case Not Ended, Oriental Son Got into Trouble Again," *Beijing Modern Business Newspaper*, November 13, 2003.

18 Fu Weiyan, "Why Do MNCs Hate Chinese Enterprises Which Have Their Own IPRs?" *Beijing Modern Business Newspaper*, May 8, 2004.

19 "GM Daewoo Finally Accused Chery of Unfair Competition," *SINA Auto*, December 16, 2004.

20 In Chinese, *meiri* means America and Japan.

21 Shanghai Volkswagen is a JV between Volkswagen and SAIC.

22 The compensation had been paid by SAIC.

23 Li Yuan, "Wuling Fight to Win or Die, Chery Conquers International Market Alone," *Southern Weekend*, October 15, 2004.

24 David Welch, Dexter Roberts, and Gail Edmondson, "GM: Gunning It in China," *Business Week*, June 21, 2004.

Chapter 6
Chinese consumers:
The new kids on the block

INTRODUCTION

China's population, which is the largest in the world, is already translating into the largest market for many products. Now, China is the number one market for cellular phones, TVs, and many other products. It will become the leading market for beer, medicine, automobiles, computers and air travel, not to mention the unlimited thirst for natural resources. Naturally, no multinational can afford to miss the golden opportunity that China represents. On the other hand, China is not an easy market. According to data from the US Chamber of Commerce, around one-third of US enterprises are losing money in China (see Exhibit 6.1).[1] China's rapid economic growth is accompanied by rapid changes and uncertainty in consumer behavior. As one saying goes, "everything is possible in China but nothing is easy." Multinationals who want to win in China should first of all understand Chinese consumers.

What are the main characteristics of Chinese consumers? It is difficult to isolate them, especially when their mores and needs are changing so rapidly. Here are some of those characteristics that we consider important.

EXHIBIT 6.1: THE PROFITABILITY OF US COMPANIES IN CHINA (2002–2004)
Source: The American Chamber of Commerce, P.R. China, American Business in China: White Paper 2005.

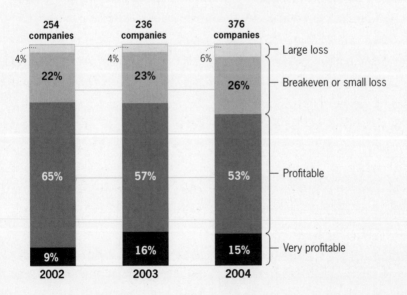

Consumer behaviors with Chinese characteristics

Research shows that differences in consumer behaviors are closely connected to the value systems across various cultures (Hampton and Gent 1984; McCort and Malhotra 1993). Consumer behavior in China is strongly influenced by its unique culture, as well as its long history. Most important of all, Chinese people are deeply influenced by the Confucian doctrine, which includes respect for authority, desire for harmony, conservatism, tolerance, and filial piety. Another important aspect of the Chinese culture is the concept of "face." "Face" means to be sensitive to other people's expectations and comments. An excellent illustration of "face" is that the Chinese tend to order an excessive number of dishes when they eat out with friends. The idea is to impress rather than to feed them.

For thousands of years, the Chinese were used to judging people by what they wore. It is no wonder that luxury goods producers such as Louis Vuitton are putting extraordinary passion into the mainland China market. According to a report published by Goldman Sachs in 2006, China is already the third-largest market for luxury goods in the world, and its demand is increasing at an annual rate of 25%.[2] This feature of the Chinese consumer means that advertising plays an extremely important role in purchasing decisions. Sometimes people buy something not because they like it, but because of the power of the marketing campaigns. In China, many healthcare products boast about their amazing, almost magic results. Despite the abundant negative results of healthcare products, Chinese consumers are still easily captured by the publicity. In fact, the real difference among various healthcare products lies in their marketing rather than in their functions. In this sense, the Chinese are still naive consumers.

However, the Chinese are now realizing that they are kings when it comes to buying. During the time before reform and opening up, the Chinese suffered from serious shortages of consumer goods. Producers did not have to worry about selling their products, even if they were of low quality – Chinese consumers bought everything. When Zhang Ruimin, the CEO of Haier Group, destroyed inferior refrigerators in the early 1980s in front of his employees, they thought he was mad. However, due to the emergence of private enterprises and the invasion of multinationals, China's market has transformed from a sellers' to a buyers' market. Producers, if they want to sell, must constantly improve quality and reduce prices just to be in the market. Simultaneously, new laws have been passed to protect consumers. In 1984 the China Consumers' Association was established as a vehicle to enhance consumer protection. In 1993 China passed its Law for Consumer Protection.

Chinese consumers are learning to use both legal and media weapons to defend their rights. The Mercedes-Benz case presented in this chapter is only one illustration of how explicitly consumers can present their claims. However, Chinese consumers in general are still much more easygoing than Western consumers. Many of them are still not well aware of their rights. Besides, lawsuits are discouraged by the low efficiency of the local courts and the small amount of compensation plaintiffs usually receive. However, in some cases, their frustration and disappointment when they don't get what they expect may lead to disproportionate reactions, as in the Benz case.

In this process of China's opening to the world, the Western lifestyle is finding its way. Although the country has a deep-rooted culture with a long history, Chinese people show a preference for Western products and lifestyles. This is especially true among the young Chinese. They prefer US movies, Western brands, and even celebrate Western holidays such as Halloween. Young Chinese now have more passion for Christmas than for Chinese New Year. Starbucks is having an amazing success in a country famous for its tea culture, presumably not because of the taste of coffee but because of the lifestyle Starbucks represents. The Chinese have a certain respect for foreign brands; in their mind, they represent quality and reliability.

In general, Chinese consumers give great value to foreign brands. They had their first contact with foreign brands early in the 1900s. Many elderly Chinese still call a box of matches "foreign match." As a Chinese saying goes, "the moon in foreign countries is brighter than that in China." For them, foreign brands not only represent quality and fashion, but also a symbol of social status. Even for home appliances, dominated by Chinese companies, foreign brands like Sony and Philips are still considered the best and thus enjoy a certain price premium.

This phenomenon applies to many industries such as clothing, automobiles, notebooks, cell phones, hotels, and so on. Interestingly, local firms also take advantage of this blind preference for foreign products. For example, a local clothing manufacturer named itself Metersbonwe, which sounds like a foreign name, and hired Taiwan and Hong Kong stars to appear on its advertisements. It turned out to be a big hit. Many customers, mostly teenagers, still do not know that Metersbonwe is a local brand. When you walk through the famous East Nanjing Road in Shanghai, you find many stores promoting their clothes by labeling them as "domestic sales of commodities originally produced for export." However, this high expectation on foreign brands is a double-edged sword, as we can see from the Benz case.

In China, the only constant rule is that every rule is changing. Despite China's long history, the market economy is a very recent phenomenon. With the opening of the country to the rest of the world and progressive market reforms, Chinese consumers are also learning quickly. As a result, what worked yesterday might turn out to be wrong today. In such a dynamic environment, foreign enterprises cannot rely on repeating what worked in the past. Instead, they should adjust products, strategies, and marketing in quick response to changes in consumer requirements.

Another element that adds up to the rapid change comes from local competitors who are quickly catching up with foreign rivals. Even in the automotive industry, previously monopolized by foreign brands such as Audi and Volkswagen, local car makers like Chery and Geely have experienced dramatic success. In contrast, Volkswagen, which once enjoyed a market share of more than half of China's car market, is giving way to local firms and other foreign brands. In the PC industry, Lenovo was irrelevant to giants such as IBM or HP since it only ranked number 10 in China's PC market in 1995. Today, Lenovo is China's leading brand. Ironically, it ended up acquiring IBM's PC business in 2004. Similarly, Whirlpool, once the world leader in microwave ovens, was easily beaten by Galanz, which now accounts for one-third of the microwave oven global market.

Some foreign companies assumed that China was an under-developed market. As a result, they brought outdated products to China. Volkswagen was a good example of this. In the early 1980s, Volkswagen established two JVs in China. Thanks to strong support from local governments and the lack of competitors, Volkswagen occupied nearly half of the car market in China. Santana and Audi were widely used by officials and the taxi industry. However, the huge success blinded Volkswagen to the increasing competition from other foreign and local firms. Today, compared to its rivals like Honda and General Motors, its car models are now considered outdated by the Chinese. No wonder Chinese consumers gradually abandoned Volkswagen since they now have many more choices. By 2005 its market share had dropped sharply to 19%. Meanwhile, its profit in China decreased from around 700 million euros in 2003 to 220 million euros in 2004, and there were even losses in 2005.[3] Volkswagen's experience demonstrated the dynamic and challenging nature of the market in mainland China. Foreign enterprises also tend to underestimate how fast China's market can grow. For example, China's cell phone users exploded from 24.48 million in 1999 to 339.79 million in 2005, increasing by 1,288%. China's auto industry has experienced a similar growth in the past decade.

National pride is another danger for multinationals. In its modern history, China has been invaded by many Western countries and by Japan. With the peaceful rising of China, national pride has also picked up. After all, China, as the Middle Kingdom, was once much more powerful in the world than the United States today. The Chinese people are becoming more and more sensitive to issues connected with national dignity. Given Japan's attitudes toward past wars, Japanese companies are especially vulnerable to this reemerging pride. In recent years, many Japanese cars have been damaged during street protests every time the Japanese prime minister visited the War Heroes Shrine. Another example is a Toyota advertisement, in which a lion bows to a Toyota car. This advertisement irritated the Chinese public since the lion, which represents China,

EXHIBIT 6.2: TOYOTA'S ADVERTISEMENT IN CHINA
Source: Li Jia, "Why the Lion Salutes to Toyota: An Analysis of Toyota's Advertisement Crisis," Beijing Star Daily, December 3, 2003.

is bowing to Toyota, which represents Japan. The advertisement made people recall the terrible Japanese invasion of World War 2.

In brief, Chinese consumers are deemed "the new kids on the block" to many Western companies. They "hug" Western products while having strong national pride. They are easygoing but are getting tougher. They trust foreign products but overreact when they feel cheated. Marketing in China is like an interesting adventure, and foreign companies must be flexible, responsible, and responsive to gain the hearts and pockets of Chinese consumers.

In China, "nothing is easy, everything is possible." Sometimes people do not trust the courts or time-consuming negotiations, especially when companies' reactions seem bureaucratic. The following case, Mercedes-Benz and Wuhan Wild Animal Park, demonstrates many points discussed in this chapter. In the morning of December 25, 2001, many people in Wuhan, a large city in middle China, were surprised to see a Mercedes SLK230 sports coupe being towed by a water buffalo in the street. The next day the car was wrecked by five men in the Wuhan Wild Animal Park (WWAP) on behalf of the owner, publicly humiliating Mercedes. After the negotiation between WWAP and Mercedes failed, WWAP threatened to smash another Mercedes car. Why did such a terrible incident happen? What makes the car owner resort to such an extreme reaction? How should Mercedes handle this situation? Could Mercedes prevent this incident repeating itself again? Mercedes would have to act fast.

Following the case, you will find two commentaries: the first by Dongsheng Zhou, Professor of Marketing, CEIBS; and the second by Yufeng Zhao, GM, Progress Strategy Consulting Co., Ltd. Both commentators focus on what are the right responses for Benz. They also provide insights into key elements of crisis management.

CASE STUDY
MERCEDES-BENZ AND WUHAN WILD ANIMAL PARK[4]

It seemed that winter turbulence would continue unabated for Mercedes-Benz managers trying to resolve a customer complaint in Wuhan, China (see CS Exhibit 6.1). On February 27, 2002, the owner of a Mercedes S320 had threatened to smash his car with sledgehammers at Wuhan Wild Animal Park (WWAP) in the presence of spectators and journalists. If carried out, this would be the second Mercedes-Benz automobile destroyed at the park within three months. The first car – owned by WWAP – had been smashed in December at the direction of park managers who complained of poor quality and insufficient repair servicing. The event built strong public awareness of WWAP's complaints, but also sparked a debate about the propriety of the park managers' actions. Some considered the product destruction extreme and unproductive, especially in view of Mercedes' repeated attempts to find a solution at cost to itself. Others sympathized with the park managers and considered Mercedes insensitive to the needs of Chinese buyers. To fully resolve the problem, managers would have to consider the public's views as well as those of the disgruntled WWAP managers. The threat of another imminent car smashing meant they would have to act fast.

CS EXHIBIT 6.1: MAP OF CHINA

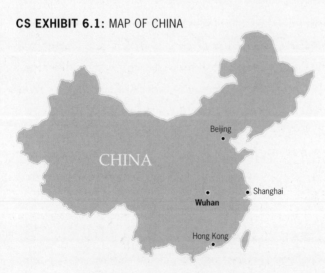

Company and customers disagree

The situation first gained widespread attention on December 25, 2001, when Wang Sheng, Chairman of WWAP, had his Mercedes SLK230 sports coupe towed by a water buffalo through the city of Wuhan to protest what he claimed was insufficient servicing of a defective product. The car had been purchased for RMB700,000[5] from the Bingshi Car Sales Center of Beijing (Bingshi) on December 19, 2000, and was one of four Mercedes autos owned by the park. Sheng claimed that repeated repairs had failed to fix a problem with the car's fuel system. In protest, he wrote on the car in bold letters, "No quality, no service" and "This is Mercedes, let's kick it." He then had the car towed through the town accompanied by journalists and photographers.

On the following day Sheng held a press conference at the animal park's entrance where the vehicle was parked. Journalists were told that the car's problems had started a few weeks after its purchase. Although Bingshi technicians had traveled to Wuhan repeatedly for repair servicing, Sheng felt that problems persisted. Because the car's warranty had expired on December 19, and a consumer association was unwilling to help,[6] Sheng felt that a public event was his only possible recourse.[7] Thus, when the press conference ended, hired men were ordered to pound the car with hammers and sticks until the exterior shell was mangled. Journalists loved the inherent drama of the story, and media reports in subsequent days showed images of the car being towed and ultimately smashed.

WWAP claimed it had sent faxes to the retailer and manufacturer prior to the warranty expiration demanding the car's exchange or return, and warning of drastic action in the event of refusal. To justify these demands, park managers cited a US "lemon law" (see CS Exhibit 6.2) that allows consumers to return a car for replacement if a problem persists after three attempted repairs.[8] Mercedes, however, disagreed with WWAP's claims of poor quality and, instead, believed that the problems were caused by the customer's use of inferior, low octane fuel that did not match the car's specifications. Therefore, the solution that was offered to WWAP did not extend to a full refund or replacement of the vehicle. Company statements indicated that Beijing engineers who examined the car's fuel tank found dark colored fuel and dregs that had blocked the car's oil spray nozzle.[9] The car had already been serviced repeatedly and the nozzle replaced

CASE STUDY: MERCEDES-BENZ AND WUHAN WILD ANIMAL PARK

at Bingshi's expense, for a cumulative total cost of more than RMB100,000.[10] Mercedes concluded that "impurities contained in the fuel affected the perform- ance of the car … [and] we cannot replace the car [when problems stem from] external factors rather than a quality problem of the car itself."[11] Nevertheless, the company offered to clean the car's fuel system at no charge, redeemable through the end of January 2002.[12]

Despite the extension of time for repairs under warranty conditions, WWAP refused the offer and on December 26 the car was smashed. Only the windscreen, headlights, and exterior shell were destroyed, leaving the engine intact. Ms Liu Yueling, assistant to Sheng, told reporters that damage was limited to the car's ex- terior surface so that key parts could be used as evidence in a future law suit.[13]

The Chinese press ran the story widely (see CS Exhibit 6.3), with some deliv- ering editorial commentary and quotes from WWAP managers that described Mercedes products and service in unfavorable, and even inflammatory, terms. In one story, Ms Liu stated that "Mercedes has discriminated against Chinese customers."[14] Stories in the international press were more muted and careful in presenting product quality evaluations as the views of park managers rather than established fact. Stories differed as well in describing the car's ailments. Most centered on trouble with the fuel system, but some cited problems with the computer and steering systems. In one report Bingshi management was said

CS EXHIBIT 6.2: US LEMON LAW

Although details vary across individual states and the District of Columbia, the underlying principles of the U.S. lemon law are the same. In the state of Ohio, for example, a car is considered a lemon if it has one or several problems incongruent with the quality warranty. Customers who have identified problems related to performance, value and safety in the first year of purchase or the first 18,000 miles of driving can report to the manufacturer and request that the problems be solved. The car will be regarded as a lemon if its problems can't be repaired by the manufacturer when given the proper opportunity. In this event the customer has the right to demand a refund of the purchase price or a return of the vehicle for a new one.

CASE STUDY: MERCEDES-BENZ AND WUHAN WILD ANIMAL PARK

CS EXHIBIT 6.3: SAMPLE NEWSPAPER REPORTS OF THE WUHAN EVENT

Park Rangers in Car-Smashing Frenzy

By Xing Bao, *Shanghai Star*,
January 3, 2002
Reproduced with permission

Five people publicly smashed up a Mercedes-Benz SLK230 in Wuhan, Hubei province on December 26. The furious owner, Wuhan Wildlife Park, said they trashed the car because it still had problems after being fixed five times over the course of one year. At 11:00 a.m. the park's general manager Zhao Jun yelled 'Start!' and five young employees proceeded to smash up the luxury automobile with sticks and hammers. Glass from the car broke into pieces and flew in all directions. The smooth shell of the car was mangled beyond recognition.

It is the first case of car-cracking following a quality-related complaint by a consumer that has been recorded in China. "We've got to destroy the car," explained Zaho Jun. "We have no other way to complain about this low-quality product. Even the consumer's association refused to accept our complaint because it is related to a private company."

The owner bought the import-

ed Mercedes-Benz on December 19, 2000, from the Bingshi Vehicle Sales Company in Beijing. But after less than three months the car turned out to be a lemon, with a leaking gasoline line, weak pickup, and other assorted problems. "The computer system went haywire, causing the warning lamp to continuously light up," Zhao said. The problems remained after a fifth trip to the repair shop on December 12. The guarantee expired seven days later. The Mercedes-Benz authorities said the problems had nothing to do with the car, but were related to the use of sub-standard gasoline.

The park faxed the sales company and two agencies of Mercedes-Benz in China and demanded the company take back the car and give them a refund. The angry owner first mentioned his plan to publicly pulverize the car in a fax to the Mercedes-Benz agency on December 11 if the refund demand was not met. But by December 20 Mercedes-Benz was still refusing to yield and continued to assert that low-quality gasoline was the source

of the car's manifold problems and state of disorder.

Two staff members of Mercedes-Benz who went to repair the car said they were not doing so on behalf of Mercedes-Benz, but only represented themselves when answering questions from the media on December 19. "Their behavior helped us make the final decision to lay waste to the car in public," Zhao added. The car-cracking stunt attracted large numbers of interested onlookers.

The Beijing office of Mercedes-Benz released a statement on December 27. It reiterated that the underlying reason for the car's catastrophic condition was that the consumer had failed to use the

appropriate gasoline. "We have offered to clean the gasoline system for the consumer," the Mercedes-Benz statement announced. "The service will be available until the end of January of 2002. But the consumer refused this suggestion. We feel deeply sorry that they have rejected our offers of help," the statement said.

Duan Zhigang, deputy general manager of the park, pooh-poohed the suggestion that low-quality gasoline was to blame. "We have another three Mercedes-Benz cars, all of which use the same fuel and none of which have encountered any problems," he said. "If the gasoline quality is low in Wujan, why did the producer sell Mercedes-Benz cars

in the city? Don't they know how to respect the Chinese consumers?"

Not all local residents were in favor of taking such violent revolutionary action against the offending car. One young woman told the local media that she thought it was "unbelievable." However, another woman expressed the view that the action would likely harm the reputation of Mercedes-Benz. Yin Yan, a lawyer at Beijing Jingyi Lawyer's Office, said knocking the car to bits was definitely the wrong thing to do. "Though people have the right to destroy their own property, it is better for them to find a solution through legal procedures according to the laws concerned," he argued.

Mercedes-Benz deplores car-wrecking "stunt"

By Mark O'Neill, *South China Morning Post*, December 29, 2001
Reproduced with permission

Mercedes-Benz yesterday accused a man who destroyed one of its cars, to protest against defective parts, of staging a groundless publicity stunt. Wang Sheng, chairman of the Wuhan Wild Animal Park, ordered five men to smash the SLK230 he bought for 700,000 yuan (HK$660,000) a year ago. Wednesday's demolition in Wuhan, Hubei province, was watched by hundreds of spectators and the press. [Mr Wang] said the car had serious defects that had been repaired several times, to no avail and that the company refused to change or give him a new one.

"This was a publicity stunt," said a spokeswoman for Mercedes-Benz, a unit of Daimler-Chrysler. "It smacks of sensationalism. He had no grounds to do this. It was an extreme act and unwarranted." A company statement said the cause of the problems was the customer's use of fuel other than that specified by the manufacturer.

"It is unfortunate that the customer has chosen to decline our goodwill offer to clean his fuel system free of charge," the statement said. "We stress that Mercedes-

Benz strives to deal with all reasonable issues and concerns with care and thoroughness for our customer ... and feel it is a pity that in this case such an extreme, unnecessary action has been taken." The spokeswoman said the company refused to exchange the car because oil and fuel not recommended for the car was used.

The Bingshi Car Sales Centre of Beijing, where Mr Wang bought the car, said its engineers examined the fuel tank and found fuel of a darker colour than recommended and many dregs, which blocked the oil spray nozzle.

Mercedes faces a tough time from the Chinese media, which picked up a similar story about consumer complaints over Mitsubishi Pajeros. The press has run many stories about injuries which victims blamed on faulty Pajeros, damaging the company's reputation.

According to a front-page article in the *Beijing Youth Daily*, while consumers had the right to do what they pleased with their properties, the destruction of the car will definitely make solving the problem more difficult. It said the consumer committee of the China Quality Association had received a complaint from Mr Wang.

Why is Mercedes-Benz tough on its Chinese customer?

Translated from *Beijing Youth Daily*, January 24, 2002
Reproduced with permission

By playing a tough hand against a Chinese customer, Mercedes-Benz Company recently caused a big stir in China's car market, leading the customer to angrily smash his shoddy "Benz" because of the manufacturer's intransigence. Among news reports of various quality disputes in modern days there has never been a car manufacturer like Benz Company being so intransigent and unyielding, even showing an escalated angry mood in handling the quality problem of its car. People can observe the following three announcements made by the manufacturer:

December 27, 2001, "We are very sorry the customer refused our offered help, and for the most extreme unnecessary action he has taken."

January 8, 2002, "The car owner's action is irrational and regrettable."

January 17, 2002, Benz simply requested "an open letter of apology by Wuhan Wildlife Zoo for their unnecessary action taken in harming the rights and interests of our company and that it must make sure every new medium has a copy of the letter for carrying related news coverage".

How can the Benz Company be so forceful and show no scruples in playing a tough hand?

First, Benz's previous practice shows no Chinese customer has ever won out. It is common sense that an ordinary quality problem

should not have raised a big uproar for Benz or any other car company from the very outset. On December 26, 2001, before the Benz was smashed, the car owner held a press conference at Wuhan and had meanwhile given Benz Company the message that he would "smash his Benz" if his problem was not resolved. Different car manufacturers would have vastly different and varied means for handling such a problem. Personnel could be sent to patch things up by repairing the problem or improving relations to hush the matter. This has been done before by some Chinese manufacturers, as well as Korean. Japanese manufacturers act in a similar way. They would apologize sincerely and quickly send repairmen to help comfort customers. Added to the list could be various procrastinator-like moves to keep matters essentially the same and unresolved.

German manufacturers seem not to apply these techniques since their inborn rigidity and intransigence in work excludes any possible modifications or policy shifts. Of the various quality disputes we have learned about the concerned Benz Company, not a single Chinese customer has won.

Second, Benz as a luxury car enjoys the biggest sales among world brands. In 2001 Benz commanded sales of over 5,000 luxury cars in China and most of these are of the S-grade, leaving other brands far behind. The only threat posed to its market size is BMW. Why don't the manufacturers of Chi-

nese cars, or those from Korea or Japan, dare to challenge their customers over quality disputes? Because of their intense worries that sales would be affected. In other words, a quality dispute like the shoddy smashed Benz can in no way disfigure the image of luxury Benz or its market. This makes Benz bullish.

Third, corporate strength finds no match in individuals short of legal protection. Essentially, the blame is China's lack of laws ensuring car quality, orderly market sales, and consumption. It is reported that concerned central departments are currently mulling over specific laws or regulations to provide a legal basis for consumer protections.

But how will the case of the shoddy Benz that has been smashed end? Let's choose from among these alternatives:

One, Benz explicitly rules out any quality problems with its car and retains its right to countercharge the customer. Naturally, nothing comes out of the customer's half-year of effort and he will have to take his smashed car home from Beijing at long last. The chance of such an ending is 60%.

Two, Benz strikes an agreement with its customer after prolonged bargaining or haggling. A new Benz is provided on the sly so that the cat is not let out of the bag by news media. This stands a 40% chance.

Three, Benz admits its quality problem and openly apologizes. This would be a windfall.

to have claimed that the car's owner drove "too fast and used the steering wheel too violently" in addition to using low-quality fuel.[15]

Official statements from Mercedes to the press raised two major points. First, WWAP's actions were characterized as a "publicity stunt [that] smacks of sensationalism."[16] In support, a Mercedes spokesperson noted that WWAP had increased the park entry fee from 35 to 65 RMB on December 27, just after the car had been smashed. WWAP later called this a seasonal price adjustment that had nothing to do with the car incident. Second, Mercedes insisted that problems with the car's fuel system arose from the customer's use of inappropriate fuel rather than any inherent quality weakness. A spokesperson said that "many old Chinese gas stations are dirty in the petrol storehouse and petrol pump, and the petrol they sell is inferior in quality. We have constantly advised our customers to pay attention to this point."[17] The company asserted its "confidence that the vehicle [did] not have a quality problem," and called it "unfortunate that the customer [chose] to decline [the] goodwill offer to clean his fuel system free of charge." They further stressed that "Mercedes-Benz strives to deal with all reasonable issues and concerns with care and thoroughness for our customers … and feels it is a pity that in this case such an extreme, unnecessary action has been taken."[18]

In defending its own claims, WWAP noted that four Mercedes-Benz vehicles were owned by the park, but that only one had experienced the presumed problem with fuel. Fuel providers in Wuhan spoke up to support WWAP's arguments. A director at Hubei Petrol Company – which owned 80% of the area's petrol stations – stated that national producer SINOPEC (Wuhan) set strict standards for purchasing and managing gasoline. It was estimated that SINOPEC supplied 90% of the region's gasoline and diesel needs. The director claimed "there are many luxury cars in Wuhan, and my company also has two Mercedes, all running well." A SINOPEC director added that "gasoline sold in the China market has to satisfy a national quality standard just like any other product, and the product provided by SINOPEC (Wuhan) complies with [that] standard."[19]

Public reaction was mixed. Five additional disgruntled owners of Mercedes-Benz vehicles sympathized with WWAP's position and decided in December to form the Association of Mercedes Quality Victims (AMQV). By March the group's membership list had expanded to 23. Other members of the general public felt that, in failing to meet the demands of AMQV members, Mercedes showed insensitivity to the needs of Chinese buyers. Some suggested that Mercedes was arrogant. In contrast, however, many people felt the park had gone too far with the publicity event, and advised taking a legal route to solving the problem. One belief shared by all parties on both sides of the debate was that China needed to do more to ensure consumer rights and protection.

The debate escalates

As January unfolded the parties remained entrenched in their respective positions, and each raised the ante of the dispute. Mercedes took a firm stance by threatening legal action against WWAP for damaging its reputation. The car maker stated that "… inappropriate action taken by WWAP has made it impossible to constructively solve this problem through normal means. … We condemn Mr. Wang and WWAP for taking such an irrational and meaningless action … [and] we are planning to take necessary legal action."[20] News reports asserted that Mercedes had requested a "… letter of apology by Wuhan Wildlife Zoo for their unnecessary action taken in harming the rights and interests of our company," further stipulating that the apology letter should be widely distributed to the Chinese media.[21] Legal experts in China agreed that Mercedes had a reasonable basis for claiming harm to its reputation since WWAP used a public arena to make statements about poor quality and service when the situation had not yet been legally assessed.[22]

WWAP meanwhile sought the support of the media in the nation's capital, Beijing. Park managers were interviewed by CCTV – China's biggest television network, and the only one with national coverage – just days prior to China's official Consumer Day. The park managers told journalists that additional Beijing media outlets were being contacted. At the same time, Ms Liu brought the damaged car to Beijing to "find out whether the problems are due to the fuel or the car itself."[23] She proposed to take the car for a test drive in Beijing after the fuel system had been cleaned and the specified petrol had been added. By the end of the month, however, WWAP abandoned this approach and took the car back to Wuhan. Ms Liu commented that "Mercedes did not send any staff to talk to me during my stay in Beijing."[24] Moreover, although WWAP wanted to take legal action against Mercedes, "no institution could help … make the technical test on the car."[25] Without evidence, park managers felt that a legal claim would fail. Thus, they switched tactics. Managers announced that "the volume of visitor traffic at WWAP is more than 500,000 per year, so the car will be exhibited to the visitors until the problem is solved."[26]

By the end of February no settlement had been reached, so WWAP again raised the stakes of the dispute. It announced that "a Mercedes owner in Beijing has offered his car to be destroyed at WWAP if Mercedes does not give WWAP a meaningful reply."[27] The car's owner remained anonymous but he claimed to be a friend of Sheng. He justified his actions by saying that, although he was proud to own a Mercedes, he felt discriminated against due to the high number of AMQV members who had problems with their cars. He further stated, "I will never again drive a Mercedes … if the problem can't be solved in China."[28]

The Chinese auto market

The Chinese auto market experienced rapid growth at the end of the 1990s and into the new millennium. Annual sales volume of domestically produced passenger cars rose from 300,000 units in 1992 to more than one million units by 2002 (see CS Exhibit 6.4 for sales volume from 2000 to 2002). Analysts projected sales of five million units by 2010, which would make China the world's third-largest passenger vehicle market behind the United States and Japan.[29] Rising incomes, greater availability of credit, improved road conditions, and competitive price pressures all contributed to double-digit growth rates that were expected to hold for the foreseeable future. In addition, imported auto sales were set to rise dramatically as tariffs fell steeply in line with WTO requirements.

The market for low-priced passenger vehicles was crowded with dozens of

CS EXHIBIT 6.4: CHINA AUTO MARKET TRENDS (UNIT VOLUMES)

	2000	2001	2002
Domestically produced passenger vehicles	607,445	703,525	1,092,762
Imported vehicles (passenger cars and others)	42,000	72,000	127,000

Note: Sales volumes closely match production and import volumes.

domestic and locally produced international brands. Volkswagen (VW) was an early entrant to the mid-market, producing the popular Santana model with JV partner Shanghai Automotive Industry (SAIC). For many years Santana had been the bestselling passenger vehicle in China, and its strong lead still held. But by 2002 the results of a sustained economic boom were visible and a market had emerged for more upscale sub-luxury and luxury brands. Most major international manufacturers were preparing for the up-market shift, either by upgrading the vehicles produced locally or increasing the levels of imports. Shanghai VW had introduced the Passat, General Motors partnered with SAIC to produce the Buick Regal, and Audi made the A6 sedan in a JV with Changchun's First Automotive Works (FAW). BMW had plans to produce models from the 3 and 5 series in China by 2003, and Toyota was in discussions with FAW to begin production of a full product line, including luxury brands.

The Mercedes-Benz parent company, DaimlerChrysler, had a partnership with the Beijing Automotive Industry (BAIC) to produce sport utility vehicles (SUVs) under the moniker of Beijing Jeep. As the first Sino-foreign auto JV, established in 1984, Beijing Jeep had taken an early lead in the sales of off-road vehicles. DaimlerChrysler also was part owner of Mitsubishi, which sold locally made and imported Pajero SUVs, and DaimlerBenz produced heavy trucks and passenger coaches through various JV arrangements. Like many makers of high-end luxury vehicles, however, DaimlerChrysler imported its Mercedes-Benz passenger cars rather than producing them locally. In 2002 Mercedes had the largest China market share of imported luxury brands with an estimated 75,000 vehicles on the road.[30] In contrast, BMW had only about 50,000 vehicles in the country at that time.[31] Despite the incident at WWAP in late 2001 Mercedes sold 870 cars in the first two months of 2002, a 40% increase over the same period the previous year.[32] The future for Mercedes passenger car sales looked bright.

DaimlerChrysler had two Mercedes subsidiaries operating in China. The first, Mercedes-Benz China Ltd, was set up in 1986 and was based in Hong Kong. This firm held the franchise for all imported Mercedes-Benz passenger vehicles in China, Hong Kong, and Macau. The second entity, DaimlerChrysler China Ltd (DCCL), was established in 2001 to support JV projects and oversee development of the China, Hong Kong, and Macau markets for passenger vehicles, vans, and trucks. In addition, three regional distributors in China and an exclusive retailer in Hong Kong provided sales and after-sales service for Mercedes-Benz vehicles. Southern Star Motor Company, Eastern Star (Shanghai) Automobile Ltd, and Northern Star (Tianjin) Automobile Ltd covered China's southern, eastern coastal and northern provinces, respectively. Zung Fu Company Ltd covered the Hong Kong and Macau SAR areas.[33]

Due to the small number of imported cars in China many brands had limited capacity for after-sales service. Hence, owners of imported brands sometimes had to wait for appointments or for delivery of parts for repair. Manufacturers worked hard to maintain high standards of service, but some service employees lacked service skills and product knowledge. The latter problem was particularly acute for recently introduced models. Compounding the problem, China's massive geographical size meant that some imported car owners had to travel long distances to reach a service outlet. Consequently, imported car owners had been heard to complain about high costs of maintenance and poor levels of service convenience. Automakers struggled to balance the needs of these buyers with the costs of servicing a market that still remained small. Mercedes-Benz China had by March 2002 established 23 Service Centers in China's mainland, and eight in the Hong Kong Special Administrative Region.[34] The number was scheduled to double by the end of 2004.

Consumerism and China's regulatory environment

China's economic reforms brought a rising sense of power to consumers. Buyers increasingly were aware of their rights and were willing to seek redress for unsatisfactory purchase outcomes. In 1984 the China Consumers' Association (CCA) had been established as an affiliate of the State Administration for Industry and Commerce (SAIC). CCA protected consumer interests through educational efforts, counseling, advice, and investigations. Over the years CCA had played a key role in raising awareness and knowledge about consumer rights, encouraging more responsible business behavior, and facilitating government adoption and revision of regulations and laws. By the year 2001 CCA had helped settle more than six million consumer complaints throughout China.

To further strengthen consumer protection, China introduced the Law on Protecting Consumers' Rights and Interests in 1994. The law specified nine consumer

CASE STUDY: MERCEDES-BENZ AND WUHAN WILD ANIMAL PARK

rights, including among others the rights to respect, safety, and fair trade, as well as compensation for violations of these principles. By raising the possibility of compensation the law provided a framework for legal action and courtroom resolution of disputes between buyers and sellers. Nevertheless, implementation problems limited the rule's effectiveness. Company ownership structures often were unclear, making it difficult for consumers to know who to sue, and which court would hold jurisdiction over a complaint. In the past, consumers had in some cases been unable to serve a subpoena when a local company claimed to be legally independent of the parent organization, which it claimed was responsible for the problem. Even in the best of cases, consumers might have had to file papers in a municipal court and then wait while the documents found their way through several layers of higher courts, bureaucratic offices and government ministries. As a consequence, Chinese consumers seldom resorted to the courts for redress. When asked how they responded to violations of their consumer rights, Chinese buyers most frequently claimed to (1) take no action, (2) complain to the selling units or the manufacturers, (3) seek assistance from the consumer associations or governmental departments, (4) go to the media, and (5) resort to legal action. Litigation was consistently ranked the lowest in frequency of usage.[35]

China's government had been discussing product recall regulations for several years, but as of early 2002 no official policy had been established. The State General Administration for Quality Supervision, Inspection, and Quarantine (AQSIQ) was working on draft regulations that would ask firms that produce, sell, import, rent, or repair cars to take back those found to be defective. Consumers supported the moves strongly due to a widely held perception that the lack of laws meant Chinese buyers were excluded from, or differentially compensated in, international recalls of foreign goods.[36] Several recalls of imported electronics and automobiles had aroused strong media attention when discrepancies were noted in the terms offered to product owners in China and elsewhere. In each of these cases the manufacturer had argued that differences in the products sold (for example, precise models or time and place of production) or in the legal requirements for compensation (which could vary within, as well as between, countries) lay behind any differences in recall policy across regions. Nevertheless, the press was quick to claim racial discrimination in these situations.[37]

China had been included in a recall of Mercedes-Benz vehicles in 1999, but was excluded from one undertaken in Europe and the Middle East during the summer of 2001 to correct a problem with air bag deployment. DaimlerChrysler announced that no problems had been detected in the China market since its earlier recall, but the *People's Daily* newspaper had carried a quote from a CCA source claiming to have several complaints about Mercedes products in its current files.[38] The 2001 Mercedes-Benz recall had not greatly aroused public sentiment, however, since Chinese press coverage had been limited. The current problem with WWAP was entirely different. Journalists had actively reported the first car-smashing incident, and the public had shown strong interest.

What next?

The immediate problem for Mercedes-Benz managers was to formulate a response to the threat of a second car-smashing episode. Neither the offer of additional repair services nor the threat of intended legal action had succeeded in defusing the situation. Indeed, WWAP seemed intent on escalation. The media had followed the first public event closely. Would a repeat action keep the problem in the public's eye or would journalists consider it "old news"? In the latter event, would WWAP do something even more drastic? The response of both the customer and the media seemed hard to predict. On the other hand, product sales did not seem to suffer because of the problem. Perhaps it was best to do nothing at all.

CASE COMMENTARIES

COMMENTARY 1
DONGSHENG ZHOU
PROFESSOR OF MARKETING
CHINA EUROPE INTERNATIONAL BUSINESS SCHOOL (CEIBS)

In this case study the worst possible scenario has happened: Mercedes-Benz received widespread negative publicity about its insensitivity to the needs of Chinese buyers, while WWAP had lost a very valuable asset.

Yet, Mercedes-Benz believed that it had done all it could to help its customer, while WWAP believed that it had given Mercedes-Benz enough opportunities to repair the vehicle and its reputation. At the end, it had to destroy the "defective" product. How could this happen? Could Mercedes-Benz have done better?

Mercedes-Benz can do better

It could be true that "the problems were caused by the customer's use of inferior, low octane fuel that did not match the car's specifications," but what Mercedes-Benz did in this incident, while justifiable, was not enough for a world-class company.

Although Mercedes-Benz did offer some extra service (for example, agreeing to clean the car's fuel system at no charge), by and large, it treated the incident as one of a normal case and handled it in a very professional but less warm-hearted way. Mercedes concluded that "impurities contained in the fuel affected the performance of the car ... [and] we cannot replace the car [when problems stem from] external factors rather than a quality problem of the car itself."

Mercedes-Benz should separate the issue of "who was responsible for the problem" from the issue of "how to best solve it." Mercedes-Benz may worry that, even though it is not responsible for the problem, by offering a car exchange (a better service than its obligation requires), it is admitting some wrongdoing. However, this worry is not necessary. As one of the best loved brands in China, Mercedes-Benz should go an extra mile to delight its customers.

Furthermore, Mercedes-Benz failed to recognize the fact that WWAP had in total purchased four Mercedes autos! How many customers in China have ever bought four or more cars from Mercedes Benz? Probably not many! My guess is that the number would be less than 1%. The fact that WWAP had purchased four cars from Mercedes-Benz suggests that WWAP is a very loyal customer and that it loves the Mercedes-Benz brand deeply. Probably it is precisely this deep affection toward the Mercedes-Benz brand that led WWAP to overact to Mercedes-Benz's handling of this incident. WWAP may have treated Mercedes-Benz as an old friend, but Mercedes-Benz's lack of "friendly" behavior in this matter (at least in the eyes of WWAP) may have shocked it and have led it to feel a sense of betrayal, all of which may have contributed to the very extreme action.

While it is important to diagnose the true cause of the problem, it is more important to solve it. The sooner it is solved the better (more people may join the AMQV – Association of Mercedes Quality Victims – if the incident is not resolved quickly).

It is still neither wise nor helpful for Mercedes-Benz to suggest that WWAP used the car incident to increase its entry fee from 35 to 65 RMB, and to comment that "many old Chinese gas stations are dirty in the petrol storehouse and petrol pump, and the petrol they sell is inferior in quality." (By doing so it has brought in additional parties to the incident – the fuel provider – and it has made things more complicated).

Mercedes-Benz should meet with WWAP's demand for the car to be exchanged, and as soon as possible. Of course, there are costs of doing this – first, the opportunity cost of selling a new car. However, while the retail price of a new Mercedes-Benz is around RMB700,000, the cost for a Mercedes-Benz in a car exchange is the wholesale price to the distributor, which will be much less than that. Further, the WWAP's used car still has some value. So the real cost of the car exchange is far less than RMB700,000. By doing so, Mercedes-Benz can prevent the widespread negative publicity (it may cost Mercedes-Benz millions of RMB to correct this negative image). The second possible cost of the car exchange is that other customers may follow suit and make all kinds of unreasonable demands. Mercedes-Benz can prevent these potential costs by using the following strategy: Emphasizing that this is a reward policy for loyal customers only (for example, any customers who have purchased three or more Mercedes-Benzs). I believe the chance for other customers to follow suit and make unreasonable demands is very low as, after all, Mercedes-Benz is a very respected and high-quality product.

By offering a car exchange to WWAP there are many potential benefits. First, WWAP will become an even more loyal customer, and it will spread positive word-of-mouth to the community. Second, by offering the car exchange, Mercedes-Benz can suggest that WWAP sign a long-term maintenance contract for all its four cars with Mercedes-Benz's official partner. Given the fact that the current problem was largely due to maintenance and inappropriate use of fuel, WWAP is very likely to agree to the contract. Third, good publicity. In recent years, there has been a lot of negative publicity on multinational companies (MNC) in China. The main complaints in these reports were that MNCs were insensitive to the needs of Chinese buyers, or that they did not treat Chinese consumers in the same way as those in the developed markets. By offering the car exchange, Mercedes-Benz stands out and provides a rare good example of how a leading MNC paid close attention to Chinese consumers, and went one step further in satisfying a customer's needs, to the delight of that customer.

Even though the sales of Mercedes-Benz in China did not seem to be affected by the WWAP incident, with an increasingly competitive automobile market, it is crucial for Mercedes-Benz to maintain a good public image.

COMMENTARY 2
YUFENG ZHAO
GENERAL MANAGER
PROGRESS STRATEGY CONSULTING CO., LTD

The "Benz incident" in the WWAP was a well-known PR stunt and appeared in many newspaper headlines. Even though several years have passed, it is still widely discussed. From the case, we can see that a PR crisis can be complex, sudden, and often have significant impact on the public. On the other hand, it can be solved smoothly if handled well.

There are many kinds of crises that can affect products and services: customers, finance, public image, and so on. From the "Benz case" we can see how a service problem created a misunderstanding with a customer that later became a media crisis. Newspapers at home and abroad, popular TV shows, and websites reported the incident. It was a service crisis as it was partially caused by the incomplete after-sales service of Mercedes-Benz. The attention and attitude of the company's staff in service delivery was also not satisfactory. It was a suing crisis as both the company and the car-owner threatened to take the other side to court. It was also a customer crisis in that some customers of Mercedes-Benz organized the AMQV, attempting to influence other Benz car users.

There are six major principles for handling this PR crisis:

- have a clear goal
- respond quickly without delay
- admit to problems or mistakes bravely rather than defend yourself in vain. Over 90% of the badly handled crises are related to improper attitudes, such as indifference, arrogance, perfunctoriness, and inefficiencies
- pay due attention to the problem
- seek evidence and proof from authorities
- avoid overreaction.

Unfortunately, Mercedes-Benz failed to handle the media crisis properly. Judging from the above six principles, the company only followed the first principle – but in the wrong direction. The company had a clear goal, knowing that they were right. But from the beginning to the end, their attitude was quite unfriendly and it didn't provide an effective solution.

First, before the crisis the company should have changed the bad engine for the customer who had complained, even if it didn't recall the car. If the same problem reoccurred after the change, it would be more convincing to say that the problem was caused by petroleum. If the company had done this, it would have prevented the problem from growing. By doing so, Mercedes-Benz would have more justification to defend itself. Second, the company should have been more understanding and sincere when handling the customer's complaints. Third, the company should have sent someone from top management to handle the problem to show that they had paid due attention to it. Fourth, it should have shown to the public that they were making great efforts to solve the problem. For example, they could have issued an inspection report by its engineers, or have received better proof from a third party in order to clarify the issues. And last, right after it discovered that the ticket price of the zoo was raised after the incident, the company should have fought back by gathering the media and holding a press conference, or using other PR methods, to attack the other side's intention to manipulate the issue for its own economic benefits. Thus, it could have diverted the media and the public's attention to the commercial behavior of WWAP.

Compared to Mercedes-Benz, Toyota seemed much more mature when handling a similar crisis. In December 2003, two Toyota ads belittled the stone lions, a traditional symbol of power in China. The ads had drawn widespread indignation and criticism, and roused resentment from the Chinese people. However, the company minimized the impact of the crisis by using four tactics. First, they quickly responded and communicated with the media. On December 4, right after the media reported the incident, the company immediately held a press conference with participation of several top executives. It then published a letter to apologize for the inappropriate ads. Such a move helped the public to ease their anger and thus prevented an escalation of the crisis. Second, Toyota was honest and brave enough to take responsibility. In a letter, Toyota apologized with honesty and sincerity rather than defending itself with various excuses. When mentioning Saatchi & Saatchi Co., which designed the two ads for Toyota, the GM of FAW Toyota Motor Sales Co. said, "It is our fault. We should take the full responsibility." The company's positive attitude was widely welcome. Third, top management played an active role in seeking understanding from both the media and the public. A number of Toyota company executives apologized openly for the incident at a press conference. The involvement of top leaders indicated that the company's apologies were sincere. Finally, they ensured that all stakeholders demonstrated the same attitudes when communicating with the public. After the ads incident, all stakeholders, including the Toyota Company, the media which released the ads, and the ad agency, apologized to the public without making any excuses. In addition, Toyota appointed a spokesperson to represent it. When others in the company were asked about the matter, they would only apologize without making any comments on it. In fact, Toyota set a good model for other companies to adopt in handling PR crises.

Of course, companies can also take advantage of the crisis for their own benefit. For example, if Mercedes-Benz could make clear that WWAP was simply manipulating the incident to attract more visitors, and apologize sincerely during the crisis-handling process, it would have helped to eliminate the negative impacts and even boost the company's reputation and image.

NOTES

1   The American Chamber of Commerce, P.R. China, *American Business in China: White Paper 2005.*

2   http://www.cctv.com/program/cbn/20060221/100376.shtml.

3   "List of Top Five Car Producers in China Changes and Volkswagen's Position is Shaken" ("Zhongguo Jiaoche Wu Qiang Chong Pai Zuoci, Dazhong Qiche Diwei Dongyao") *Beijing Evening Post (Beijing Wanbao)*, April 21, 2005.

4   This case study was prepared by Dr Junsong Chen and Professor Lydia J. Price at CEIBS. The case was prepared on the basis of class discussion rather than to illustrate either effective or ineffective handling of an administrative situation. Certain names and other identifying information may have been disguised to protect confidentiality. The information in the case is based entirely on published news reports. The case was originally published by CEIBS in 2004. Published with permission.

5   Approximately equal to US$85,000. In 2001, US$1 = RMB8.3 approx.
6   China's main consumer association, CCA, assists individual product owners to resolve product-related disputes, but does not assist corporate or other commercial product owners.
7   "Mercedes Wants to Solve the Incident Privately," *www.xinhua.org*, March 9, 2002.
8   "China's Sledgehammer Activists," *www.csmonitor.com,* March 28, 2002.
9   "Mercedes-Benz Deplores Car-wrecking 'Stunt'", *South China Morning Post*, December 29, 2001.
10 "Mercedes Reacts to the Incident," *Beijing Youth Daily*, December 28, 2001.
11 "Mercedes Smashed, Who is Hurt?" *China Economic Times*, December 29, 2001.
12 Ibid.
13 "Whether Mercedes or Not, Wuhan Wild Animal Park Just Smashes It," *www.qianlong.com*, December 28, 2001.
14 "Mr. Wang and His Mercedes Car," *Frankfurter Rundschau*, January 23, 2002.
15 "Demolish My Mercedes, Orders Angry Owner," *South China Morning Post*, December 28, 2001.
16 "Mercedes-Benz Deplores Car-wrecking 'Stunt'," *South China Morning Post*, December 29, 2001.
17 "Mr. Wang and his Mercedes Car," *Frankfurter Rundschau*, January 23, 2002.
18 "Mercedes-Benz Deplores Car-wrecking 'Stunt'," *South China Morning Post,* December 29, 2001.
19 "Car Owner Smashes Mercedes, Leading to a Chain Lawsuit," *Beijing Youth Daily*, December 30, 2001.
20 "Another Statement from Mercedes," *Beijing Youth Daily*, January 10, 2002.
21 "The Wrecked Mercedes Comes to Beijing for a Test," *Beijing Youth Daily*, January 18, 2002.
22 "Car Owner Smashes Mercedes, Leading to a Chain Lawsuit," *Beijing Youth Daily*, December 30, 2001.
23 "The Wrecked Mercedes Comes to Beijing for a Test," *Beijing Youth Daily*, January 18, 2002.
24 "The Latest Progress of the Incident," *China Youth*, January 25, 2002.
25 "The Wrecked Mercedes Will Return to Wuhan," *Beijing Youth Daily*, January 25, 2002.
26 "The Wrecked Mercedes Will be Exhibited in Wuhan Animal Park," *www.chinanews.com.cn*, January 29, 2002.
27 "The Negotiation Breaks Up," *Wuhan Morning Post*, March 9, 2002.
28 Ibid.
29 "Toyota Secures Approval for $2b Car Engine Plant," *South China Morning Post*, November 17, 2003.
30 "The After-sales Service of Imported Car Enters 'Sunny Zone'," *Beijing Business Today*, October 17, 2002.
31 "What Could You Use to Repair Arrogant BMW and Mercedes?" *www.qianlong.com*, December 15, 2003.
32 "An Exclusive Talk with Mercedes," *Beijing Morning Post*, March 13, 2002.
33 Abstracted from "New and Events/About Us," http://www.mercedes-benz.com.cn/amw/emb/zh.
34 "The After-sales Service of Imported Car Enters 'Sunny Zone'," *Beijing Business Today*, October 17, 2002.
35 "Close to 50 Million Consumers Had Their Rights Infringed," *China Consumer Journal*, March 15, 1997.
36 "Car Industry to Test-drive Official Recall Plan," *South China Morning Post*, January 9, 2004.
37 "Car Recalls Threaten Japan's Reputation in China," *Asia Times Online*, www.atimes.com, March 6, 2004.
38 "China Not on Benz Recall List," *People's Daily Online*, http://fpeng.peopledaily.com.cn, July 17, 2001.

REFERENCES

1   Chan, Hui-Chun 1999, *A Study of Consumer Behavior in the Department Stores of Taiwan, Hong Kong, and Shanghai: Applications on Fuzzy Set and Gray Theory,* unpublished Masters thesis, Soochow University, Taipei, Taiwan (in Chinese).

2   Hampton, Gerald, M. and Gent, Aart, P. 1984, *Marketing Aspects of International Business,* Boston and Hingham, Mass.: Kluwer-Nijhoff Publications.

3   McCort, D.J. and Malhotra, N. 1993, "Culture and Consumer Behaviour: Towards an Understanding of Cross-Cultural Consumer Behaviour in International Marketing," *Journal of International Consumer Marketing,* Vol. 6, pp. 91–128.

Chapter 7
Government relationship: Playing Chinese poker

INTRODUCTION

The imperfect legal system, fierce competition, prevalence of counterfeiters, scarcity of talent, and other factors make China a very challenging business arena. One of the factors with an especially high impact on business activity is the role of the Chinese government.

Government relations are relevant in China for several reasons. First, there are still many restrictions and regulations in place with unclear guidelines. This gives a lot of leeway to local authorities in the interpretation and application of those regulations. Government officials can find a million excuses to create difficulties for your business. In China it is very difficult to find the official who will approve your project but very easy to find those who can stop it. Actually even the lowest level official can create enormous difficulties for your business. Second, the laws and regulations affecting businesses are frequently revised and reinterpreted. Subsequently, companies must constantly update their knowledge about the regulatory environment. Third, the situation is further complicated by the role that different government levels play. This creates a peculiar phenomenon of illusory compliance in which local authorities adapt to their interests those instructions emanating from Beijing. Companies may benefit from this situation but, at times, they may also become its victims. Fourth, there is a certain disparity in regulatory development among the different regions of China, which means that the same rules may be applied differently depending on the locality. Finally, the government sometimes acts both as a player and a referee in the business field due to the numerous state-owned enterprises it still controls. All these points make the government at different levels a relevant element to consider when running your business.

Companies doing business in China must try to understand the political and administrative systems. However, that is not an easy task even for the Chinese. There are actually two parallel systems – the Party and the government system (see Exhibit 7.1). In China, the real decision-making power belongs to the Communist Party of China (CPC). Important decisions are typically made by the Politburo Standing Committee, then it is voted on in the Politburo, and finally in the CPC Central Committee. If required by the Constitution, the decision must be voted on in the People's Congress in order to take effect. The provincial

EXHIBIT 7.1: CHINA'S POLITICAL AND ADMINISTRATIVE STRUCTURE

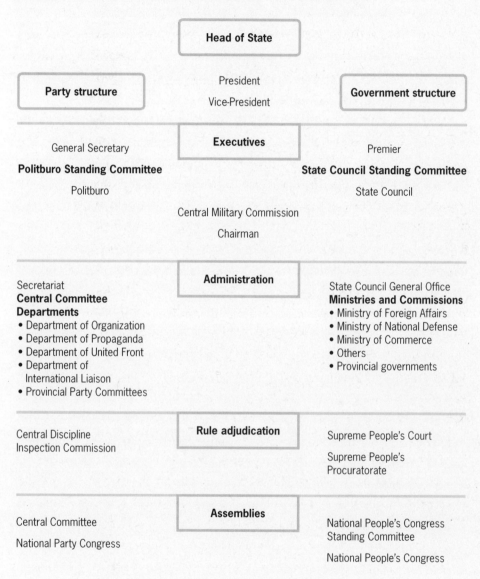

leaders are selected by the Standing Committee of CPC and then approved by the provincial people's congress.

As mentioned before, one perverse phenomenon of the system is the illusory compliance of local authorities. Local governments always try to interpret policies coming from Beijing to their own benefit. Despite its absolute power, the

Central Government rarely forces local governments to comply unless the deviant behavior is too evident and damaging for the central authority. This leads us to another phenomenon: corruption. The combined effects of economic growth and the loose control of the Central Government on local authorities have created the conditions for corruption. Deng Xiaoping once said that when you open the window, you cannot avoid the flies coming in. He was referring to corruption as one of the prices to pay for the opening of the country.

Local officials have very low salaries, and bribery or benefiting from public assets may be their main source of income. This also has its roots in history, as it has been the practice for centuries that Chinese officials enrich themselves with a moderate squeeze as a recognized privilege from their positions. Until recently few officials have been punished for corruption. Nevertheless, the selective application of anti-corruption punishment deters officials from being too corrupt by following the principle of "killing the chicken to scare the monkeys." Also, Party authorities use the threat of punishment to control those whose political allegiance has become suspect. Interestingly, the CPC, by using corruption as a way of compensation, has created a situation in which they have something they can use on almost everybody. Corrupt local officials know that higher-ups could charge them with corruption at any time. That way corruption has served the CPC as a mechanism of control on its members.

Companies resorting to corruption to gain the will of the officials can get a short-term advantage, but it does not last. Officials may be moved, retire, or fall into disgrace, and the relationship is therefore lost. In addition, the precedent created taints the company, which gives further opportunities for corrupt officials to ask for kickbacks. This problem does not affect MNCs so much as they usually have strict rules against entering into corruption practices. Government officials know this and are less inclined to ask for kickbacks from MNCs. One way corrupt officials circumvent this is to have consultants acting as intermediaries, who usually claim to have connections with the promise of obtaining favorable treatment from those authorities. A better way is for companies to build relationships in a clean and honest way.

Two elements of Chinese culture are critical in building relationships with the relevant authorities: *guanxi* (networking) and *mianzi* (face). When the government agent perceives a company as an insider, it usually provides more favors to such a company and makes more effort to support the company's interests. Calling on government officials frequently and inviting them to visit the company or to attend important occasions helps companies build and sustain relationships with the government. If government officials accept your invitation, it indicates that the officials want to build a good relationship with you or that you have already built that good *guanxi*. Through *guanxi* companies can solve administrative and regulatory issues. Inviting officials to important occasions also means that you give them *mianzi* – face. Then they will have a good impression of you and will help when you need it. *Guanxi* and *mianzi* are individual actions by companies. Usually, companies avoid collective actions to avoid being attacked by the media and being perceived as a threat to government authority.

How do companies manage the relationship with the government? Usually, companies delegate these activities to their Public Affairs (PA) departments. The PA has the mission to predict changes in regulations and sometimes to influence the political business environment in which the company operates. Due to its strategic importance, the PA is usually a senior staff position in many companies, directly reporting to the top. The responsibilities of the PA are very special and usually require a professional with the abilities and skills of a detective, diplomat, entrepreneur, orchestra conductor, and salesperson.

Typical PA responsibilities include:

- monitoring the legal environment relevant to the company
- assessing the potential impact of changes in that environment on the company's present and future activities
- planning and carrying out efforts to interact and influence the regulatory environment
- educating employees and other stakeholders about the impact of policies on company activities.

Some companies use an extended definition of PA beyond merely government relationships by combining it with PR, branding, employee communication, corporate philanthropy, and community relationship programs. PA, in that sense, becomes a fundamental instrument in building a relationship and in creating a public image among external stakeholders.

As a final advice, companies should strengthen the monitoring function of their PA government section. They should integrate their communication efforts by combining government relations, branding, and media communication. Another favorable practice is to build relationships with opinion leaders such as famous economists, influential media, and government think-tank organizations. All these actions must be undertaken with the objective in mind of building a closer relationship with those levels of government critical to your business.

PA can play a significant role in gaining strategic advantage over competitors. As the saying goes, "In China nothing is easy, but everything is possible." Sometimes, strictly following rules made by the Central Government may mean that you are giving opportunities to your rivals. The following case study, Carrefour China, shows how a good understanding and leverage of government relations could add value to the company. Admittedly, it is also risky to play games with Central Government, but the payoff may be significant.

Though China did have a plan of gradually opening the domestic market to foreign retailers, the big players had to gain fast access to the best cities and locations before their competitors. It was a race against time. As a result, many foreign retailers managed to expand by signing agreements with local authorities, bypassing the Central Government. Carrefour found that local governments were very receptive due to the job creation and taxes generated by the investment. With the help of local governments, Carrefour quickly established footholds in the best locations in China's major business cities. They quickly developed into the number one foreign retailer in China. However, this irregular expansion irritated local retailers and the Central Government. Beijing decided to teach a lesson not only to Carrefour, but also to other foreign retailers and the local authorities. They were using the principle "kill the chicken to scare the monkeys." Carrefour was the chicken to kill; other foreign retailers and the local authorities were the monkeys to be scared.

Following the case study, you will find three commentaries: the first by Thomas E. Callarman, Professor of Operations Management, CEIBS; the second by Sergiy Lesnyak, Chief Representative of Ferrexpo Group in China; and the third by Xuezheng Li, Global Sales Director of Beijing BOE Optoelectronics Technology Co., Ltd. The first commentary focuses on the first advantage gained by Carrefour despite the risks it incurred. The second commentary illustrates the philosophy of Carrefour China, and its pros and cons, and then gives instructions on what Carrefour should do next. The third commentary shows Carrefour how to react in a Chinese way to minimize the negative impact.

CASE STUDY
CARREFOUR CHINA, REVAMPING BUSINESS TO FOLLOW LOCAL RULES[1]

> *Carrefour's international experience is unequalled. It began to expand to other coun-*
> *tries very early, at a time when competition was less fierce and modern retailing was*
> *not very widespread.*
> —*Carrefour Annual Report 2001*

On February 8, 2001, the Chinese people were still immersed in the Spring Fes-tival atmosphere. Carrefour China, however, received an unpleasant gift. Reuters invoked the words of a Chinese official from the State Economic & Trade Com-mission (SETC),[2] saying Carrefour had broken rules by opening stores without permission from the Central Government. Then, on February 20, the *Financial Times* said that STEC had demanded that Carrefour China revamp its 27 stores to meet government requirements. Suddenly, the PR department of Carrefour China was weighed down with hundreds of inquiring calls and Carrefour be-came the focus of attention of the leading domestic media.

By the end of 1999, China only approved 21 JV retailers. However, the actual number of JV retailers was thought to be as high as 300 due to illegal expansion. Unfortunately, Carrefour became a target. Jean-Luc Chereau, President of Carre-four China, called for an urgent meeting to solve the coming crisis. He began to worry about the plan of opening 10 more stores in 2001. Since this was not the first time that the Central Government threatened to take action against illegal JV retailers, could Carrefour ignore the impending danger? Otherwise, what actions should be taken?

Carrefour Company

Carrefour Company was founded in 1959 and invented the "hypermarket" con-cept in the early 1960s. It was now the number one chain retailer in Europe

CASE STUDY: CARREFOUR CHINA

and only second to Wal-Mart in the world. Carrefour had 10,378 stores and 420,000 staff in 29 countries with sales of 88.7 billion euros in 2003. As the leader in hypermarkets,[3] Carrefour had 750 hypermarkets worldwide, 144 in Asia (see CS Exhibit 7.1). In fact, Carrefour was considered to be the most internationalized supermarket giant and a globalizer that was much more aggressive than Wal-Mart. In 1998, while Wal-Mart generated only 9% of its sales in

CS EXHIBIT 7.1: GEOGRAPHIC DISTRIBUTION OF CARREFOUR HYPERMARKETS (AT THE END OF 2003)

Source: www.carrefour.com.

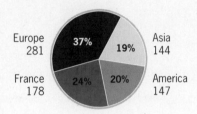

overseas markets, Carrefour achieved as much as 44%. The company was well known for its adaptation to local environments and in keeping sound relations with host governments. As an illustration, when entering the market of Porto Alegre in Brazil, Carrefour satisfied all pre-conditions of local government, including building a new road and a new nursery, dredging up a nearby river, and even building facilities for 40 small shops in that area.

Carrefour China

Carrefour entered China in 1995 by establishing hypermarkets in Beijing and Shanghai, the two most important cities in China. Thanks to the takeoff of China's retail market, the average sales of the top 100 chain retailers in China jumped from 240 million yuan in 1997 to 2.5 billion yuan in 2002, and the average number

CS EXHIBIT 7.2: GROWTH OF CHAIN RETAIL BUSINESS IN CHINA (1997–2002)

Source: China Chain Store and Franchise Association.

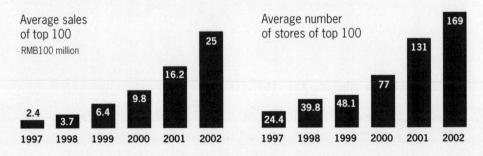

of stores also increased from 24.4 to 169 (see CS Exhibit 7.2). Carrefour successfully took advantage of this trend and developed into the number one foreign retailer with 27 stores in China by 2000, greatly outperforming Wal-Mart, its chief overseas rival. Chereau analyzed the success factors of Carrefour China:

> *We came to China nine years ago and brought our business concepts, low-price,*
> *safety, freshness, and local manufacturing into China. We found ideal partners such*
> *as Shanghai Lianhua. By now, Carrefour China has 30 local partners. Our advantage*
> *is the excellent adaptability and we have different ways in different environments.*[4]

China's door opened

Before July 1992, foreign enterprises were kept away from retail and wholesale business in China. However, according to rules for the implementation of the *Law on Chinese–Foreign Equity Joint Ventures* (1983) and *Law on Foreign-Capital Enterprises* (1990), foreign-invested manufacturers were entitled to sell part of their products in the Chinese mainland. Thus, some of them sold products within assigned quotas through corporate stores, agents, or department stores.

In July 1992, the State Council of China permitted the establishment of one or two retail Sino–foreign JVs in six business centers – Beijing, Shanghai, Tianjin, Guangzhou, Dalian, and Qingdao – and five special economic zones – Shenzhen, Zhuhai, Shantou, Xiamen, and Hainan. However, local governments must seek approval for JVs from the Central Government. Moreover, the business scope of these joint ventures was confined to retail and import and export.

In March 1993, the State Council allowed the establishment of pilot JV retailers in several designated cities. Then in June 1995, the *Catalogue for the Guidance of Foreign Investment Industries* was announced, which classified retail as a restricted field and extended the retail scope from clothing to general merchandise and from the manufacturing to the merchandising industry. By October 1995, 15 JVs were approved, including Lufthansa Shopping City and Shanghai Yaohan No.1.

In October 1995, the State Council permitted the setting up of two pilot JV chain retailers in Beijing, on condition that local partners should hold no less than 51% of equity. After, many leading retailers were lured into China to fight for a foothold in this tempting market.

CS EXHIBIT 7.3: MEASURES ON THE TRIAL OF FOREIGN-INVESTED MERCHANDISING ENTERPRISES (EXCERPT)

The State Economic and Trade Commission
June 25, 1999

Article 2: These Measures apply to Sino–foreign joint equity merchandising enterprises and Sino–foreign cooperative merchandising enterprises (referred to as "jointly operated merchandising enterprises"), which are jointly established within the territory of China by foreign and Chinese companies and enterprises. Establishment of solely foreign-owned merchandising enterprises is not allowed in China for the time being.

Article 4: The State Council takes charge of determining the areas in which jointly operated merchandising enterprises may be established. At present, these areas are limited to the capital cities of provinces and autonomous regions, municipalities directly under the Central Government, municipalities specifically listed in the State economic plan, and the Special Economic Zones (referred to as the "trial areas").

Article 6: A jointly operated merchandising enterprise shall meet the following conditions:
(4) If the jointly operated merchandising enterprise conducts its business through more than three chain stores (except those convenience stores, specialized stores, and stores for monopolized commodities), the ratio of investment contribution by the Chinese partner must constitute at least 51% of the total investment. Where a jointly operated merchandising enterprise has a sound operation record, its foreign partner has purchased large quantities of Chinese products and the enterprise is able to increase exports of domestic Chinese products through the foreign partner's global sales network, the foreign partner in the jointly operated chain-store merchandising enterprise may, subject to the approval of the State Council, be permitted to hold controlling shares of the said enterprise. For a jointly operated merchandising enterprise with three chain stores or fewer and other convenience stores, specialized stores and stores for monopolized commodities which operate in the form of chain stores, the ratio of investment contribution by the Chinese partner must not be less than 35% of the total investment. For a jointly operated merchandising enterprise conducting wholesale business (including retailers engaging in wholesale business simultaneously), the ratio of investment contribution by the Chinese partner must reach 51% or more of the total investment.

(5) Branches of jointly operated merchandising enterprises are only permitted to operate under the direct chain-store operation method according to which the foreign partner and the Chinese partner have a direct investment and direct Control. Other forms of chain-store operation methods such as free chain stores or franchise chain stores, etc, are not allowed to develop at present.

Article 8: The following procedures shall be carried out when applying for the establishment of a jointly operated merchandising enterprise:

The Chinese partner should submit a feasibility study report (serving as a project proposal) and other relevant documents to the local economic and trade commission (the economic commission, and the planning and economic commission, the same hereinafter). The local economic and trade commission will, jointly with the local departments in charge of domestic trade, submit the feasibility study report and other documents to the State Economic and Trade Commission in accordance with prescribed procedures. The State Economic and Trade Commission will, upon consultation with the MOFTEC, conduct a final review and grant approval. After the feasibility study report (serving as a project proposal) has been approved, the local foreign trade and economic cooperation department shall submit the contract and the articles of association to the MOFTEC in accordance with prescribed procedures. The MOFTEC will conduct final examination of and approval for the contracts and articles of association. Where approval for the establishment of a jointly operated merchandising enterprise has been granted, the jointly operated merchandising enterprise must, with the Foreign Investment Enterprise Approval Certificate issued by the MOFTEC, carry out the registration procedures with the state industrial and commerce department within one (1) month from the date of receipt of the approval certificate.

Article 17: All regions must strictly implement the provisions of these Measures in the establishment of jointly operated merchandising enterprises. Violation of the provisions of these Measures will be jointly investigated into and punished by the State Economic and Trade Commission, the MOFTEC and the State Administration of Industry and Commerce. The economic and trade commissions and the foreign trade and economic cooperation departments in all regions shall, in conjunction with other relevant departments, pursue the trial in a timely fashion, conscientiously summarize the trial experience, and properly resolve problems arising from the trial.

In June 1999, SETC promulgated *Measures on the Trial of Foreign-invested Merchandising Enterprises* (see CS Exhibit 7.3). According to the measures, "establishment of solely foreign-owned merchandising enterprises is not allowed in China for the time being," "the State Council takes charge of determination of areas … these areas are limited to the capital cities of provinces and autonomous regions, municipalities directly under the Central Government, municipalities specifically listed in the State economic plan and the Special Economic Zones," "for a jointly operated merchandising enterprise with three chain stores or fewer and other convenient stores, specialized stores and stores for monopolized commodities which operate in the form of chain stores, the ratio of investment contribution by the Chinese partner must not be less than 35 per cent," and "branches of jointly operated merchandising enterprises are only permitted to operate under the direct chain-store operation method according to which the foreign partner and the Chinese partner have a direct investment and direct Control. Other forms of chain-store operation methods such as free chain stores or franchise chain stores, etc, are not allowed to develop at present."

Despite the strict restrictions set by the Central Government, many foreign retailers acted secretly, by taking advantage of the gaming between the Central Government and the local governments in China. By the end of 1998, the State Council only approved 20 Sino–foreign merchandising enterprises; however, the number of illegal JVs was as high as 227. By the end of 2001, China only permitted 49 foreign-invested retail projects; however, there were 316 illegal projects approved by local governments.

The gaming between the Central Government and the local governments

In order to seize market opportunities and gain first-mover advantage, many foreign enterprises managed to elude the approval of the Central Government, with the help of local governments. From the perspective of local governments, investments of multinationals could bring about significant economic benefits and even political achievements. As an illustration, the peripheral areas of the Nanfang Mart located southwest of Shanghai were originally remote areas. However, ever since the coming of Carrefour, these areas developed into prosperous sub-centers of Shanghai. Subsequently, real estate, retail, restaurants, and public transport all benefited. As one magazine described:

> *The Carrefour Gubei store in Shanghai seems to be still extremely popular. Free shuttle buses run frequently full of Carrefour shoppers. Shoppers often find it difficult to find a parking place. The tempting aroma of food spreads around the store. Walkways are filled with people eager to pay money. This flagship store of Carrefour is always as busy as a bazaar.*[5]

Driven by local interests, local governments generously gave foreign retailers many favorable terms in shareholding ratio, land, and so on. A member of the Chinese media noted the spread of illegal stores in China:

> *In China, the equity structure of most foreign-invested retail stores remained secret. Most people know that Hoyodo, Hymall, and RT-Mart are all from Taiwan. However, nobody knows for sure their equity structure. As an illustration, I investigated the background of Hoyodo. According to relevant materials, Hoyodo Management Consulting Service (Shanghai) Co. is wholly owned by Hetai Merchandising Co. However, the Hoyodo stores used the invoices of Shanghai Chengda Stores Co., which has no formal connection with Hoyodo Management Consulting.*[6]

Though WTO agreements only required that China open its retail business in four years, China had already expanded the opening to more than 30 key cities all over China. Obviously, local governments should be held responsible for those illegal expansions. Huang Hai, Assistant Minister of Commerce, pointed out:

> *Many local governments exceeded their authority and opened markets to foreign retailers ahead of schedule. In one province, seven departments invited one foreign retailer in at the same time and promised to give them the best lands for opening the store.*[7]

Tempted by short-term self-interest, many local governments exceeded their authority in helping foreign retailers enter China. It was reported that foreign investors commanded equity of more than 65% in all the 18 foreign retailing enterprises in Liaoning province. Some of the projects were even wholly owned by foreign enterprises.

Carrefour's "moss strategy"

Carrefour emphasized the huge potential of the Chinese market. A vice-president once said:

> There are plenty of opportunities in China and those French enterprises interested in China should start right away! It will be a huge loss to miss this wonderful opportunity.[8]

In order to elude the regulation of the Central Government, Carrefour China and the Zhongchuang Business Co. (hereinafter referred to as Zhongchuang), a local company, set up a JV – Beijing Jiachuang Business Administration Consulting Co., Ltd (hereinafter referred to as Jiachuang). According to the regulation, Jiachuang could only conduct business consulting and was not allowed to make investments. Thus, Carrefour could only provide management to others instead of investing in chain retail directly. To solve this problem, Zhongchuang set up a wholly owned shell company, Chuangyijia Mart, which could, of course, operate retail business without any restrictions. Then Chuangyijia Mart trusted its business to Jiachuang. Through these steps, Carrefour actually controlled chain stores and openly used its own brand. In this model, Carrefour was "manager" rather than owner of the chain store and shared profits by means of charging management fees. This kind of secret expansion was called "moss strategy" by the local media.

Then Carrefour copied this model in other cities. Top executives of Carrefour China flew from one city to another to organize, together with local governments, various procurement activities. Taking into consideration the tax and employment benefits brought about by Carrefour stores – it promised 500 positions for each store – local governments rushed to give the green light to Carrefour.

Local governments had a sound excuse to let Carrefour pass – introducing foreign enterprises to upgrade domestic retail business and to enhance the management of domestic merchandising enterprises. When Wal-Mart still operated in Guangdong province following the regulation of the Central Government, Carrefour had made its entry into major business centers such as Shanghai and Wuhan. By the end of 1999, Carrefour became the number two chain retailer in China, only second to Shanghai Lianhua Supermarkets. In 2000, Carrefour's sales in China amounted to 8.1 billion yuan. An official of the Liaoning government made an analysis of local governments:

> *Before 1999, the maximum foreign stake in retail business was 50 percent and all investments were to be approved by the State Council. However, the censoring procedure was rather complicated and often cost dozens of thousands of yuan. Moreover, local government usually did not have enough funds to invest into joint ventures to reach a controlling stake. As an illustration, Dalian Mycal Shopping Centre would require an investment of 700 million yuan for 51 percent of the stake. Lacking enough money, Dalian government managed to get special permission to reduce its stake to 30 percent. Due to similar problems, the Shenyang government approved Carrefour's investment in Shenyang without seeking approval from the Central Government.[9]*

Carrefour sticks its neck out

The rampant deviant behaviors posed significant negative impacts on domestic retailers. Recognizing the severity of the situation, the Central Government began to take ratifying measures. Unfortunately, but naturally, Carrefour became a key target.

In July 1996 SAIC required the Beijing Administration of Industry and Commerce to "order Jiangchuang to revise the inappropriate description of its scope of business in its articles of association and contract, and to report the revision results to the SAIC" (see CS Exhibit 7.4).

In August 1997 the State Council ordered that "those non-pilot foreign-invested merchandizing enterprises which resort to deceit, concealment, or negligence, shall be shut down and the persons liable and their leaders be called to account" (see CS Exhibit 7.5).

In July 1998, the State Council pointed out in a Circular that "199 foreign-invested retailing enterprises should make rectifications. Specific requirements for rectification are: the percentage of contribution and profit-sharing by the

CS EXHIBIT 7.4: REPLY OF THE SAIC ON THE ISSUE OF WHETHER ENTERPRISES WITH FOREIGN INVESTMENT MAY CONTRACT AND OPERATE DOMESTIC-FUNDED COMMERCIAL ENTERPRISES

July 8, 1996

I. Registered enterprises with foreign investment should perform their duty of the capital appropriation requirement and operate in accordance with the laws and regulations. Therefore, Beijing Jiachuang Business Administration Consulting Co., Ltd (hereinafter referred to as Jiachuang) should appropriate investment funds in compliance with the above-mentioned principle and operate within the scope of business approved by the competent registration authority.

II. In the case of Jiangchuang, which contracted domestic-funded enterprises and engaged itself in commercial retailing and wholesaling activities without the approval of, and registration with, the competent authorities, your administration is therefore requested to order for the termination of the contract and submit a criticism of its activities in writing.

As regards the issue of "commercial property management" in Jiachuang's scope of business, the content of commercial property management should be specific management of commercial facilities (such as renting, maintenance, and security protection of commercial facilities and other relevant items), and thus does not cover commercial retailing and wholesaling. Your administration is requested to work together with the Beijing Development Planning Commission and the Beijing Foreign Trade and Economic Commission, and jointly order Jiangchuang to revise the inappropriate description of its scope of business in its articles of association and contract and report the revision results to the State Administration of Industry and Commerce.

Chinese side in a foreign business invested commercial enterprise must be over 50% (over 40% in the mid-west region), holdings of chain stores and warehouse marts must be controlled by the Chinese side ... Some local governments ignored the state policy on foreign investment in the commercial sector. The governments in Chongqing, Chengdu, Xi'an, and Nanchang went even further in that they still approved the establishment of non-experimental foreign-invested commercial

CS EXHIBIT 7.5: NOTICE ON ISSUES CONCERNING THE CLEANING-UP AND RECTIFICATION OF NON-PILOT FOREIGN-INVESTED RETAIL ENTERPRISES (EXCERPT)

The General Office of the State Council

August 5, 1997

A. Prior to the issuing of the "Urgent Notice by the General Office of State Council on Putting an End to the Unauthorized Approval to the Establishment of Foreign-Invested Merchandizing Enterprises by Local Authorities," all the foreign-invested merchandizing enterprises established with the unauthorized approval of local governments or departments shall be cleaned up and rectified.

B. In the course of cleaning up and rectifying the non-pilot foreign-invested merchandizing enterprises, the people's governments of all provinces, autonomous regions, municipalities directly under the Central Government, and the municipalities specifically listed in the State economic plan as well as the relevant departments of the State Council shall ... conduct careful investigation and examination focusing on the conditions of shareholders, provisions of contracts, scope of business, operational mode, conditions on technological transfers and the technical commissions, the present status of operation, and the results of annual inspection of these enterprises. On this basis, they shall produce the reports on the cleaning-up and rectification, and carefully fill out the registration forms.

D. The people's governments of all provinces, autonomous regions, municipalities directly under the Central Government, and the municipalities specifically listed in the State economic plan, as well as the relevant departments of the State Council shall strengthen the leadership of this cleaning-up and rectification program, and organize a specific working team with the participation of the planning departments, departments in charge of domestic trade, foreign trade and economic cooperation department, as well as administration of industry and commerce or the relevant organizations. They shall, in accordance with the requirements of this "Notice," proceed from actual conditions, attentively conduct the work, and timely and adequately accomplish the task. Those non-pilot foreign-invested merchandizing enterprises that resort to deceit, concealment, or negligence, shall be shut down and the persons liable and their leaders be called to account.

CS EXHIBIT 7.6: CIRCULAR OF THE GENERAL OFFICE OF THE STATE COUNCIL CONCERNING THE STATE OF SORTING OUT AND CONSOLIDATION OF NON-EXPERIMENTAL FOREIGN BUSINESS-INVESTED COMMERCIAL ENTERPRISES (EXCERPT)

July 1, 1998

In order to defend the seriousness of the state policy on foreign investment in the commercial sector, several ministries established a taskforce in August 1997. These taskforces tried to sort out and consolidate foreign-invested commercial enterprises approved by local governments beyond their mandates. Upon the approval of the State Council, the state of sorting out and consolidation is hereby notified as follows:

I. Permission has been granted to 42 foreign business invested commercial enterprises to continue operations within the duration of joint operations after examination and verification of the percentage of contribution made by foreign businesses, the status of capital in place, duration of joint operations, business scope, and status of operations in accordance with relevant state policy of absorbing foreign business investment in the commercial sector.

II. 199 foreign business invested commercial enterprises need to make rectifications after sorting out. Specific requirements for rectification are: the percentage of contribution and profit-sharing of the Chinese side in a foreign business invested commercial enterprise must be over 50% (over 40% in the mid-west region), holdings of chain stores and warehouse marts must be controlled by the Chinese side, duration of joint operations shall not exceed 30 years (not exceeding 40 years in the mid-west region) and they shall not operate wholesale business; commercial enterprises of sole foreign business investment shall, in accordance with the above-mentioned standards, be transformed into Sino–foreign joint ventures or Sino–foreign cooperative commercial enterprises. Sorting out and consolidation groups formed in all localities should, by the end of 1998 and in pursuance of the requirements, complete rectification of the above-mentioned enterprises and submit reports to the State Development and Planning Commission, the Ministry of Foreign Economic Relations and Trade, the State Administration of Industry and Commerce, and the State Administration of Domestic Trade for examination and verification.

IV. With respect to the 36 foreign business invested commercial enterprises examined and approved after the issuance of the "Urgent Circular of the General Office of the State

Council Concerning the Immediate Stoppage of Examination and Approval of Foreign Business Invested Commercial Enterprises by Localities on their own" (Kuo Ban Fa Plain Code Telegram No.[1997]15), capital not injected in accordance with the time prescribed, that have failed to pass annual inspection or failed to take part in annual inspection, as well as those foreign business invested commercial enterprises that fall within the scope of sorting out and consolidation but have failed to submit a report shall be revoked the original approval certificates by departments of foreign economic relations and trade and departments of industry and commerce administration at the provincial level, and formalities of nullification of registration or revocation of business licenses completed.

V. The State Development and Planning Commission, the Ministry of Foreign Economic Relations and Trade, the State Administration of Industry and Commerce, and the State Administration of Domestic Trade shall jointly issue a document notifying all localities of detailed list of the aforesaid non-experimental foreign business invested commercial enterprises retained, rectified, and revoked, and shall be responsible for the supervision of implementation.

VI. Local people's governments that arbitrarily exceeded the mandate of examination and approval of foreign business invested commercial enterprises in contravention of the state policy of experiment in absorbing foreign business investment in the commercial sector and in particular the People's Governments of the Municipalities of Chongqing, Chengdu, Xian, and Nanchang that still approved the establishment of non-experimental foreign business invested commercial enterprises on their own after the issuance of the "Urgent Notice" are meted out criticism in the circular. All localities should learn a lesson and do the work well of successful handling of rectification and correction, and nullification (revocation) of non-experimental foreign business invested commercial enterprises in accordance with the requirements of this Circular. China will continue to implement the policy of actively, rationally and effectively make use of foreign investment in the light of the spirit of the 15th National Congress of the Chinese Communist Party and expand the opening up to the outside world in the commercial sector step-by-step on the basis of summing up the experiences in experiment. People's governments of all localities should carry out their work in pursuance of the state policy and the unified arrangement of the State Council and each shall not act in its own way, be strict in the execution of orders and prohibitions, and jointly uphold the seriousness of the state policy so as to ensure that the work of absorption of foreign business investment proceeds in a sound and orderly way.

enterprises after the previous notice. These local governments are hereby criticized" (see CS Exhibit 7.6).

In June 1999, *Measures on the Trial of Foreign-invested Merchandising Enterprises* stipulated that "for a jointly operated merchandising enterprise with three chain stores or fewer and other convenient stores, specialized stores and stores for monopolized commodities which operate in the form of chain stores, the ratio of investment contribution by the Chinese partner must not be less than 35 per cent of the total investment. For a jointly operated merchandising enterprise conducting wholesale business (including retailers engaging in wholesale business simultaneously), the ratio of investment contribution by the Chinese partner

CS EXHIBIT 7.7: NOTICE ON PUTTING AN END TO THE APPROVAL BEYOND THE AUTHORITY OF THE FOREIGN-INVESTED MERCHANDISING ENTERPRISES AND THE ESTABLISHMENT OF SUCH ENTERPRISES IN DISGUISED FORM (EXCERPT)

December 1, 2000

... the General Office of State Council issued the "Notice on Cleaning-up and Rectification of Non-pilot Foreign-Invested Merchandising Enterprises" in 1998 ... However, there still exists in some places the approval beyond authority of the establishment of foreign-invested merchandising enterprises or the setting up of such enterprises in disguised form, resulting in ill effects on the utilization of foreign investment in our commercial sector. To safeguard the authority of rules and policies of the State, the relevant matters are hereby given as follows:

A. Following the issuing of the "Notice," it is wrong for a few local authorities to ratify beyond their powers the establishment of foreign-invested merchandising enterprises or their branch firms. This practice must be put to an end immediately. For those that hadn't yet started business upon the issuing of this Notice, the departments concerned shall cancel their project approval documents and the approval certificate; and the administration of industry and commerce shall nullify their registrations or revoke their business license. ... Local authorities shall clear up these projects and report the results to STEC, MOFTEC, and SAIC before November 30. From now on, the must reach 51 per cent or more of the total investment ... The State Economic and Trade Commission will, upon consultation with the MOFTEC, conduct a final review and grant approval."

In December 2000, *Notice on Putting an End to the Approval Beyond the Authority of the Foreign-Invested Merchandising Enterprises and the Establishment of Such Enterprises in Disguised Form* said that "if, after the issuing of the procedures, there are still authorities who, in spite of the provisions, approve the establishment of foreign-invested merchandising enterprises and their branch firms, or to approve the foreign investors to participate in disguised form in the domestic commercial business projects, the related responsible personnel shall be called to account.

application for establishing new foreign-invested merchandising enterprises shall ... be submitted to SETC and MOFTEC for examination and approval. These enterprises shall also register with SAIC or with its authorized local organs.

B. The relevant departments of the State Council are now working on administrative procedures to strengthen the administration of all kinds of forms resulting in the participation of foreign investments in the domestic commercial activities, including foreign-funded investment management companies, management consulting companies, franchises operations, and reinvestment by foreign-invested companies. Before the issuing of such procedures, the local government shall suspend the approval of these kinds of projects, and shall execute in accordance with the provisions specified in the procedures after they are promulgated.

C. If, after the issuing of the procedures, there are still authorities that, in spite of the provisions, approve the establishment of foreign-invested merchandising enterprises and their branch firms, or approve of the foreign investors to participate in disguised form in the domestic commercial business projects, the related responsible personnel shall be called to account. The departments concerned shall cancel their project approval documents and the approval certificate, and the administration of industry and commerce shall nullify their registrations or revoke their business license.

The departments concerned shall cancel their project approval documents and the approval certificate and the administration of industry and commerce shall nullify their registrations or revoke their business license" (see CS Exhibit 7.7).

Taking these types of deviate behaviors into consideration was actually common in China. Why was Carrefour chosen as the number one target when the Central Government decided to rectify the illegal projects? An article analyzed the situation:

> Carrefour was in too much of a hurry and expanded too quickly. Though Wal-Mart confined its business primarily in the Guangdong province – 8 of its 11 stores were in Guangdong – Carrefour signed contracts one after another with local governments, including Chongqing, Wuhan, Shenyang, Qingtao, and of course Beijing and Shanghai. It has 10 stores in the last two cities. ... Actually, the State Council began to rectify the retail industry beginning from as early as August 1997. Obviously, Carrefour stuck its neck out in front of the rule.[10]

Public criticism

Carrefour was thrown into the focus of the media. As pointed out by an analysis:

> Why is Carrefour so brave? The company has a good knowledge of the Chinese way of the world and established strong relations with local governments. It successfully took advantage of the desires of local governments to attract Fortune 500 companies. Local governments rushed to meet its requirements and even generously entitled it to tax or land benefits. There seemed to be a lot of rules and regulations in China. However, companies that follow all these regulations may be later surprised to discover that other companies have seized market opportunities by secretly bypassing such rules.[11]

Ironically, after issuing many regulations and circulars, SETC found it difficult to punish those deviate behaviors due to the lack of detailed regulations and the involvement of local governments. Local governments seemed to turn a blind eye to the warning of the Central Government. "Carrefour" means crossroads in French and Carrefour now seemed to stand at a crossroad in China.

CASE COMMENTARIES

COMMENTARY 1
THOMAS E. CALLARMAN
PROFESSOR OF OPERATIONS MANAGEMENT
CHINA EUROPE INTERNATIONAL BUSINESS SCHOOL (CEIBS)

This is a classic case of international location of facilities. When a manufacturing company wants to locate new factories, a logistics company wants to locate new warehouses or distribution centers, or when a retail establishment wants to locate new stores, there are a number of objective and subjective criteria that must be taken into consideration. The objective criteria include the costs, expected volumes, and expected profits involved in the decision, while the subjective criteria include social, cultural, political, and governmental issues.

The most obvious cost of opening new facilities is that of obtaining land and the physical facilities needed to provide the product or service. In the case of Carrefour, locating new stores in China and the costs of obtaining these physical facilities was rapidly growing, and it made it necessary for Carrefour to act quickly to acquire land and buildings in the prime growth areas, so that it could realize a profit. In addition to the costs of acquiring the land and the facilities, there were also such costs as licensing by the government and other governmental fees that may need to be paid. At the time of writing this case study, the local governments, cities, districts, and so on, did not have consistent licensing requirements or fee structures, and the individual government Carrefour worked with could also significantly impact the costs and profits it would realize. To complicate matters further, the local governments' fee structures and licensing requirements did not always match with the provincial or Chinese government structures. Because the new requirements developed by the Chinese government and reported in the case were widely publicized, it is difficult to imagine that Carrefour was unaware of the risk it was taking by working with local governments, seemingly outside the letter of the law. Another factor that has come into play more recently is the impact of the ascension to the World Trade Organization, which has increased the pressure on the governments to become more consistent in their application of regulations.

Carrefour, through its extensive network of foreign investments, had a great deal of experience with cultures and social environments other than its own, so it would seem that these factors would have less impact on their operation. Contrast this with Carrefour's biggest competitor, Wal-Mart, and its initial forays into foreign investment. Most of Wal-Mart's stores are still in the United States. One of the early attempts to locate stores elsewhere was in Brazil. Wal-Mart management essentially ignored the buying habits of Brazilian customers and assumed that they would buy products similarly to the way customers buy products in the United States. In addition, Wal-Mart did not take into consideration the differences in logistics that they would face in Brazil. As a result, the early attempts at locating facilities in Brazil were failures. Carrefour had enough experience to avoid making similar social and cultural mistakes in China, and modified its stores and practices to take local environments into consideration.

Going back to the governmental issues, two things seem obvious from the case. First, the Chinese government needed to make certain that its regulations and policies regarding ownership of companies doing business in China were followed consistently by all local governments and by businesses. Who better to make an example of than one of the two largest retail companies in the world? By going after and fining Carrefour, the government sent a strong signal that no one, large or small, is exempt from the regulations and licensing requirements. Second, because of Carrefour's extensive experience in international operations, it was also unlikely that they were unaware of the regulations and, more importantly, of the potential consequences of violating them. It seems clear that Carrefour felt that the government would not shut down the operation of so many new stores, but would more likely level fines against the company. It also seems clear that Carrefour would have factored the costs associated with such fines into its "equation" for cost and profit. As such, it seems highly likely that Carrefour estimated the potential cost of the risk it was taking and made the economic decision that the reduced costs of being early in the market, as well as having "first-mover" advantages with customers, outweighed the potential costs of violating the regulations.

COMMENTARY 2
SERGIY LESNYAK
CHIEF REPRESENTATIVE
FERREXPO GROUP IN CHINA

Obviously, Carrefour's strategy in China is very effective in terms of a good understanding of localization practices. It is quite understandable why the Carrefour strategy was called "moss strategy": moss can reproduce itself by a number of different methods, and even with very few shoots it can stick to unfriendly ground or stone and develop into a colony.

The strategy of market penetration shows that Carrefour is very familiar with Chinese practices; probably sometimes it is too Chinese. The familiarity came with the experience of the top executive, who had experience in Taiwan (see below). Jean-Luc Chéreau, CEO of Carrefour, has described in one of his recent interviews a situation that he experienced in Taiwan:

> Another aspect was Chinese business dealing. When I arrived in Taiwan, my former boss told me I was lucky: I was set for the first year because he had already signed five contracts for five new stores. Then I started talking with one of our Chinese partners who had signed those contracts, and nothing seemed to be happening. Finally, my assistant told me, "Just because he signed a 20-year contract two years ago with your former boss – a person who is not you – does not mean he will respect the contract." That was a big shock to me since the contract was notarized. But we started to renegotiate article by article. Five years later, during the Asian Financial Crisis, I invited this

> *same partner to my office and said, "Just because I signed a contract with you*
> *does not mean I will respect it. We are in a crisis." So he said, "Fine," and we*
> *started to renegotiate to reduce the rent.*[12]

Chereau describes the situation as an aspect of Chinese dealing, but in fact through the experience he has learned a lot, and his style became "Chinese" as well. Probably his attitude toward "breach of contract," which was shocking to him before, is acceptable and appropriate as long as it brings some real results.

In an interview by *McKinsey Quarterly*, Chéreau mentioned that Carrefour was successful from day one in China because local governments pushed it to open stores everywhere. And after the seventeenth Carrefour store opened, the Central Government decided to establish some rules. (From Chereau's position, these rules weren't established earlier; see CS Exhibits 7.4 to 7.8). Carrefour's position is clear: if you want to be effective you need to break the rules: "So together, the Central Government and Carrefour solved the problem because if you operated 100% by the official rules of that time, you couldn't do business."[13]

Probably, companies like Carrefour view China purely from a commercial perspective: leveraging skillfully the differences between local and central governments. China is acting around the world in a similar way. Probably this is one of the reasons why some global companies are trying to play *"real politics,"* carefully watching Chinese business practices abroad.

It seems that Carrefour feels mature enough to be a player comparable to local governments, but this position can be very vulnerable. It is better to avoid any inappropriate practices, especially corruption issues in business, because if you are connected to corrupt officials, the company can be affected by measures taken by the Central Government and the company's business could vanish.

To illustrate the lesson we can use an extract from James McGregor's book: *One Billion Customers: Lessons from the Front Lines of Doing Business in China*, Free Press, NY, 2005.

Conclusions

1 As Carrefour's strategy was a little bit ahead of time, "stuck its neck out in front of the rule," the company was able to predict that in "turbulent times" you can gain more than lose if you are brave enough. But to keep up with new conditions, Carrefour must change its business behavior.

2 Therefore the development strategy of Carrefour for the coming years should focus on improving its image in the local community and among Central Government officials, introducing advanced management knowledge and applying it to the local market situation, and setting up some moral and ethical standards for the industry.

3 Carrefour can establish the goal of being the leader in applying transparent practices in cooperation with local governments, in an effort to avoid leveraging the differences between central and local governments.

4 Carrefour cannot be criticized too much for being effective in an uncertain environment; this case study is the description of many systems' coexistence and interaction. The role of Carrefour in setting the standards and enhancing the management of local retail business is huge. Carrefour is definitely an industry leader, so the company can communicate and address important issues with the Central Government on behalf of the whole industry.

REFERENCES

Child, Peter N. 2006, "Lessons From a Global Retailer: An Interview with the President of Carrefour China," *The McKinsey Quarterly*, October, 2006.

McGregor, J. 2005, *One Billion Customers: Lessons from the Front Lines of Doing Business in China*, Free Press, NY.

COMMENTARY 3

XUEZHENG LI

GLOBAL SALES DIRECTOR

BEIJING BOE OPTOELECTRONICS TECHNOLOGY CO., LTD

FORMER CHIEF PUBLIC RELATIONS OFFICER

BOE TECHNOLOGY GROUP CO., LTD

During the past decade, foreign retailer giants like Carrefour and Wal-Mart competed head to head in China, the fastest growing retail market in the world. However, the retail market was highly regulated by the Central Government in order to protect domestic companies. MNC retailers adopted a very aggressive expansion strategy to get a foothold ahead of competitors in the major China metropolitan cities. Their objective was to gain a first-mover advantage. Once a hypermarket was in a location, there was no room for a second.

In order to circumvent the restrictions imposed by the Central Government, foreign companies use a number of tactics:

- obtaining local government favor by promising economic growth, taxation, and employment for locals
- partnering with local companies who can influence local government in the granting of the necessary licenses and the provision of prime locations for the stores
- establishing consulting companies jointly with local partners to indirectly operate new supermarkets.

Through the successful use of such tactics, some foreign retailers enjoyed fantastic business growth and expansion in China. Carrefour was one of them. This rapid expansion by foreign companies irritated domestic supermarkets. They began to put pressure on the Central Government and to criticize local authorities for granting privileges to foreign retailers. There were 316 supermarkets operated by foreign retailers by end of year 2001, but only 49 stores were officially approved according to statistics published by the government. According to prevalent regulations, retailers had to obtain approval from central ministries before opening a new store. Thus Carrefour became the main target of the public and was continuously criticized by the major local media.

Though it was not the first time that the Central Government warned Carrefour, this occasion proved different in several ways. First, Central Government officials intentionally leaked possible action to important media like the *Financial Times,* and this can be considered a clear signal of impending punishment. However, it also implied the willingness of the Central Government to reach reconciliation with Carrefour. In Chinese culture, harmony brings wealth. Generally speaking, the Central Government is reluctant to be too tough on MNCs because it heavily depends on foreign direct investment to fuel its fast growth. However, if Carrefour just turned a deaf ear to all these signals, the Central Government would think that Carrefour is unfriendly for not "giving face." Therefore, this is the last chance for Carrefour to correct its past mistakes. Second, the coming punishment had been spread all over China through media reports. This also forced the Central Government to get serious with Carrefour.

What should Carrefour do in order to sustain its business growth and market leadership in China? A business–government relationship should be considered by Carrefour to promote its image of corporate citizenship. Although Carrefour was the target of the media and public in past years, there were few direct and proactive responses from Carrefour to improve its public image.

On one hand, the company should tell the public of its contributions to the local economy, which may include jobs for the locals, local economic growth, benefits to local suppliers, and so on. On the other hand, Carrefour's top management should strengthen communications with Central Government ministries. This is critical for any MNC business success in China. China is in transition from a planned economy to a market-oriented economy. Many laws and regulations were reviewed and modified to accommodate such transitions, especially after China joined the WTO in December 2001. Both domestic and MNC companies have had to adjust their strategies and respond proactively to changes in the legal environment. Smart companies know when and how to act by strengthening their communications with both central and local government agencies.

In terms of business–government relationships, Carrefour should consider the following actions. First, it should publicly admit its mistakes and declare its willingness to follow the government policy in the future. In China, an apology is much more effective than lawyers. It would be highly recommended that the Carrefour Global CEO could fly to Beijing to meet with central authorities. This would surely be interpreted as a gesture of regretting past mistakes, something the Chinese appreciate. Second, Carrefour should press local authorities to explain to the Central Government the importance of Carrefour to the local economy. Such explanations will give the Central Government more reasons to forgive Carrefour. Third, Carrefour should adjust the ownership structure of its stores in line with government policy. It should have patience. After all, the stores use the Carrefour brand. Carrefour could increase its shareholding step by step in the future. Finally, Carrefour should try to establish a good relationship with the media so that their image is portrayed in a more favorable light.

Through these actions, Carrefour should survive the crisis. As one Chinese saying goes, "Try first to make the mistake sound less serious and then to reduce it to nothing at all" (*Da shi hua xiao, xiao shi hua liao*).

NOTES

1   This case was prepared by Dr. Shengjun Liu under the supervision of Professor Juan Antonio Fernandez at CEIBS. The case was prepared on the basis of class discussion rather than to illustrate either effective or ineffective handling of an administrative situation. The case was based on public source documents. The case was originally published by CEIBS in 2004. Published with permission.

2   In 2003, SETC and MOFTEC (Ministry of Foreign Trade and Economic Cooperation) were combined to form the new Ministry of Commerce.

3   Carrefour had several types of businesses, including hypermarkets, supermarkets, hard discount, convenience stores, and "cash and carry."

4   Zhou Yiting and Zhu Rui, "Carrefour: First Come, First Served," *Economic Observer* (经济观察报), May 14, 2004.

5   Xiang Wen, "Carrefour at the Crossroad," *Global Entrepreneurs* (环球企业家), December 2003.

6   Zhou Yiting, "New Policy Announced, Can Foreign Retailers Like Carrefour Still Open New Stores?" *Economic Observer* (经济观察报), December 31, 2003.

7   Zhou Yiting, "New Policy Announced, Can Foreign Retailers like Carrefour Still Open New Stores?" *Economic Observer* (经济观察报), December 31, 2003.

8   Wang Zhen, "Carrefour's Face Off," www.globrand.com.

9   Ibid.

10 Wang Zhen, "Carrefour Changing Face," Think Tank (Zhinang), April, 2005.

11 Ba Shusong, "Carrefour and Informal Rules," *China Economy Weekly* (中国经济周刊), July 8, 2004.

12 Peter N. Child, "Carrefour China: Lessons From A Global Retailer," *The McKinsey Quarterly,* McKinsey & Co. July 19, 2006.

13 Ibid.

Chapter 8
Expatriates in China:
Lost in translation[1]

INTRODUCTION

Professional success for an expatriate in China is not as easy as elsewhere. What people generally mean by success in an expatriate assignment is the achievement or surpassing of results expected by HQ. These expectations are usually expressed in measurable terms such as sales growth, market share, and profits. However, the hard data only depict part of the reality about success; they do not include the personal side of expatriate living in China. Needs such as career progression and professional development must also be taken into account. Finally, family is also an important element of that success. As one expatriate told us, "It is very difficult to be productive at work when a storm is waiting at home." In that sense, a more thorough way to measure success should include the needs of the organization, the expatriate, and his/her family in a kind of triangular relationship, represented in Exhibit 8.1.

EXHIBIT 8.1: THE EXPATRIATE "TRIANGLE"

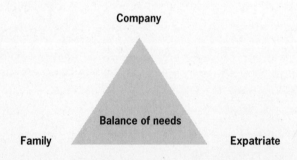

We can analyze each of these elements in turn.

Company needs

Expatriates are very expensive employees for companies. Besides their salary, companies must cover housing, schooling, cars plus drivers, medical insurance, home trips, and so on. For international companies, the total expatriate cost usually represents the biggest percentage of their total payroll in China. Despite the high costs, companies employ expatriates for several reasons. First, operations abroad need their technical and managerial expertise, which is still not available in the local market. Second, expatriates serve as missionaries propagating the company culture. Finally, they are perceived as trustworthy employees as they have served the company for years. As long as the local Chinese cannot meet the above criteria, it is reasonable to have expatriates working in China or anywhere else.

On the other hand, there is a tendency to localize the expatriate positions with Chinese managers whenever possible. Localization benefits the company not only for the obvious reduction in labor costs, but also for the reduction in the turnover of local talent as they are given more opportunities for promotion.

In that sense, companies must work on two fronts simultaneously. On one front, they have to develop the local talent capable of taking greater responsibilities in the future. On another front, they have to develop talent at home in order to keep the global operations running. In this process of global talent development, companies must constantly hire young managers who are interested in other cultures, who can speak foreign languages, and who are willing to travel and work abroad. The companies must also have processes in place to develop the international talent pool by instituting cross-cultural teams, job rotation among different country operations, and other systems to expose the talent pool to the international environment and its practices.

As expatriates are expensive, companies are contemplating other sources of candidates to replace them. What are some of the potential substitutes?

- Local Chinese are the right substitutes in the long run. However, it takes time to develop them to the right level, and it is a problem to retain them. Once they are ready for the position they become the poaching target of another company. Despite all the challenges, they are no doubt the natural substitutes for "expats."
- Oversees Chinese are another option. They usually get as good economic packages as expatriates do. What is then their advantage over other expatriates? Basically, they speak Chinese and supposedly adapt better to the business environment. Paradoxically, sometimes they are not so well received by the Chinese when they are seen as arrogant. Moreover, it is difficult to justify in the eyes of the local Chinese the huge salary gap.
- Returnees – that is, Chinese who study abroad and come back to China

after graduation – speak good English and have been exposed to a foreign culture. Their compensation packages are in general lower than that of an expatriate, as they don't usually get extra benefits such as housing and schooling for children. Furthermore, personal and family adaptation to China is not a question. They are most probably the best substitute for expatriates after local Chinese.

- Long-term expats, some of whom adapt so well in China that they do not want to return home. One common reason is that they marry a local Chinese. They usually have to give up certain privileges, such as the housing allowance and schooling for their children. They occupy an intermediate position between locals and expats mentioned above.

Expatriate needs

There are many reasons for an expatriate to accept an international assignment: better career prospects, more autonomy, the chance to experience a different culture, a fatter paycheck, and increasing professional value in the foreseeable future. On the cons side, they have to work long hours with less time after work for family and private life. Research shows expatriates and their families go through a culture shock cycle as shown in Exhibit 8.2. Initially, there is a phase of excitement immediately after they settle down in the new environment. After a few months, there is a decline in mood when they are confronted with frustrations, loneliness, and other difficult aspects of life in an alien culture.

EXHIBIT 8.2: THE EXPATRIATE CULTURE SHOCK CYCLE
Source: Nancy J. Adler 2002, International Dimensions of Organizational Behavior, Thomson Learning: South West, Cincinnati. Ohio.

Probably, one of the biggest challenges for an expatriate is the return after they have finished their assignment. Companies usually include return clauses in their contracts, but these do not address the problem. After spending several years on the international assignment, the situation may change back at HQ. People there and the company's priorities may change; these are the factors that may strongly affect the conditions when the expatriate returns. The so-called "out of sight out of mind" syndrome might be a consideration for rejecting an internal assignment.

In the end, expatriates become entrapped in their international careers and have no better choice but to become a kind of professional expatriate ready for another international position in the same or a different company.

Family needs

Success at the family level implies that the family – spouse and children – are well adapted to living in China. This depends very much on things like housing, education, and social life. More importantly, a stable and healthy relationship in the marriage is a crucial condition before accepting the assignment. Some potential candidates for foreign posts have rejected the assignment due to family considerations.

On the positive side, China can be a great learning experience for the family, but it can impose a heavy burden on the trailing spouse and children. The negative side includes the emotional suffering, the loneliness, boredom, frustrations, and depression of the spouses, especially for those that have to give up their own professional career.

Exhibit 8.3 represents a phenomenon that affects the relationship during the initial months in a new posting. Usually, the expatriates are fully immersed in the demands of their jobs at the time when their spouses require the most attention. This gap between needs and availability can cause disagreements and quarrels that will further affect the health of the relationship.

Companies can facilitate the adaptation process by offering pre-move preparation and helping with housing, schooling, and medical coverage, but at the end, the adaptation depends very much on the personality of the spouse.

What are the desired qualities of the spouse? Basically, spouses that adapt well are sociable and able to make new friends. Spouses adapt well when they have

EXHIBIT 8.3: EXPATRIATE AVAILABILITY AND NEEDS CURVES
Source: Nancy J. Adler 2002, International Dimensions of Organizational Behavior, Thomson Learning.

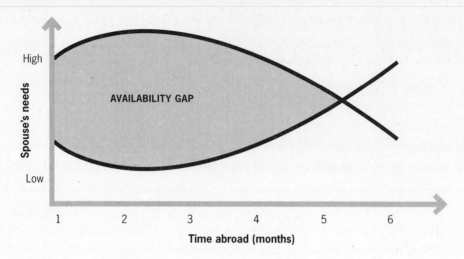

an interest in the local culture and are eager to learn a new language. Working in China does not usually break a happy marriage, but it would deteriorate an already problematic one. Therefore, good communication and understanding between the couple are very important for the success, not only of the marriage, but also of the expatriate's assignment.

The case study included in this chapter describes the experience of an expatriate couple in China. The case takes the perspective of Alain, the husband, who decides to take a challenging assignment in China. Montserrat, the wife, follows him but has to give up her own career. Once in China, things do not go as expected. After the case, you will find two commentaries: the first by Bala Ramasamy, Professor of Economics, CEIBS; and the second by Bettina Ganghofer, Deputy General Manager, Shanghai Pudong International Airport Cargo Terminal Co. Ltd (Lufthansa JV). Both commentators relate the case study to their own experiences and give suggestions, with clear logic, to Alain and Montserrat.

CASE STUDY
THE LOLLYPOP THAT TURNED BITTER,[2] THE EXPERIENCE OF AN EXPATRIATE COUPLE IN CHINA

When Alain told his wife, Montserrat, he had to close down the company in China she felt as if a glass of ice water had been poured over her head. "We'll have to move soon," Alain said with a grave tone. His wife could not believe her ears; "You must be kidding! I've only been here half a year. I quit my job to come to China. Our daughters have just started in the new school. How can we move again?"

"Montserrat, calm down. We'll find a solution," Alain replied.

It was June 2002 when they received the terrible news.

Alain and Montserrat were an expatriate family working and living in Shanghai, one of the biggest cities and the business hub of China. One year ago, Alain had received an offer from Chupa Chups, a Spanish company well known for its lollypops, to become its next GM in China. It was Alain's dream position. After consultation with his wife, he accepted the challenge. Alain had great hopes to grow the business in China and to become the new VP for Asia Pacific of the company. Now, all his dreams had vanished. Jose Luis Becerra, the CEO who had asked him to come to China, had left the position. The newly appointed CEO changed everything. He asked Alain to close down the company's operation. It was a nightmare.

An international couple

Both Alain Rauh and Montserrat Garrido had extensive international experience before coming to China. Alain, born in France, had completed his undergraduate studies in Germany and France, and obtained an MBA in the United States from the Tuck School of Business at Dartmouth College. His professional career enabled him to work for multinationals such as Braun and Sony in Germany, and Chupa Chups in Spain and in China. Montserrat also had an international background. She was born in Spain and had obtained a Bachelor of Business

CASE STUDY: THE LOLLYPOP THAT TURNED BITTER

Administration from the Florida Atlantic University in the United States. After graduation, she worked for Fidelity Investments in Boston, one of the biggest mutual funds, and at Quaker Oats, a unit of PepsiCo in Florida. Later, she went back to Spain and joined an affiliate of Andersen Consulting in the executive education section. At the time she decided to complete an MBA at IESE Business School in Barcelona. There she met Alain, who was an exchange student at IESE from the Tuck School of Business. During one of their first dates they spoke about their future career plans. Montserrat asked Alain about his dream job. "GM of a subsidiary in a foreign country," he replied without hesitation.

After finishing her MBA, Montserrat accepted a job offer at A T Kearney, a consulting firm in London. Alain found a job as business manager in Germany at Braun, a unit of Gillette, P&G group. They reached an agreement to both look for work in the other's city. Montserrat got an offer from Citigroup in Frankfurt, where Alain was living. They married and lived in Frankfurt for almost five years. Later on, Montserrat was offered a position at IESE Business School and moved back to Spain. Alain soon after found a job in Spain at Chupa Chups. It was 1999.

Chupa Chups is a Spanish company founded by Enrique Bernat in 1958. Bernat developed an innovative idea of a candy with a stick in it. He created the concept that is now known around the world as the lollypop (see CS Exhibit 8.1). This innovation quickly became tremendously popular in the Spanish market. Based on a dominant presence in the domestic market, Chupa Chups aggressively explored new parts of the world. In 2000 Chupa Chups traded in more than 150 countries and had 2,000 employees; its sales amounted to 450 million euros, 90% coming from outside Spain.

CS EXHIBIT 8.1:
CHUPA CHUPS LOLLYPOPS

Soon after starting in Chupa Chups, Alain was promoted to marketing director for the Candy & Toys division. He was then given even larger responsibilities for the Chupa Chups and Smint brands. Alain felt he was getting closer to his long-time cherished dream of becoming country manager.

CASE STUDY: THE LOLLYPOP THAT TURNED BITTER

Alain's dream came true

He had never expected his career dream to be realized by the age of 38. At the beginning of 2001 Jose Luis Becerra, the former GM of Chupa Chups Russia, the group's most successful subsidiary, was appointed CEO. Xavier Bernat, the founder's son, decided to step down from his executive role and remain as the company chairman. One day in March 2001, Jose personally invited Alain to lunch. Alain immediately sensed that something important was about to happen.

Alain's intuition was correct. During the lunch, Jose asked him, "Do you want to become country manager?" Alain firmly replied, "Yes." The boss continued, "In which country would you like to work?" After a short hesitation, Alain replied, "Any English-speaking country." He thought it would be easier for his wife to find a job in such a country. "Well, I'm not thinking about any English-speaking country," said the boss, "What about China?"

This proposal was a big surprise to Alain. China was totally strange to him. Alain had only a limited knowledge of China and he could not speak any Chinese. Working in an emerging country with such high cultural and linguistic barriers was certainly a risky career move. On the other hand, he had heard about the changes and tremendous growth of the Chinese economy. He knew that China was of strategic importance for any company. Therefore, he thought it would be a great professional experience and a boost to his international career. Furthermore, it was Alain's dream to be a country manager, a position he had longed for for many years.

Jose Luis, the CEO, told Alain that their business in China was not going very well. He needed somebody he could trust to replace the current GM, to streamline the organization and grow the business from there. The proposed duration of the expatriation, Jose Luis told him, was seven years in total. Alain had two years to turn around the China business plus five more years with extended responsibilities for the Asia Pacific.

"The assignment is very exciting but I have to discuss it with my wife first. I'll let you know my final decision in three days," Alain told his boss,

The boss agreed, but still pushed on him, "Three days? That's too long. What about telling me tomorrow?"

After the meeting with the CEO, Alain was anxious to share the good news with his wife. He called her from his office. Montserrat was astonished, "China? I don't think so." Alain realized that his wife didn't share the same enthusiasm, but he wanted to persuade her. Alain understood his wife's strong reaction. She was really enjoying her job at IESE as marketing director. Besides, they had two small daughters and Montserrat was pregnant. She considered that their life was perfect in Barcelona. Why would she consider moving to China, a land so alien to both of them? But Alain didn't want to lose this career opportunity. If things went well, he would be promoted to VP of Chupa Chups Asia Pacific. This promising future excited him.

To his surprise, Montserrat was calm when he met her at home. She understood that it was a big opportunity for her husband. They talked about all the pros and cons of the decision. They concluded that it could be a great learning experience for them and the children. Montserrat could spend more time with the kids and maybe later find a job there. The discussion lasted till late that night. Finally, he got the green light from Montserrat, but she suggested that Alain get more information about Chupa Chups in China in order to be sure they were making the right decision.

Chupa Chups' problems in China

When Jose Luis, the CEO, offered Alain the GM position in China, he said it was very confidential and asked him not to tell anybody from the China operation. As it was such an important decision for him, Alain decided to talk to someone in the export department who knew about Chupa Chups China. The information he got was rather negative.

Chupa Chups started its operation in China in 1994 as a JV with Quan Sheng Yuan, a well-known Chinese candy-maker based in Shanghai. Initially, the business developed very well. The local partner was in charge of production and administration, while Chupa Chups focused on marketing and distribution. Yet, the communication with the local JV partner was not smooth. With sales growing at double-digit rates, Chupa Chups decided to set up its own company, build a state-of-the-art plant, and bring in new machinery. The investment also included the introduction of SAP, a business management software system, and the opening of sales offices in 20 cities all over the country. The challenge was

CASE STUDY: THE LOLLYPOP THAT TURNED BITTER

then to utilize the new production capacity, and leverage the investment in sales force and management systems. The company had big investment plans concerning China's huge population to counter the still low candy consumption rate. However, results were very disappointing.

From the conversation with his colleagues, Alain learnt that the situation in China was quite difficult. Some even suggested that he not take the position. They thought it was too much of a risk. However, Alain was not deterred by what he was told. According to him, problems mainly came from the management of the unit. He was confident that he could do a better job than the incumbent GM and improve the situation.

He also trusted Jose Luis, the CEO, who Alain considered his mentor. Jose Luis had been the GM of Chupa Chups Russia before becoming the CEO. The Russia unit was at the time the most successful operation of the group, accounting for 25% of the whole company's profit. The CEO believed that his achievement in Russia could be replicated in China. In his mind, the two countries shared a lot of similarities. Both were large, emerging markets in the process of economic and political transformation. Jose Luis had personally come to China, spent two weeks auditing the entire operation and formulated a detailed plan for the turn around. He considered Alain the right person to go to China to execute his business plan.

Alain now had two different versions of the situation. It would be a "mission impossible" as his colleagues told him, or a great career opportunity as Jose Luis described it. As a believer in "high risk, high return," Alain decided to take the risk.

He officially informed Jose Luis of his decision to accept the position in China. In May 2001 HR organized a look-and-see trip for the couple. Alain and Montserrat spent a week in Shanghai. They toured the city and visited apartments in search of a future home and they checked out schools for their daughters. They were also provided with an excellent introduction to the practical details of life in Shanghai. The trip took away a lot of their concerns and strengthened the determination to move. They even finalized the contract for housing and schooling for their children. Montserrat, thinking of the trip, admitted, "It was very important for us to make this decision. I think the HR manager was very competent and aware of the type of support we needed. That helped us to accept the position."

Alain decided to move first. Montserrat would stay behind for a few months. She needed time to hand over her job and to give birth in Spain, where she felt more secure and had the support of her family. If things went well, Montserrat would move to Shanghai with the rest of the family later that year.

Alain's first six months

Alain moved to China on June 17, 2001. He was accompanied by Giorgio Maritan, his direct boss and head of Sales & Marketing for Northern Europe, Africa, the Middle East, and Asia. On the plane, Alain was told that not only did he have to fire the current China GM, but almost the entire management team, which included the three expatriates in charge of Finance, Marketing, and Operations. He was also asked to close all the sales offices and distribution centers, and to use only local distributors. He was surprised by the plans and the dimension of the changes he was expected to execute. He said to Giorgio, "I thought you were only going to change the GM. I didn't expect that I had to lay off the whole management team." Giorgio replied that the company was determined to clean house as a necessary preparation for a healthy growth.

Alain thought it was a daunting job to lay off so many people and simultaneously introduce the new strategy. He recalled this difficult moment: "The first day we went to a restaurant and had dinner together with the management team in China. The next day they were all fired. I tried to be nice and respectful, but I was seen as a killer. The employees were scared of me as I kept firing people." He also had to close down sales offices. The company had more than 20 in various cities. Alain traveled to all of them to restructure the commercial operations. He closed the offices in the secondary cities and streamlined those in the first-tier cities in order to cut costs.

Alain worked around the clock during those first six months. He saw a lot of problems in Chupa Chups China: obsolete inventories, de-motivated people, and a lack of money for any marketing activities. But he was eager to implement the new business plan and was motivated by the support from his CEO. He felt confident that he could improve Chupa Chups China. He described his feeling at that time: "I was so happy to be GM. I felt like a young man with great dreams. I wanted to be Jack Welch. I knew the situation was bad, but I tried to tell people that there was light at the end of the tunnel. I fired many people, but tried to give them hope. I managed the situation with a lot of care and respect."

Alain devoted himself wholeheartedly to the restructuring of the company. In six months, Alain completed the restructuring according to the plan his CEO gave him. Difficult as it was, the first six months were a success for Alain. Even with the reduced advertising expenditure, sales climbed in the fall and reached a peak in December. The satisfactory market result made Alain optimistic about the success of the restructuring. Finally, Alain called Montserrat and said, "Come with the children. Things are not easy, but I believe I can fix them!" In December 2001, only 10 days after giving birth, Montserrat came to Shanghai with the newborn baby girl and their other two daughters; the oldest was only three and a half. Montserrat was mentally prepared to start a new life in China together with Alain.

Montserrat's first months

Montserrat rented out their house in Barcelona and moved to China with her three little daughters. She only brought some personal belongings. The first months for her were very busy. There was so much change in her life all at once. She had to look for a new *ayi*[3] to help her with the house and the children. The two older daughters soon started at a new school. Everything was new to her: the city, the language, and the people. It was December. Shanghai was cold and rainy. In the first month, Montserrat and the girls caught a flu that lasted a long time. Montserrat had never been sick like that before and had to stay in bed. She was helpless but said to herself, "No, you can't get sick now! You have so much to do!"

Despite the difficulties, Montserrat didn't feel down. What enlightened her were the people who lived in the same compound. They offered her great support. Montserrat realized that she was not alone, as everybody had basically gone through the same difficult times. She built up a circle with the wives of the expatriates, people from all over the world. Most of them were from Western countries, others were from Hong Kong and Singapore. They all had similar responsibilities, taking care of their husbands, family, and the house. They exchanged information, went shopping together, and offered open ears and good advice when she had problems. Montserrat recalled the happy moments with them; "In spring, when our children came back from school, we sat on the grass. Children played together and we talked about how our days went. They were very supportive. They made me feel at home."

Montserrat was also happy with her daughters' school. It taught in two languages, English and Chinese. As the kids were very young, they learned the two languages very rapidly. The school was not big, but it was very professional and gave the children plenty of personal attention. However, not everything was perfect. Carmen, the eldest daughter, broke her leg and shoulder in different accidents at school. Montserrat was very concerned but luckily everything worked out well.

With friends' help, Montserrat got to know Shanghai more and more. She also started to learn Chinese. She felt Shanghai was her new home and wanted to have a good life here for her and her family. Even though she had made a tremendous sacrifice by quitting her job and moving all the way to China, she felt it was worthwhile as long as Alain could achieve big success in his career.

The lollypop turns bitter

Despite great hopes and efforts, Alain's plans at Chupa Chups did not produce the expected results. The good performance in the first six months turned out to be a mirage. The Russia model advocated by Jose Luis did not work well in China; the two markets had significant differences. In Russia, Chupa Chups was one of the few foreign companies that remained in the country after the 1998 crash and therefore gained a tremendous distribution advantage. They even distributed products and brands from other companies such as Halls from Warner Lambert. By sharing the distribution costs among more products and with less competition from premium brands, Chupa Chups Russia was tremendously successful. This is a practice that the Chinese law does not permit. Foreign companies can only sell and distribute what they produce in China.

From June to December, Alain was able to maintain the sell-in[4] at the level of the previous years. However, due to the lofty investment in previous years in the new plant, the integrated IT system, sales offices, and three distribution centers, he had no money left to use in advertising. Therefore, head office decided to cancel all advertising in China to save costs. This had a tremendous impact on future sales. Chupa Chups in China had always sold at a premium price and had dedicated 20% of net sales to advertising and promotion.

The trade was fully loaded with products, but the up-take from consumers turned out to be much lower than in previous years. As of January 2002, distributors sat on high inventories and stopped re-ordering. That came at a moment when many new confectionery competitors entered the market with massive launch campaigns. The situation got worse with the arrival in the market of cheap local brands. On top of that, multiple copycats in second-tier cities appeared. Consequently, retail sales prices dropped. It took time for Alain to understand what was really going on due to the lack of reliable nationwide market data, regional market differences, the loss of knowledge due to the restructuring, and Alain's inexperience in the Chinese market.

The reduction in advertising expenses decreased Chupa Chups' brand recognition and sales drastically dropped. At group level, the situation was becoming tight. Between 1999 and 2001 the company had opened plants in Russia, Mexico, Brazil, and China. The financial burden of the investments was so heavy that the group was no longer able to provide its China operation with financial support for marketing activities when it most needed it.

In fact, the group was undergoing a financial crisis. Under pressure from the banks, the chairman appointed a new CEO. Jose Luis went back to lead the Russia unit. The new CEO, Juan Jose Perez Cuesta, changed the strategy of the group. His objective was to save the core business. The new strategic plan was to concentrate on key markets where the brand was well established and profits were high. In subsequent years, worldwide sales went from 450 million euros to 250 million euros, but they finally returned to financial equilibrium. In an effort to reduce costs, the company decided to concentrate production in the Spanish plants. Finally, in spring of 2002, the decision was taken to close down the operations in Brazil, the United States, and China.

The new CEO told Alain that he had to close down the China operation as soon as possible. Alain had to find a partner in China and establish a JV. The JV partner would take care of management, advertising, and the distribution, and Chupa Chups would contribute with the plant and its brand name. The objective was to continue operating in China with minimum operating costs.

CASE STUDY: THE LOLLYPOP THAT TURNED BITTER

For Alain, it meant a career death sentence. He had to lay off all the people, including himself.

It was a shock for Alain when he received the news. He was initially confused and later upset. "It was so difficult to describe my feelings at the time. I couldn't believe the decision, but had to accept it. I even said to myself, 'I wish I hadn't come to China.' But I knew there was no time for regrets. I had to save myself and take care of my family." Alain thought about his options. Should he go back to work at HQ? His contract allowed him to resume his previous position as marketing director. After being a GM in such a challenging position, it was hard for him to go back to his old job. It would be a step down in his career. Should he go to another operation of Chupa Chups such as Russia? Should he find another job in another country? Montserrat would be outraged. She had given up so much to move to China with him. She now enjoyed life in Shanghai very much. Furthermore, if they moved again to another country, their daughters would lose the chance to learn Chinese, which was an increasingly important language in the world.

Alain didn't know which direction to take. His career dream of becoming a country manager is dissolving; the lollypop had turned bitter. After talking to Montserrat on the phone, he knew it would be 10 times harder to persuade her to move again. But he believed Montserrat would give him constructive ideas as she always did. He decided to go back home early and have a long talk with her.

REFLECTIONS

Alain Rauh

If your ultimate goal is to go back to your home country, most probably you should never take an international assignment. Everything at home may change – the people, the company – after your stay in another country for two or three years. The situation will not be the same as before. Similarly, you also change after some years abroad. It's like doing an MBA. You can always go back to your former company, but most people leave because an MBA changes your priorities and the way you see things.

Coming to China as an expatriate is not like taking a vacation. It is a big commitment. You must be really serious. It's almost like getting married. You know how it starts, but you never know how it will end. You should not come here only for the job the company offers you, but for a number of considerations. I came to China because I was interested in the country, the professional experience, and the possible benefits to my family.

If you decide to be an expatriate, you will be taking a risk with your job and also with your family. For instance, your wife might not be able to find a job in the new country and will have to be a housewife. That can be an enormous sacrifice for her. When you decide to go back home, she might have lost her connections and ability to find a new job. She would then feel frustrated or even be resentful. Your decision will also have an effect on your children. In our case, our three daughters were very small when we came to China. After staying there for years, they will not speak French or Spanish well. Their mother tongues will be English and Chinese. It might sound great that my daughters speak these important languages, but on the other hand it means it will be difficult to go back home. If we go back to Spain or France, they will have to adapt to a foreign country and culture for them. They cannot even attend the normal school, but have to go to an international school, which is very expensive. But then, we wouldn't have the typical expatriate package that covers that. I feel I have locked myself into a career as an expatriate. I have practically no choice but to continue as one if I want to keep the type of life we are used to.

As an expatriate, you need to have a genuine interest in other people and cultures. I was rather adventurous even as a child; it's something in my personality. China has been the sixth country where I've lived for more than six months. Coming to China was a continuation of my journey around the world. France is where I was born and raised, but I have spent more time in other countries than there. It's great to be in a different country because I can learn a new language, a new culture, and meet new friends. But if you are not adventurous you will never enjoy this type of life.

Despite my adventurous spirit and eagerness to learn, I must confess that I have had periods of deep frustration in China. It's too hard to learn Chinese, to penetrate their culture, to make Chinese friends, and to understand what's going on. Generally speaking, it would be much easier to move from one European country to another, or even to go to the United States. Even without a good level of English, you can always watch American movies or American sports, and eventually fit into their culture. But in China it is very difficult to fully adapt unless you learn the language or marry a Chinese.

So far, no Chinese have invited me to their home. Maybe people feel ashamed to invite a foreigner to their home, maybe there are some other reasons that I don't know. Communicating with my Chinese colleagues is also a challenge. We have different problems, so it's difficult to exchange views and share thoughts. I sometimes compare it to oil and water. You try to mix the two things by shaking them but after a while the oil separates. I have to say that all these things make my life in China difficult.

I would say that my biggest concerns and problems are not so much adapting to China and communicating with the Chinese, but dealing with HQ's expectations. It can be a very frustrating relationship. In China, the gap between the expectations of a Western company and the local circumstance is so big that it takes tremendous effort and patience to achieve the expected results. I find it difficult to get HQ to understand the real situation. For instance, I can hardly find any 45-year-old who can speak good English and understand the Western way of doing business. You have no choice but to hire managers in their late 20s or early 30s, and to give them tremendous responsibility. This would never happen in Europe.

It's also difficult for expatriates to communicate with all the people in the office, because foreigners don't usually speak Chinese and workers rarely speak English. It's difficult to explain all these things to the people at HQ. They don't understand it. When they come to Shanghai, there are picked up at the airport by the company driver and go to a five-star hotel where everybody speaks English. They think they know China but China is not like the Jin Mao Tower.[5] The ability to communicate with HQ and to explain your situation is very important. You should change their expectations and let them accept the reality here; otherwise, your life can be rather difficult.

People say "out of sight, out of mind." This is especially true in your relationship with HQ. At the beginning, when you leave you know everybody. Then you visit them every four or six months. Gradually you feel like an outsider. People change, bosses leave, and your contacts move to other companies. You lose track of the politics at HQ. You become a stranger after a few years.

My wife has been very supportive. I could not have achieved so much without

CASE STUDY: THE LOLLYPOP THAT TURNED BITTER

her. As the saying goes, "behind a successful man, there is a great woman." Often, the spouse is the only true confidant you have in hard times, since acquaintances made in China are very volatile. If your wife is not happy, it can be a big problem. My wife has done a great job supporting me and getting her own life organized. She has made a lot of friends, especially in the compound where we live. We are lucky to live in a good and safe community with lots of foreigners like us. Children can play together and the mothers can chat and help each other. I find that the wives of the other expatriates are very interesting people. Most of them are equally competent and as daring as their husbands. It is very easy to communicate with them because they are highly educated and open-minded. It's easy to make friends with them. There are some extraordinary spouses. I know one who is now studying a PhD on Chinese Civilization in Tong Ji University. Some do charity work, some take art classes, and others learn the language.

Another important concern is our children. When we came to China, my oldest daughter was only three and a half, the second was two, and the little one was only 10 days old. Children so little never complain about anything. This is normal life for them as it's the only life they know. However, things will be difficult when they get older. Children who are 12 or over have a difficult time here because they are cut away from their roots and their friends. At 16 it is critical because they will soon start their college education. You need to get them into a good international school, but there are few good schools for that age in Shanghai.

A lot of expatriates send their children to boarding schools back home. Then the mother is alone, which may create a lot of tension in the couple. The husband is busy all day at work. He has his own problems. His old friends are far away and nobody here can offer him an open ear. After working long hours, the exhausted husband goes back home and starts telling his wife his problems. Without letting him finish the desperate wife claims, "I also have problems, but you never listen to me. You only think of yourself." This is how some families get into trouble.

The future can be a big question mark. Nobody will guarantee you a good job after you have concluded your expatriate assignment. Smaller companies have no real career track for expatriates, since they only have very limited international postings. Let me give you an example. I know an expatriate who works as R&D manager for a foreign company in China. He had an agreement with his company that after two years here, he could go back to the R&D center at head office. The problem was that after one year in China, head office closed the R&D unit there. He couldn't go back because the department did not exist anymore. What could he do? Look for another job. The company could offer him some position like plant supervisor, but that is not his expertise and professional interest. The company had its good reasons for the closure, but he had to swallow the consequences.

Another factor to consider is age. When one is young, going abroad sounds so exciting. It's a beautiful adventure. However, I'm now 40 and I'm getting worried about it. In Europe, when you approach your late 40s it gets harder to get a good job. People at that age cannot change companies very easily. At my age I have to be extremely careful about my career moves.

Montserrat Garrido

The life of a trailing spouse should not be bad in principle if the husband is working for a good company. A serious company will make the family adaptation very smooth, simply because they offer a benefits package that will make the life of the family much easier.

The two most important things that allow the family to settle down well are housing and schooling for the children. It is very important to find a comfortable house, a place you can feel at home. Equally important is to find a good school for your children. You should also be able to travel back home once or twice a year to keep the family ties strong. If you are able to secure this, life can be quite good.

I know many "professional" expatriate spouses. They follow their husbands around the world. In a certain way that's their job. The husbands might have assignments of two or three years in one country, and then move to another one. These wives are just incredible global dwellers. They have the know-how and expertise of getting to know what's important in a new city. They have the intuition of going to good places, meeting the right people, and building their social network. They have done this for many years and are quite professional about it.

In my case, China was not my first foreign country, but it was my first

CASE STUDY: THE LOLLYPOP THAT TURNED BITTER

experience in an emerging economy. When you have been in other countries before, it is relatively easy to adapt to a new one.

Communication in the new country may be difficult if you have never lived abroad before and don't know the local language. The first thing to do is to learn some key survival vocabulary in Chinese. You also need to get to know your city quickly and find your way around.

My advice for any spouse coming to China for the first time is to be prepared. Learn as much as you can about the country, take some Chinese lessons, and most important, talk to other expatriates before coming here. You should try to come with a list of people who are already here and reach out to them as soon as you arrive. They can give you advice and orientation. These people will make a difference in your life. You husband will be working or traveling most of the time. He will be home usually on weekends. That is the only time to be with the family and meet other friends.

The expatriate community in Shanghai is growing and is extremely supportive and vibrant. It is very easy to create a bond with them as most expatriates experience very similar situations. They are generally very open and friendly. I feel that my family away from home is my neighbors and the friends I have made here.

CASE COMMENTARIES

COMMENTARY 1
BALA RAMASAMY
PROFESSOR OF ECONOMICS
CHINA EUROPE INTERNATIONAL BUSINESS SCHOOL (CEIBS)

This case study highlights two aspects of risk. First, it deals with the risks an expatriate faces. Second, it shows the risks of engaging in international business in general, and China in particular.

Literature on international HRM is filled with case studies and surveys that point to the qualities of a successful expatriate. High on that list is the cultural adaptability of an expatriate. Still, more often than not, the technical competencies of the manager are the main criteria that companies look for. This is proven in the case of Chupa Chups. Although Alain might have international experience, his technical competencies – that is, managing the marketing activities at HQ level – most likely influenced Jose Becerra. Alain's international experience is predominantly in Western countries. These countries have a cultural distance that is closer to his native France than China. The fact that Jose did not consider the effects on Alain's family as a result of the expatriate assignment is perhaps typical among senior executives who put company interests ahead of individual family interests. Alain is lucky because he has a wife who is supportive. Despite not having a proper country and cultural orientation in China, Alain, on the whole, fulfilled the expectations of his superiors. He removed the management team and closed down sales offices. In this sense, Alain was not the one who failed. Jose's expectation that China can follow the strategies implemented in Russia was perhaps the problem. It is here that the risks of expatriation highlighted in this case emerge. HQ changing the strategies of its international subsidiary is not uncommon. While expansion strategies are welcomed, shutting down and divesting is painful. One could appoint the best international manager, but if the manager is not given the time and resources to build a business, failure is imminent.

International business is riskier than domestic business. As returns are higher in international business, so are the risks. Foreign markets may be more volatile politically and economically. International markets could be more complicated for a foreigner to understand as it is meshed in with culture. It is perhaps for this reason that not all foreign ventures are successful. This is particularly true for emerging markets like China and India. No doubt, China has been opened to foreign enterprises for more than a quarter of a century; direct access to the Chinese customer, however, is relatively new for foreign enterprises. At the same time, foreign businesses are beginning to realize that the average Chinese consumer is more complicated than expected. The competition from other foreign players, as well as domestic firms, is on the increase. Early mover advantages are fading. What works in the home market or other foreign markets may not necessarily be replicated in China with equal success. Chupa Chups realized this, at the expense of Alain and his colleagues. The experience curve has its limitations.

As for Alain, he has two important qualities. He is an operations person in that he gets the job done; and he also has a long-term vision. Managers with both qualities are scarce. I would recommend that Alain stay in China after he completes his job at Chupa Chups. It is clear his family wants to stay and it would also be beneficial for his career. In today's globalized world, no manager could claim international experience if he or she has not served a reasonable amount of time in China. It is not easy to get an expatriate job when you are already in China. Perhaps Alain has to give up some benefits, but the costs would be higher if he goes back to Europe.

As a foreigner in China, I can relate to the issues raised by Alain. An experienced expatriate once told me that it takes 18 months to "get over" China. I am beginning to think that this observation is correct. I moved to Shanghai with my wife and two teenage daughters about 10 months ago. We are Malaysian by nationality, but we had lived in Macau (about eight years) and New Zealand (four years) in the past, and felt that we could "survive" Shanghai. However, we soon realized that teenagers have great difficulties handling a different environment. Being far away from friends and families affects them harder than adults. My two daughters were able to make friends in Shanghai, particularly with their classmates who were also expatriates. Since they attended a local high school that had an international section, most of their classmates were foreign Chinese. We provided as much support as possible – allowing them to invite their friends over for dinner and so on. However, the differences in the education system were a little too much to handle. I was worried that this may affect the performance of my eldest daughter, who was in the final stages of high school. Being an economist, I avoided the risk, and decided that my family should move back to Kuala Lumpur (KL). My eldest daughter managed to get a scholarship at a college in KL to finish her high school, while my younger daughter went back to the school she'd left. A familiar environment helped them get back to speed.

My advice to expatriates with teenage children is this: It's not only a good school that matters, but also the similarities in the system of education. International schools in Shanghai tend to follow an American education system or the International Baccalaureate. This could be quite different from the British system at an advanced level. It is important to ensure that teenagers are able to cope with the differences.

My wife, who is a Malaysian Chinese, enjoyed her stay in Shanghai. She is adventurous. While I was at school, she would cycle around Pudong discovering new places to shop, or ride buses to determine their routes. Not knowing how to read Chinese was a big handicap for her, but she got around as she spoke some Putonghua.

I am lucky in that I work in an environment where English is widely spoken – faculty, staff, and students. While it was tough going at the initial stages, once I started teaching, it was more comfortable as one begins to know more people. I make frequent visits to KL to be close with the family. My wife also visits occasionally. I have an Internet connection at home and with VOIP and Skype, I talk to my family every day. It has been tough but manageable for the last four months. Will I survive Shanghai? Ask me in another four months!

COMMENTARY 2

BETTINA GANGHOFER

DEPUTY GENERAL MANAGER

SHANGHAI PUDONG INTERNATIONAL AIRPORT CARGO TERMINAL CO. LTD

(LUFTHANSA JV)

The main issue I see is the *unconditional* "obedience" of Alain in following HQ demands on *how to* execute his new job. Alain may have feared for his lifelong dream not coming true, but to be a successful GM in a foreign country (especially in China) simply requires one's knowledge of the local situation and one's understanding of things.

His CEO thinks he knows better, based on a two-week audit. As we see later, HQ assumptions – that is, that things work in China similarly to Russia – were not only profoundly wrong, but also damaging. Similarly, the demand to fire the complete management team (beyond the former GM – which by the way should be done by the company and not by the succeeding GM) from day one and to leave him completely alone was outrageous and should have been denied on the spot. Alain and the company paid dearly for the consequences, robbed of all internal knowledge, market insights, and possible positive recommendations from the experienced staff.

Alain captures well the ever-present conflict between the expatriate manager and HQ expectations. You have to be relentless in your efforts to make yourself and your local environment understood. It requires networking, building trust, solid preparation of information, and decision-making options, as well as recommendations. And overall, it is all about communication, communication, and communication, also in view of getting the required support.

Would it have made a difference to clearly outline his expectations on how to run the business? I believe Alain would have had a better standing back at HQ if he'd argued more convincingly, and it would have been more "his company" that he'd tried to defend. Whether this would have avoided the final decision on closing down the company remains open.

The situation of Alain and Montserrat is at that specific moment unpleasant at least. I do not recommend that he return to HQ to his previous position; this would probably be a career-killer. The couple may want to consider staying in China – it is challenging, but it is also a great place to be. I am confident that with his (and even her) résumé, he (and she) will find something interesting and adequate. I know several examples of friends of ours who did exactly that, and quite successfully.

Whatever their decision, Alain and Montserrat have a huge advantage in their respective commitment to each other and understanding of each others' needs and dreams. Without the support of his spouse, Alain indeed would have had a much harder time.

I personally have a unique situation as I am the expatriate manager and my husband and our two kids "followed" me to China. The situation for each of us presented its own difficulties. For me, in the new job environment, it was the understanding of the different rules of the game. It helped a lot (and still does) not to be the only expatriate in the company, but also the Chinese colleagues have been and still are very helpful.

The children – then four and six years old – were quite excited in the beginning and only sometimes a little homesick. As they did not know many other kids (our compound was quite new then and not too many families lived there) they focused very much on each other. Being at school made life easier and they made new friends from all over the world. They easily mastered English, which they both now speak fluently, as well as some Chinese.

In the beginning it was probably much more frustrating for my husband, dealing with the everyday challenges of traffic, where to go and where not to; the shopping, especially at local markets; getting something repaired (especially when the workers arrive with one tool only, if any); and endless discussions with compound management and workers, on what could be the possible cause of a malfunction. You sort of struggle through each of those situations and you have to have plenty of humor and someone to share your experiences with. When he was able to add some male friends to his daily exchange circle, it became much easier for him. Right now, Shanghai is for all of us our home, and we really like it here.

I shared the case study with my husband and we both agree completely

COMMENTARY 2: BETTINA GANGHOFER

on Montserrat's reflections. The ever-growing international community is really helpful and people – to a much larger extent than back home – are always offering advice and support. It simply takes some time to orient yourself, and to gain some understanding of how things work differently here. And it is, indeed, necessary to speak at least some Chinese, as it makes life considerably easier.

The biggest door-openers in this country are, from our point of view, the children. The Chinese have a great attitude toward them and they try to do everything possible to make them feel comfortable. As we both value this very highly, this has helped us immensely through many little storms.

NOTES

1   The movie *Lost in Translation* presents the life of a foreigner visiting Japan. The main role was played by Bill Murray, who won the Oscar for his interpretation.
2   This case study has been prepared by Professor Juan Antonio Fernandez and Research Assistant Dongmei Song at CEIBS, October 2006. The case was prepared on the basis of class discussion rather than to illustrate either effective or ineffective handling of an administrative situation. Certain names and other identifying information may have been disguised to protect confidentiality. The case was published in 2006. Published with permission.
3   *Ayi*, which means "auntie," is the commonly used expression in China for household helpers, who are hired to clean, cook, and take care of the kids.
4   Sell-in refers to sales to distributors.
5   The 88-storey building is the tallest in Shanghai with the world's highest hotel rooms.

Chapter 9
Foreign entrepreneurs: Chasing the China dream

INTRODUCTION

The *Financial Times*,[1] **in a recently published article,** related the problems of Mark Kitto, a foreign entrepreneur in China. Mark Kitto is the founder of That's Magazines, a very successful group of magazines for the expatriate community in China. By 2004 his group had achieved a yearly turnover of almost US$4 million and employed more than 100 staff. However, Mark Kitto was confronting a very critical situation that could endanger the continuation of his publications: in China foreigners are not allowed to own magazines. Foreigners can distribute and sell advertising, but cannot be responsible for content. His company was in a kind of legal limbo. Kitto, in order to protect his investment, reached an agreement with a Chinese official to provide him with a license and therefore get the legal coverage he needed. The two started cooperating in July 2002. The license was to the Chinese official's name, which left Kitto as a shadow partner of his own company. The Chinese partner provided a legal façade to the company. However, problems between them started to emerge. When the conflict between them escalated, the Chinese partner decided to take over the magazine, asking Kitto to leave. To his surprise, Kitto found himself disposed of by the company he had created. He is now entangled in a legal battle with little chance of winning.

This story is not uncommon, especially in those areas in which the government still keeps a strict limitation on foreign investors. Kitto saw an opportunity and took advantage of it by circumventing the law. That gave his Chinese partner the power to take advantage in case of conflict. Why did the Chinese authorities not simply stop Kitto from starting his business in the first place? The Chinese authorities are sometimes lenient, especially when they want to test new business areas with foreigners. However, this circumstance gives unscrupulous "partners" the opportunity to take advantage of the irregular and uncertain situation and to take control of a business they did not create.

In a way, the list of problems that entrepreneurs face is somehow different from those faced by multinationals: MNCs have resources and influence that small companies do not have. If country managers of MNCs can be compared to orchestra conductors with a team of professionals playing the instruments, foreign entrepreneurs are more similar to one-man orchestras, in which they compose the music, conduct the orchestra, and play the instruments. International corporations have the benefit of size, their management teams, the power of their brands, and, last but not least, their deep pockets. Entrepreneurs find themselves disadvantaged when confronting many of the same problems MNCs experience.

Let's list some of the typical problems that entrepreneurs may endure in China.

Bank financing

Getting bank financing to start your business is almost a mission impossible. It is as difficult in China as anywhere else in the world. Most entrepreneurs start their businesses using their own funds and those of family and friends. A few still resort to venture capitalists. Getting bank loans to finance the company in its growth phase is also not easy in China. Banks are not professional enough to assess risks and usually resort to collaterals to protect their investments. This keeps startups and new companies out of the banks' business. A foreign entrepreneur who exported flowers to Europe once applied for a bank loan. He finally got it approved, but to his surprise the bank branch manager asked for a 20% commission on the loan as a condition for delivering the funds. At other times, such bank managers directly ask for shares in the company their bank is financing. The main victims of this behavior are not foreign businesspeople but mostly Chinese entrepreneurs. Of course, not all bank managers are alike; banks in China are improving very rapidly and the situation will hopefully change. The fact is that most foreign entrepreneurs use their own savings or the funds generated by the business to finance their operations.

Hiring and retaining talents

If the situation is difficult for MNCs, it is even worse for entrepreneurs. Small companies cannot offer international careers, lofty salaries, expensive training, and the prospect of becoming CEOs. They cannot offer a glamorous name to put on the business cards to impress relatives and classmates. All these factors make the war for talent a lost cause from the beginning.

Fighting bureaucracy

Entrepreneurs, when facing Chinese bureaucracy, do not have the power to influence decisions. Most investors remain at the mercy of the bureaucrats and their interpretation of the law. Officials can decide what is legal and what is not; they can have great power over the future of any venture. Of course, they are more cautious before using that power against the big MNCs, but this is not the case with small businesses. The best advice, as one foreign entrepreneur told us, is to follow all the regulations as much as possible, and to try to slip under the radar. Do not attract attention by complaining too loudly or showing off how much money you are making.

But bureaucrats represent another type of danger to the entrepreneur. It is not unusual that the government official becomes your direct competitor. Once these officials identify a successful business, they will try to enter the competition with the advantage that they are playing on two sides as players and as referees. One entrepreneur in the passenger transportation service industry worked very hard to get a license to open a bus line between Beijing and Tianjin. Painstakingly, they managed to get the line approved by the authorities and started operating the route. When they proved the route was profitable, the same officials that granted them the license started a bus company to serve the same route.

Finding reliable partners

As we saw in the opening anecdote of this chapter, your Chinese partner can become your worst enemy. Partners who help you to start a business and obtain the license in their name may decide to get rid of you once the business is working out. Partners may transfer company funds to their private accounts or hire family members. It is not unusual that partners learn your technology and start a business next door to compete against you.

IPR protection

MNCs have legal teams and other resources to fight counterfeiting and prevent piracy. Entrepreneurs, unfortunately, are usually helpless in the same situation. One foreign entrepreneur literally told us that he was leaving China after losing all his investment due to IPR problems. Counterfeiters had copied his product and were selling it at such a low price that he could not make any profit. Another entrepreneur asked the authorities to inspect a company that was copying his product. He provided all the details for the convenience of inspection. The official in charge told him that his company was too small to bother and asked him to pay before taking any action against the infringer.

Dealing with local suppliers

Suppliers can be unreliable and sometimes dangerous for the business. A case was reported by EuroBiz[2] concerning a foreign entrepreneur who was producing furniture very successfully in China. The name of the company was Trayton Furniture. Simon Lichtenberg, founder of the company, bought leather for a total value of RMB37 million from a company in Sichuan. Some of the material was defective so Lichtenberg returned it and asked for new material to be sent. As the Chinese company refused, the entrepreneur decided to hold back payment for RMB3 million to put pressure on the supplier. Soon after he received a court order from a judge in the locality of the supplier freezing RMB3 million of Trayton's accounts, plus RMB4 million in company assets. The supplier was using his local *guanxi* to win the case. As Lichtenberg said, "You can have a contract but people might just not do things according to the contract, because they are not used to a society being regulated by law and contracts. At the end of the day, contracts give way to a good relationship, or connections with people in the power position." He concludes, "You might run into a supplier who says his factory is the biggest in China, and 'we can do this and we can do that,' but it might not even be his own factory – he's just an agent. There are tons of stories of this kind in China."

Collecting payments

One of the most critical challenges for entrepreneurs is to get paid. For a small business, lack of payment means the death of that business.

* * *

Entrepreneurs must deal with many of the previous situations without the support of professional teams. They are practically alone. On top of that, they do not have the luxury of holidays or weekends. The work life of entrepreneurs is very demanding. One entrepreneur confessed that he had renounced having a family to dedicate all his energies to the business.

The previous list of problems may seem a little scary. However, being an entrepreneur is the lifestyle one chooses to have. Some of the problems are also common to entrepreneurs in many other countries. Besides, Chinese entrepreneurs are also facing similar challenges. Anyway, entrepreneurs are playing a fundamental role in the rapid transformation of China.

When talking about the Chinese transformation, experts usually focus on the reform of the state-owned enterprises (SOEs) and the political system. However, the greatest success of China's reform is in its private sector. When Deng Xiaoping started the opening and reform process in China, he unleashed the enormous entrepreneurial energies of the Chinese that many years of communism were not able to eliminate. The entrepreneurs are creating the jobs that China needs. Some experts calculate that 15 million new jobs are needed each year. Exhibit 9.1 gives a partial picture of how this is taking place.

EXHIBIT 9.1: THE NUMBER OF EMPLOYED PERSONS IN URBAN AREAS (IN MILLIONS)
Source: China Statistical Yearbook 2005.

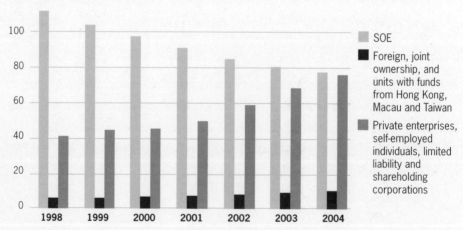

When one looks at the above exhibit, there are several conclusions to draw. First is the declining weight of SOEs in the job creation process and the small weight of foreign investment companies (FIEs). The contribution of FIEs to Chinese reform is mostly in terms of technology, high value-added exports, and modern management practices. In a certain way, FIEs are forming the future business leaders of China. The SOE contribution to job creation is negative and will continue on that path. It is the Chinese private sector that has the task of creating the jobs and the prosperity that will keep the China engine going.

In the following case study you will have the opportunity to read the real stories told by three foreign entrepreneurs in China. The first protagonist came to China as an expatriate and later became a supplier of his previous employer. Later, he started a new company quite successfully. The second protagonist started her China experience as a diplomat. After trying a low-risk but small business, she made a new move with help from a venture capitalist. The third protagonist went to China, attracted by its culture. He learnt the language and even studied in a Chinese university. He later founded several companies with his classmates. Though these three foreign entrepreneurs had different growth paths and met different challenges in their ventures, they did share a lot of best practices and lessons for doing business in China.

Following the case study, you will find two commentaries: the first by Ding–kun Ge, Professor of Strategy & Entrepreneurship, CEIBS; and the second by Shaun Rein, Managing Director, China Market Research Group (CMR). Both commentators analyze key success factors for starting up, and give useful advice on how to do business in China.

CASE STUDY
PERSONAL REFLECTIONS OF THREE FOREIGN ENTREPRENEURS IN CHINA[3]

Reflection 1: Robert A. Bilodeau

My name is Rob. I am an American. I moved to Shanghai more than 12 years ago and started my first business here in 1996. That I took the path of an entrepreneur does not surprise me – it is almost a genetic trait. As a child I spent most of my summers either working at my father's own entrepreneurial businesses, or pursuing my own simple businesses, so it was inevitable that "like father, like son" I became an entrepreneur myself.

I did not get to start my own business right after college, however. I first graduated with my degree in Economics and subsequently joined the Executive Training program of a large US department store chain. I was trained initially as a department sales manager and quickly moved up the ranks to the Merchandising Division as a buyer. By the middle of my fourth year, however, I had become disillusioned with "corporate life" and left to work for one of my suppliers. The new employer was a much smaller, family-owned company that manufactured small bags, gifts, and accessories, and whose initial success had come from the early outsourcing of its production to China. In fact, the company had been fully engaged with China since the early 1980s.

After working for the company's New York City office for several years, I was offered the opportunity to move to China and run the operations there in 1994. I had never anticipated such a transition, and the New York City lifestyle was addictive, but ultimately the timing was perfect. At the time I was 30 years old, recently divorced, and free of any binding obligations. China was most definitely considered a "hardship" assignment at the time, and it certainly didn't generate the "buzz" that it does today, but the challenge was too irresistible to forgo. Here was an opportunity to learn new skills, to explore an entirely new environment, and to do it with an employer that I respected and trusted. Moreover, while it still wasn't my "own" company, I did get to look forward to running my "own" operation within the company. I knew that if I did not accept the offer I would have regretted it for the rest of my life. I packed my belongings and blindly moved to China within two months of the offer.

My initial "assignment" was a handshake agreement for two years. The company's betting pool had me lasting only six months – in the end the assignment lasted six years. To this day, I feel especially fortunate to have had this opportunity. It let me explore a whole new world of business opportunities. It allowed me to earn and save the money that would become the capital for my own business. It taught me the skills I needed to successfully operate my own firm.

When I arrived in 1994, all of the company's products were "assembled" in China, yet most of the raw materials were still imported from outside mainland China, in places such as the United States, Japan, Taiwan, and Hong Kong. The majority of my first two years were spent developing, often from scratch, a local supply chain that could produce the quality we required. It was the "developing from scratch" stage that was particularly interesting – after all, if we were going to help set up new suppliers to achieve the quality/price objectives, why not set one of these up by myself? I discussed the possibilities with some well-trusted Chinese friends and we determined it was not only possible, but a plausible win–win scenario for the company and ourselves.

When I first accepted the China assignment, my employer was aware that I would be barraged with opportunities, and asked only that I commit two years to the project without distraction. He even stated that after the initial two-year period, he would be willing to look at participating in opportunities that I might propose. I approached him in 1996 with a proposal to open up a small factory to supply locally produced components for the accessories. In reality it was a mutually beneficial proposal – I would remain in China and devote the majority of my time to my current position, while establishing an independent supply factory on the side. This relationship would be considered unorthodox in many companies, but in this instance it was mutually advantageous – I received a great incentive to remain in China, and the company received a new "local" supplier that provided the quality needed at 10% to 40% less than the usual cost.

So, with the full support of my employer, I started a small factory with two Chinese partners whom I knew I could trust implicitly. I supplied the startup capital and marketing capability, while my partners effectively "built" the factory and the management team. We registered the company as a wholly owned foreign invested enterprise (WOFIE), shared ownership, and managed the company together. By the end of 1996, we had the factory up, a supply chain established, and we began taking orders. The company has since grown to 35+ employees and generates nearly US$1 million in annual turnover. All of the partners were well-rewarded – not only in generating capital to be used for new ventures, but also in helping us to develop business methods that merged the best of the Western and Chinese ways of doing business.

My second business venture started as a simple friendship. Shortly after my arrival in 1994, I met a fellow American expatriate who was working for a large MNC. He too had a strong entrepreneurial streak, having built and sold several companies before taking on his current role. He returned to the United States in 1996, where he had allied himself with a small US-based specialty chemical supplier to the automotive industry.

We kept in touch, and by 2000 began discussing mutual business ideas. He had developed an interesting strategy that would catapult his new company into the "big league." I had reached the point in my company of having pretty much localized myself out of a job. The timing was right! I bought into my friend's strategy and using the capital I had saved in the previous six years, I also bought into the company. Together we initially invested more than US$1 million to grow the company from a small specialty chemical supplier to a large tier-one supplier to the automotive industry – a figure that has since grown more than tenfold.

The company's strategy hinged on the recognition that a global consolidation of automotive OEMs had forced a similar consolidation on its supplier base. New vendors were shunned and existing vendors were cut or merged into preferred tier-one "mega-suppliers" that could support worldwide operations. This strategy did grow profits and yield stability for years, but innovation was stifled. As the consolidation opportunities evaporated and profits came under pressure, the mega-suppliers reacted "logically" by cutting overheads, slashing R&D, reducing customer support, raising prices, and discontinuing marginally profitable or niche markets.

Our strategy was to gain vendor status by stepping into those abandoned markets, and China was the ideal entry point. Although automotive specialty chemicals is a US$1.2 billion global market, the tier-one vendors supported only the largest segments of it in their China strategy, leaving numerous "niche" markets worth tens of millions of dollars "exposed." If the mega-suppliers even serviced these niche markets at all, then it was typically done on an import basis with "stepchild" status in the head offices. We would take advantage of this shortcoming by establishing a China subsidiary to supply high-quality, domestically produced specialty chemicals to the automotive OEMs in China.

Establishing the company itself was a relatively straightforward process. Both of the companies I've established are registered as wholly foreign owned enterprises (WFOE), a decision made very simple by the fact that we could handle this by ourselves. Foreign-invested JVs are riskier because of the difficulties in finding a reliable partner and the challenges in bridging different business "styles", not to mention the time limitations typically imposed on a JV contract. (Typically, JVs are undertaken now only in specific situations where the government requires it.) Setting up the legal structures was bureaucratic but not necessarily difficult. China has a lot of qualified agents, lawyers, and consultants that are able to provide the varying levels of service required. Read all the regulations and documents thoroughly in order to make sure you are aware of all the limitations and representations. While rules may be "bent" in order to make something happen, you have to be very careful that these different interpretations don't impose some future unforeseen liabilities on the company.

We also had the advantage that as a relatively small enterprise, our company was "under the radar." Our business was not directly involved in any of the sectors that China deemed "critical," so we were not subject to the extra levels of provincial and national approvals that the telecoms, banks, insurance companies, and of course the auto OEMs had to endure. Nonetheless, as a chemical provider, we still have to comply with the environmental and safety regulations. This is a manageable task as we established our factory to Western standards; but contrary to common belief, China does have a strict regulatory regimen on the books. While enforcement may be spotty, as the economy matures it is becoming increasingly thorough. When presented with the temptation to ignore a regulation, always keep in mind that this "oversight" can very well come back and club you later!

Ultimately we invested in the China operation and quickly began providing localized production with both "US quality" and a "China price" – the very same strategy used in my first company. With a now booming market, and a lack of competitive offerings from the global suppliers, our product was welcomed. In fact, we acquired our very first customer as a result of a cold call – the customer had just been irritated by its former supplier who had decided to enter the customer's line of business and compete directly. In this case, we were welcomed not only because of our product portfolio, but for our ethics. As it happens, it was a US company and through the relationship we also sold to its US operations.

In this respect, the China operation was established not only as a profitable stand-alone company, but also as a backdoor entry to an otherwise "closed" customer base. In fact, our China operation generated a great deal of opportunities in the United States. As we secured OEM approvals in China, we were able to use that established vendor status to bring our business back to the home markets. These new relationships were then used as a launching pad for additional products (many of them developed or tested in China) through the same channels. In some segments of our business, as much as 90% of our US business can be traced back to the relationship we first established in China. I now spend a healthy part of my time in the United States visiting these clients, whom we may have never acquired had it not been for our China initiative.

Ultimately, however, the China business is the launching pad for the domestic China market. The automotive market has grown from 500,000 vehicles annually when we started business, to the more than five million vehicles it will produce in the following year. China is already the third-largest manufacturer of automobiles behind the United States and Japan, and it has recently overtaken Japan as the number two consumer market. The China company already exceeds US$1 million in annual turnover, even as much of the attention is still focused on its support of the US business. The business is growing fast, and since the China market will likely exceed 50 million vehicles per year, we expect high compounded growth rates for many years to come.

We have since expanded our operations in China and established a wholly owned R&D center in the university area of Beijing. This facility not only develops new products for the China business, but it is also instrumental in the development of innovative products and technologies for our US customer base. Of course, "cost" was an important consideration in choosing China over the

United States, but ultimately the decision was based on China's deep pool of highly qualified personnel. Even more importantly, in our years of experience here, we had also met the one "right" person to manage it. For a company of our size, we may have been "early to the game," but we've already seen the payoffs from the investment with low operating costs, diligent project management, and rapid development.

China offers the entrepreneur unparalleled opportunities, but in order to succeed, it helps to know the "rules." A friend from Vancouver once joked, "Before I moved to China, I thought the drivers in Richmond (a predominately Chinese section of Vancouver) were crazy drivers. But now that I've lived here, I realized it's just that I didn't know the 'rules' they were driving by." You must both understand and *accept* that they may be very different from what you are used to.

In order to understand the rules, it definitely helps to speak Chinese at least conversationally. I never studied Chinese prior to the assignment, but once accepting the offer I was able to manage several weeks of intensive language training before making the move. The training gave me enough understanding of the basic grammar and pronunciation that I was then able to focus on learning the vocabulary. Since I was the only foreigner in the workplace I had no choice but to learn the language quickly. Interestingly enough it was this learning process that helped to build the friendships that would become so important later on, and it was the best way to build the respect of my colleagues. Also, it helped me to get inside the mind of the way things worked in China. It was the beginning of the process of developing *guanxi*.

When I first arrived, everybody talked about *guanxi*. It simply refers to combined business/personal relationships that entail a sort of positively reinforced "tit for tat," but it can also carry the connotation of "corruption." While I found that the *guanxi* based on personal relationships could be very helpful, the *guanxi* offered up for sale was typically over-promised and over-rated. The best success came from politely declining such offers to instead focusing on building our own network of genuine relationships, and opening business channels that way. I feel relationships that form the basis of *guanxi* are important – after all, a "trusted" supplier is treasured in even the most advanced economies – but I also feel that the corrupted form of *guanxi* is becoming less and less important.

Hiring the right people is essential to the company's success, both in navigating the circles of *guanxi* and Chinese business practices, and also in understanding and implementing your development strategy. Alas, finding that "right" person is as much an art as it is a science. When a company is small, it is like a family – every time you add a new employee, you need to make sure he or she works well with the others because a faulty hire can quickly spoil the morale for the entire group. It's always better to find the one outstanding performer, compensate them well, and retain them, than it is to hire a handful of average performers. The "right" person will add to your management resources, whereas average performers will inevitably be a drain on them. In fact, the "right" person becomes a key asset in recruiting and establishing the rest of the management team.

In our case, my GM is a Chinese woman whom I have known and worked with for more than 10 years. I met her at a "labor market" as she was applying for a position in my old company; she clearly stood out from all the other interviewees. For a young woman just out of college, she had remarkable confidence, impressive English skills, and an extremely well-organized thought process. Although she didn't know it at the time, our team had effectively made the decision to hire her within five minutes of meeting her – a decision that we never regretted. It was no surprise that I recruited her as soon as she became available. The lesson learned is not about "where" or "how" to hire the right individual, but rather the importance of looking for the right person, recognizing it when he or she is available, and then doing everything possible to retain that person.

Entrepreneurial life is not always easy. Establishing a company, funding and staffing it, developing a customer base, and turning a profit are difficult challenges in and of themselves. Doing it in a foreign country as an entrepreneur takes the mission to an entirely new level.

It might best be compared to "being in a war." You battle every day for survival against a powerful foe, and at the end of the day you often feel lucky to be left standing. Entrepreneurs do not jump intentionally into this war zone, but the battle is usually brought to the doorstep by circumstances beyond their control. Yet, as in any battle, they face the odds, forge new tactics, establish unique alliances, and develop innovative strategies that give them the upper hand. Then suddenly (and perhaps unexpectedly) the fighting stops, the war is over, and victory is at hand. It's only then that they begin to really grasp the struggles they have endured, and it's only then that they really begin to enjoy the things they have fought so hard for.

If asked six years ago to do what I have now accomplished, my reply would have been, "No way. It's impossible." But looking back, I can't think of it being possible any other way. The entrepreneurial challenge is a true test of spirit that pits you against your own fears, drains you incredibly, yet still somehow concludes leaving you fully charged!

Now, when offered senior positions in other companies I can, in good conscience, politely and quickly decline. I recognize all too well, that while stability and monetary compensation are nice, they simply cannot compensate for the "thrill of the ride" that one experiences as an entrepreneur. At a certain point, financial compensation is no longer important for the comforts it can provide; rather, it is important simply as a tool to measure your *ability* to provide – in other words, as a measurement of your ability to succeed in creating something new. If someone were to come along and offer to buy the company for US$5–10 million, I would decline because the inherent value of the company as it commercializes more of its technologies in the coming years is worth many multiples of that. If the offer were for US$100 million, I would be more inclined to take up the offer but the "payout" would simply become the capital to take advantage of the next opportunity – this time only bigger, better, and hopefully just as exciting.

After more than 12 years, China, and Shanghai in particular, still excites and energizes me. I feel lucky to be a part of it. There is a line in the movie *2010* (the 1984 sequel to Stanley Kubrick's *2001: Space Odyssey*) where the Hal 9000 computer converses with the deified spirit of his former commander "Dave".

Hal 9000: *"What is going to happen, Dave?"*

Dave: *"Something wonderful."*

Those who have seen the movie and recognize the enormous understatement in the reply will understand when I describe that "this is often the way I feel about Shanghai." I'm never quite sure what is going to happen, but I am always sure that it will be "something wonderful."

Reflection 2: Gabrielle Chou

I was born in France and educated there till I left for Italy at the age of 20. I later went to England to complete a Master of Laws specializing in International Trade and particularly Trade with China. I wanted to become a lawyer, specialized in Chinese business law, so I took additional courses in Chinese Law when I was in the University of London. I wanted to do something different.

I have been studying Chinese since I was 13 years old. After the few years of experience in England, I arrived in China in 1992 to complete my doctorate research in Chinese Intellectual Property Law. The French government subsidized my study for my Doctor of Laws (LLD). I worked as a diplomat in China upon graduation. I worked in the French Trade Commission for three years, doing some consulting for big companies. Those companies were constantly asking for the same kind of service: how can we target the right Chinese consumer? They couldn't do it through the media, because the media in China was not sophisticated enough. Being a foreign lawyer in China had its limits, so when I finished my assignment with the French Trade Commission, I started my own company, ChinaLOOP.

When I completed my doctorate, I had my first entrepreneurial experience because I set up a consulting firm in IPR in China. Although I was only 25, the business was very successful. Many large companies with reputable trademarks came to me because I was probably one of the few foreign lawyers who could speak Chinese and understand the complex IPR challenges. I provided many services to my clients in legal matters and IPR-related affairs.

My experience with the French Trade Commission did not help much when I started ChinaLOOP. For many, swapping the career of diplomat for that of entrepreneur was a crazy idea. Some commented, "You're not going to make money." There are always people who encourage you and those who don't.

ChinaLOOP is my second entrepreneurial experience in China, but this one is different from the previous. Unlike the first IPR consulting firm, it does not totally depend on my own skills. The first company could not grow much as it was very dependent on my own knowledge. This second company relies on the know-how of a team and it has a solid IT infrastructure, so that it can grow much faster.

Business in China is not fundamentally different from elsewhere. Basically, you need to create networks and to be recognized for your expertise. One difference in China compared to other markets could be the lack of sophistication. We specialize in the management of consumer databases. We help our customers to reach the right target consumers and we market them efficiently. Most of our clients are not new to the Chinese market; they are large multinationals who are trying to bring some consistency to their consumer acquisition and retention. If they are launching a new product, they need to know which segment of the Chinese consumers to target and how to reach them. They need to know whether they should contact them by telephone, by email, by direct mail, or by SMS. They need to customize their services according to the different needs of their customers. We help our customers acquire new customers and retain them through customized data management solutions.

We are set up as a WFOE (wholly foreign-owned enterprise). This means that although the company initially only had business in China, we first set up a foreign company abroad, then made an investment here. Why did I choose a WFOE structure? After 10 years in China, I simply did not believe in JVs anymore. I'm talking about the real JV. A silent partner is another issue. In the service sector, Chinese partners sell their connections. You can develop the connection yourself or through the right people. As a lawyer, I paid a lot of attention to the legal settings and particularly to the business license. New entrepreneurs should be extremely careful with their business scope in China. If the business scope on your license does not fit to your real business activity, you may have a lot of trouble.

We could get a loan from the bank to start the business but we did not attempt to do it. I was not interested in it and did not have particular experience in that. When I started the business, I invested personally, but it was not enough. We needed an investment of several million dollars to create such a structure. I did not have that much, so I raised the money abroad from venture capital firms that specialize in my area.

There are two kinds of entrepreneurs. People who totally believe in what they do and do not listen to anybody else, and people who are very humble and listen to others. I am more of the second kind. Maybe I listened too much to my investors. In fact, they did not know more about the business here than I did. They could not give me the right direction.

In the first year, in order to raise money to start the business, I had to prepare business plans. When I talked to investors of the plan they said, "No, no, no, this is the Internet era. You should focus on the Internet. Change your business plan! I did and they invested on this basis." After the initial year, I told them, "There is not much money in the Internet right now. Let's go back to the first version of the business plan." I had to accept a lot of things from them at first, and then I gained their confidence and had more to say ... I proposed a new way of running the business and it was successful. Listening to people who know your business but who have never practiced it in your particular location is not very helpful. It's a lesson for me, and it will follow me elsewhere, not only in China.

Four years after creating the business, we were frequently approached by potential buyers. The business was profitable and serving over 50 multination-als. In October 2004 we sold ChinaLOOP to Acxiom, the global leader in data management. For me and for the team it was an achievement and five-star rec-ognition to be purchased by the expert in the field. To have sold the business to a similar but bigger player was important as it enabled us to integrate with Acxiom with success. We now have more that 80 associates in China and have offices in Shanghai and Beijing, as well as in the Asia-Pacific region.

Our largest challenge is to find the right associates. Chinese candidates are not yet very specialized and often want to become entrepreneurs themselves. So it is quite difficult to find the right people. Costs for recruiting in China are also high. Often the compensations required by candidates are not in line with their capacity and productivity. You need to decide whether you need that person, whether they can bring you enough value.

Associates are one of our biggest challenges. In other parts of the world our business is less reliant on people skills, but here in China many of our clients require strong hand-holding. If we do not have the right people, we cannot satisfy our clients. We rely a lot on our associates. But once they are in, most of them stay. We have a very good team. People get along well. Of course, like everybody else, we are losing some people. But compared with other companies, our turnover rate is very low. We must have a very good management team who is dedicated to the company. Our aim is to have more of these types of people to join us as a group of entrepreneurs.

It is difficult to start a business like ours. We needed to collect a lot of consumer data to set up a good database. It also requires advanced information technology

CASE STUDY: PERSONAL REFLECTIONS OF THREE FOREIGN ENTREPRENEURS

(IT). So it is very expensive. The key thing is that you need to sell the service to your clients. Selling a service like ours is not easy. When you start a business, you are likely to be obsessed with your product and neglect the benefit it can bring to your clients. We learned that through the first year and switched our attention to our customers.

I did have some connections and knew some potential clients for years before starting the business. But when we tried to sell them something it was difficult. We found our first long-term client eight months after the company was set up. It was a very important client for us. Since this first large contract was with Motorola, it helped us grow the morale of our team and the reputation of our company.

Eighty percent of our customers are foreign companies and 20% are Chinese. The business is growing, but the percentage does not change. Our major customers are multinationals. In general, they tend to pay late, 60 days after we deliver our service. In some cases what we have seen is that some very large companies had been extremely unethical, but the management of these large companies was not aware. We had to set clear guidelines to our associates to explain that we could not enter into that type of deal. I think one of the challenges of running a business here is ethics. Some people in the companies just pull strength to get personal benefit. It is not just money under the table. It can be much more sophisticated than that. I knew it could happen in small companies, but didn't expect it with some large companies.

Our business is growing, but the number of players in the market is increasing as well. It is the story in China. When we started the market was not big. Through active marketing and education the business grew. Other players realized it and are now trying to compete for market share. Compared to our competitors, we have first-mover advantage. We have been here for years with solutions. We are very close to the market. But we have to remain better than the others. It is a challenge for us.

If you want to set up your own business in China and are asking me for advice, my three recommendations would be:

- You may need to perform a market test to try your business concept. A market test is a great way to learn and convince investors. You will realize that even on a very small scale, things in practice can work differently than expected. Do not invest money in a business without testing it. It is very important that you know how to control the risk. On the general picture, one needs to understand how things work in China. Even after more than 14 years here, I cannot pretend to predict the market.

- Be extremely careful with the legal structure and the business's scope. It is very difficult to change your business settings later. Once your investment is made you can lose much of your bargaining power with the local authorities.

- You have to spend a lot of time training and caring for your team. It is very difficult to recruit in China, especially in Shanghai and Beijing. Candidates are legion, but few have sophisticated initial skills. It is very difficult to identify the people with particular skills. New graduates are more flexible than people with three or four years' work experience. Compensation increases very fast and career-minded people are very good at bargaining. They also get many phone calls from headhunters. It is not like in Europe or the United States, where you have such a large pool of talent with skills and experience even coming out of college. In China, things taught in school are very theoretical, so new graduates usually do not have any experience before work. If you spend time training and caring for the team, associates eventually grow and develop a relationship with your company.

That's it. Good luck in China!

Reflection 3: Tomas Casas i Klett

Before landing in China a decade ago I was fortunate to experience academic and professional challenges around the world. After completing my basic education in Barcelona, the United States became my destination. I specialized in finance at the Wharton School. The original dream upon graduation was to follow my classmates into a lucrative Wall Street career. Instead the bet was on discontinuity and I moved to Japan; after a stint at Sophia University I went to work for the HQ of a Japanese electronics multinational. Three years into this intense and very enriching experience it was time to return to my beloved Spain ... yet before

CASE STUDY: PERSONAL REFLECTIONS OF THREE FOREIGN ENTREPRENEURS

doing so I decided on a short stop-over in China. The idea was to get acquainted with Chinese culture and face a nation and a people in the midst of spectacular changes. What follows is my reflection on these years as an entrepreneur in China. I hope my experience can help other would-be entrepreneurs.

In China first and foremost one finds *tremendous freedom*. In the business arena the PRC offers its energetic citizens more opportunities for self-realization and mobility than do Europe, Japan, and even the United States. Look at firm founders in Germany or France; in consideration for the risks they undertake they are burdened by rigid regulation and unyielding industry structures. Moreover, when they succeed they must transfer a vast majority of their earnings to the state courtesy of direct and indirect taxation. China, by contrast, offers its citizens a much more flexible environment and grants them unparalleled business freedom as they go about realizing their dreams. It helps, of course, that the country is undergoing rapid economic growth; growth that is precisely fuelled by unburdened entrepreneurs.

The first objective in China was to learn the language. After studying for over one year, I gained admittance to a Master's program in Economic Science (in Chinese) at Fudan University. I made many friends there, including the ones with whom I would later on venture. China is a country filled with opportunities for young people, so I started various ventures with different groups of classmates. One such proto-entrepreneurial group – specializing in IT, software, and related service projects – took off, but not without hiccups: two firms in that group went bankrupt, losing most of the money made in the early years. On the other hand, we sold a firm at a reasonable valuation early on and two more recently. Today, the core companies are going strong. We are getting closer to realizing our dreams. But it is not only successful exits that motivate us … it is something quite different …

Most learning comes from *failure*. An important lesson was that it is difficult to develop IP (intellectual property) in China. Not because of IP protection issues or lack of talent, but because of a lack of executives able to manage IP creation processes. Our failures were predictable in hindsight: We were too optimistic and overestimated our management and technical capabilities, our vision was unfocused and size too large. We also misjudged the market and underestimated the competition. We almost deserved to fail.

What do our firms do, what core competence have we built? We are good at developing business solutions around software technologies in the ERP, financial software, business intelligence, BPM, portal, data warehousing, unstructured data management, security, balance scorecard, integration, statistics, and data-mining fields. By now we excel in the sales, distribution, technical support, and localization (both linguistically and otherwise) of these technologies. Moreover, we have built proprietary IP on the basis of these technologies and our Chinese client requirements. An important part of our model today is based on long-term partnerships with selected international vendors – many of them are global names and some NASDAQ-listed firms that rely on us to enter the China market. We build tremendous brand equity for them in China, a sophistical channel network, a client base with recurring revenue potential, and an effective technology support and deployment infrastructure. As we make our principals succeed we build significant value for ourselves. It is an extremely exciting experience. We have quite a number of top tier clients, such as China Telecom, China Construction Bank, Bank of China, and so on. We have offices in Beijing, Taiwan, Hong Kong, Guangzhou, Shanghai, and now in Manila.

We are a group of firms and each firm, or operational company (Opco), is independently run and managed. The value of the group grows with each Opco, and the value of the group to each Opco is tremendous. A new Opco can be up and running within weeks. Opcos are usually JVs with our principals or WFOEs. Starting a WFOE in China is now very convenient; the government also promotes high-tech in many ways. As to financing, up to now we have mostly relied on retained earnings and did not take on debt or external capital. Concerning external funding, however, now that we have a solid size and profits, we may contemplate seeking outside synergies, possibly with US or European venture capitalists that could in various ways add new value. As for debt my Chinese partners have always been adverse – they almost would prefer the firm to go bankrupt rather than incur such obligations! This is interesting, since we often need fresh capital as we grow, and our retained earnings cannot always cover all needs. A new Opco requires an investment as high as US$1 million – a huge gap from the US$60,000 with which we started our first outlet. Incidentally, our principals, the US or European IT firms, realize that if they set up shop directly in China they would easily spend US$3 million (and more!), for the same results

..: and then at a much higher risk. That calculation reflects part of the value that our group brings to the table.

Selling is key to start a new business. But A/R management, collection, which relates to cash flows, is the biggest issue for small and mid-sized private firms in China. Local customers are famously reluctant to pay in a timely manner, and sometimes they are over 400 days late (some of the most reputable clients in the country!). Customers must see the value you offer to have an incentive to pay earlier. In the first years, 90% of our customers were foreign enterprises in China; today 90% of the customers are Chinese. Our firm value relates to our ability to acquire and collect from Chinese firms; even though foreign customers know better what they want and pay on time, they are obviously much smaller than Chinese firms in China. Think about it: the largest foreign companies here, GM or Siemens, are smaller compared to the locals like China Mobile, Sinopec, or ICBC.

In order to boost sales, we built, support and manage an array of channels, specialized by industry and geographically dispersed. Our challenge is to wave them into a coherent, non-cannibalizing, and effective channel network. China is immense and has many markets – for each segment, for each province and even cities, for each industry and name account, we must relay on channel partners to service, sell, and collect. Again, *channels are the commercial key to China*. We need to nurture them: we have intense contacts and feedback loops at the highest levels, to train their people, carry out joint-marketing activities, and constantly ensure quality control so that they provide good pre-sales and after-sales services. Establishing solid relationships with channels is a function of time and commitment.

For a foreign firm founder wanting to venture to China, business partners are all important. There is no need to dwell on the primacy of *guanxi*; like elsewhere one must go into business with reliable and trustworthy partners. In my case I found them at Fudan University, and later through business engagements, like in Taiwan. You hear many stories, though, of partner risk. There is the example of my friend from Shanghai who dispatched his partner to Beijing to set up the North China subsidiary. Not only was he unable to sell and ended up losing the initial investment … the guy bought a luxurious car, rented an expensive office, and in general spent money unwisely, if not dubiously. Moreover, without consulting with my friend, his own partner, he made bad and far-reaching business decisions that came back to impede the well-run East China operation. Really getting to know your partner may take new challenges; it is a learning process … often a costly one.

Interestingly, our worst experience was not with a Chinese business partner, but with a foreign principal, a very successful and otherwise great listed company. We helped them introduce their software into the country, spend an inordinate amount of money sending engineers to Paris, and localizing their product; indeed, we orchestrated a very successful China entry. We had a superb channel network, strong customer references, and the pipeline of potential clients was huge. When we least expected it, and after a change in management at the regional Singapore HQs, they got rid of us in a rather thuggish way. The new Asia-Pacific GM simply said: "You guys did a great job, thanks for the clients and the prospects, your channels, your employees. The market is indeed great and we will go direct; sorry we do not need you any more." Then they hired away most of our team, or helped them start their own firms, took on our channels, and went on developing our clients and prospects. That was a terrible blow; fortunately it happened some years ago … and in China you are too busy to ever look back – so it was no satisfaction when recently the firm had to restate earnings because of a revenue recognition China issue and dismissed the Asia-Pacific GM. The larger point we are making here is that many troubles in China are not with China partners; rather, like many executives and expatriates here will attest, trust issues and related difficulties often occur with HQ and partners abroad who want to be involved but are clueless and out of touch with the local realities.

After all those years in China, and while I have often not resided here, it is finally possible for me to recognize with a minimum degree of confidence whether the individual I am facing across the table is meaning what he says. That is, whether moral hazard could be an issue or not. Clear feelings now instruct me about whether I am wasting my time with somebody. These sentiments are by no means explicit, nor are they easy to articulate. They are a type of acquired *tacit knowledge*, like the ability to recognize and classify a certain smell. Effective Chinese entrepreneurs are masters of tacit knowledge and do possess very, very fine noses – mine is still in the training stage.

Yes, regional cultural differences matter a lot! As for employees, managing and nourishing them in Shanghai is very different than doing so in Beijing or Guangzhou. Some local peculiarities are obvious even to the newcomer. In Shanghai bosses monitor their employees very tightly. They do not get an inch of freedom. Employees are surprisingly adroit and opinionated, and often their ideas (and actions!) conflict with the interests of the firm. Maybe it is because of their capabilities – flexible, quick, professional – that they are prone to challenge their bosses. In Beijing, on the other hand, workers possess larger scopes of vision and are much better team players. They are also more loyal. But often they promise more than they will deliver. Surely when it comes to IT, Beijing is ahead of Shanghai with many firms having grown to over 5,000 employees in size. These workers cooperate and share information. Knowledge creation is not the key, the key is *knowledge sharing*, and Beijing beats its rivals at that. In Guangzhou, employees are very independent, like cowboys. They go, get a deal, come back, get their commission, and get out for another deal. They seem not to care about anything except how much money they will make, although they are not as extreme and do not have the "take-no-prisoners" touch of the Hong Kong people. In general the Cantonese are seen as very pragmatic and effective. They do not want to waste their or anybody's time, and you do not have to push them much for results. But they are seen as lacking the skills to move into high value-added activities. We could go on and on with local insights and biases. One of the best ways to learn about China's regional business practices is to listen to the prejudices Chinese businessmen have about areas outside their own. In this respect they all do possess near encyclopedic knowledge!

Employee retention is a problem. Competitors with bigger budgets and more powerful brands constantly attempt to "steal away" our team – the more we have invested in somebody, the higher the likelihood that he or she will be enticed away. We once had a marketing assistant, a regular graduate from an average university. We offered her RMB1,500 at entry level and then took care to develop and train her. She responded well, so we increased her salary to RMB3,000, and then increased it again to RMB4,500 – all within 18 months. The pay was commensurate, generous indeed in relation to her productivity and background. But a competitor came and offered her a whooping RMB15,000 – the idea was not only to benefit from her skills, but also to access key knowledge about our company, including mailing lists and client base. So one day she said "good-bye" and left, telling us that she needed a vacation and was going on a long trip to Tibet with her boyfriend. About two days later she was calling up our clients and prospects. Employees are attracted to higher pay, and one cannot do much to counter excessive offers – we accept the nature of the market economy. However, people remain the most critical aspect of our business. Fortunately in China, and that is especially true for higher management, it is possible to motivate key people by means of non-financial considerations. That is, by working the heart.

Foreigners who start a business in China should choose a familiar industry and compensate for being an outsider, in the nationality sense, with being an industry insider. Experience and contacts, including global ones, can be leveraged. Embedded in an industry network they will be able to deal with regulators, clients, relevant government officials, channels, partners, competitors, suppliers, managers, salespeople, and so on. Relationships are also a function of time. In our case, all ventures have been in the IT industry – only now and given our size, we may very cautiously diversify. Anyway, the more we understand the industry the quicker we will grow – today we are growing quite fast – maybe too fast. For instance, the Solvento Group is expanding from 100 to 200 people in 12 months. We expect 80% revenue growth next year, but we might end up expanding only 30% … or by 120%. Unpredictability – the inability to forecast accurately – seems to be, incidentally, the trademark of entrepreneurial projects in China.

Language skills are essential like elsewhere. Even though my Chinese is worse than during my university days, it suffices to read contracts and carry out negotiations. Life in China is fraught with pitfalls for foreign entrepreneurs who do not know the language – unless they possess a tremendous idea, are very well capitalized, or have acquired a Chinese spouse. Good translators are difficult to find and you cannot always rely on them. Usually translators are not experts in any field other than the English language, and they invariably mess up figures and number calculations in price negotiations!

The Chinese government has done an amazing, first-class job. They have made China a safe and promising place to invest and to undertake risk. China's economy is growing fast and it provides entrepreneurs with a unique, opportunity-filled business environment. Interestingly – along with competition – taxes and regulations are becoming more demanding, and some firm founders are starting to complain, yet overall the burdens are still reasonable. China will continue to

CASE STUDY: PERSONAL REFLECTIONS OF THREE FOREIGN ENTREPRENEURS

modernize economically and socially while maintaining the present liberal regime that welcomes entrepreneurial wealth creation.

If in the future I return to the corporate career track, the rich learning derived from founding new firms will be an asset. The life of an entrepreneur is different to that of workers and executives of established firms. As an entrepreneur you are extremely risk adverse, since you are brutally exposed to risk; you are playing with your own money and so are deeply concerned about failure. You become extremely careful and meticulous in management, financial controls, and general decision-making. All the while you are juggling with forces that you cannot fully control. You do feel like an artist; instinct provides key guidance. Often you do not sleep well as your mind is never blank, your emotions are always active. Your challenge is to create something out of nothing – "value beyond the tangible resources you control." At times this magical trick does work; statistically speaking, most of the time it will not. You are clearly in a "bounded luck" paradigm. Yet regardless of the outcome, the work is heavy and so is the sacrifice; as a Catalan, blessed with an understanding of entrepreneurship since Phoenician times, I know this all too well. Work routines till midnight and limited or no personal time are part of the price to pay for this apprenticeship. This is the life of many entrepreneurs: wonderful learning, the certainty of pain, and maybe extreme rewards of the tangible kind.

CASE COMMENTARIES

COMMENTARY 1

DINGKUN GE

PROFESSOR OF STRATEGY & ENTREPRENEURSHIP

CHINA EUROPE INTERNATIONAL BUSINESS SCHOOL (CEIBS)

Thanks to the continuous growth of its economy, China is becoming a hotspot for entrepreneurship, or the "land of opportunities" as termed by one of my former students from Korea. Tax and other incentives from local and central governments, an almost unlimited supply of talent at low cost, increasing domestic demand … all these make China an ideal place to start one's company. As the case studies indicate, the "land of opportunities" is not for the Chinese alone, but for everyone from everywhere, as long as they harbor an entrepreneurial dream, identify the best point of entry, and most importantly, follow some of the important tips offered by the three entrepreneurs in this chapter. Three foreigners, from different parts of the world, came to China to realize their entrepreneurial dreams. While their exact experiences may differ, they offer very valuable advice and tips to would-be entrepreneurs who want to replicate their success story in China. I will comment on three of the key critical areas of entrepreneurship: opportunity evaluation, market entry strategy, and managing people.

To start a new business, one of the key items an entrepreneur needs to pay close attention to is the identification and thorough evaluation of the right opportunity. Pursuing the wrong opportunity at the wrong time and the wrong place is the single most frequently cited reason for startup failure. This is as critical in China as in any other part of the world. Even though China's munificent environment may offer more entrepreneurial opportunities, the ability to identify a manageable opportunity at the right time and at the right place is still a challenge. The experiences of the three successful entrepreneurs suggest at least two ways to ensure that the opportunity is right. One way is to immerse yourself in China for quite some time before you start your business.

The three entrepreneurs Bilodeau, Klett, and Chou, did just that – they got a job or studied in China. They learnt "the rules [the Chinese] were driving by" through daily interactions with Chinese employees, suppliers, and channel partners. While learning typically incurs costs, fortunately, their employers "covered" the tuition of the initial learning cost for two of the entrepreneurs. The moral is: if you do not have a deep grasp of the economic, social, and regulatory environments in China, work for someone else first before you "do it alone." Though not a perfect substitute for "letting others pay for your tuition," the second approach is to start with a pilot project, at a much smaller scale. For example, Chou set up a small consulting firm specialized in IPR while she was finishing her doctorate research in China. Though Chou did not mention the size of her business in the case, we can reasonably assume it was a one-person shop, with a couple of local associates at most. Entering a market with a small pilot project brings tremendous benefits to the entrepreneur. Small scale means much smaller risk. Even if you screw up, it does not sink your boat. Further, a pilot project gives the first-time entrepreneur opportunities to develop and hone entrepreneurial skills. More importantly, a small pilot project allows the entrepreneur to test the market, get connected with key players in the field, and eventually identify a great opportunity with much larger potential. In addition to these two approaches to finding a good opportunity, systematic analyses of potential opportunities have also proven valuable. Systematic evaluation of entrepreneurial opportunities may consume more resources and demand different skill sets than a typical first-time entrepreneur has. If you have been in business for some years and have accumulated the necessary resources and skills, systematic analyses of an opportunity will save you money and time in getting you into the entrepreneurship game. How to systematically identify and evaluate entrepreneurial opportunities is taught in many entrepreneurship courses in business schools around the world. If you want to brush up your skills, taking one or two courses in the weekend should help.

Once the opportunity is identified and carefully evaluated, the next key issue of strategic importance is how to enter the market. Market entry strategy sometimes makes or breaks a new venture. Different market entry strategies are associated with different levels of difficulty and risk, cash-burn rates, need of resources, and so on. Entrepreneurs must carefully explore all possible "ways of attack" and settle on the one with the best chance of success. Highly constrained in resources, most entrepreneurs find that market entry strategy often boils down to how to get the first client or customer. Whoever pays the first bill directs most small new ventures to that segment or direction. Empirical research finds that most entrepreneurs find their first customer through social networking – through people they knew in college, former employers, friends' friends, and so on. This is especially true in Asian countries, where *guanxi* plays an important role in business transactions. So making more friends in China is imperative before you start your new business.

The last point to highlight is that once a business is up and running, how is it scaled up by effectively managing people? This is a universal challenge, not only to startups, but also to large established companies. How to find, train, motivate, and retain talented employees is a mix of art and science, yet no one dares to claim that they have mastered either. This is especially true in China. Thousands of universities produce millions of graduates every year, but only a small percentage are able to roll up their sleeves and get their hands dirty right after graduation. The founder/CEO of a semiconductor startup in Zhangjiang High-tech Park stated it succinctly: "You [Chinese college graduates] have a powerful CPU, very large hard drive, yet a very sluggish operating system, and almost useless application software." To work effectively in this cut-throat business, "We need to reformat your hard drive, reinstall a more powerful operating system, and hopefully you will develop a more useful application package over time." A Chinese returnee himself, the entrepreneur realized how people's mentality or mental paradigms affect their performance. All of our three entrepreneurs recognized the challenge of managing people and proposed useful advice. For example, Bilodeau offered several tips on how to pick the "right" people from the crowd – he looked for people with "remarkable confidence," "impressive English skills," and a "well-organized thought process." He tracked the whereabouts of such talented people and "snatched" them whenever they became available. Chou deemed finding the "right associates" his biggest challenge, and it is equally challenging to keep them, as many talented Chinese want to become entrepreneurs themselves. To face up to the challenge, Klett suggested that we need to "work the heart": genuinely care about employees, motivate key people with intrinsic incentives, and develop a dedicated management team, rather than a few superstars.

COMMENTARY 2

SHAUN REIN
MANAGING DIRECTOR
CHINA MARKET RESEARCH GROUP (CMR)

Over the past two decades, scores of foreign entrepreneurs have sat haplessly on the sidelines as Chinese IT entrepreneurs like Netease's William Ding Lei or real-estate tycoons like Shimao's Hui Ming Mau made fortunes taking advantage of China's "electric" economy. However, as the successes of Robert Bilodeau, Gabrielle Chou, and Tomas Klett underscore, foreigner entrepreneurs can indeed make money in China if they understand the particulars of doing business and execute sound business strategies. There are four main points that entrepreneurs conducting business in China can learn from reading the case studies presented in this chapter.

Going it alone vs partnerships

Layers of bureaucracy, fast-changing laws, fickle consumers, and the sheer size of the market often daunt foreign entrepreneurs entering China. To overcome China's challenges, many foreigners believe that it is best to cooperate with a Chinese partner in order to benefit from their expertise and gain access to their connections. Unfortunately, many partnerships fail because of mismatched cultures, pay scales, motives for conducting business, and, most importantly, lack of trust. In all three case studies the entrepreneurs established companies using the help of local Chinese with whom they had cultivated relationships and built trust.

Klett says that finding "reliable and trustworthy" partners is the key for building a good business in China. Too many foreign entrepreneurs make the mistake of partnering with people they do not know well, but who are rumored to have good connections. This route can lead to failed deals, stolen IP, or worse. Entrepreneurs should partner with people they know and trust. Klett partnered with his classmates from Fudan University. Bilodeau worked with "well-trusted Chinese friends" for his first venture, and then on his second with an American expatriate he had known for six years.

Starting a company anywhere is a struggle. In China, it is even tougher. A trusted partner can mitigate a lot of problems. Unless you are operating in a specific sector where the government forces you to establish a JV, it is always best to establish a WFOE and build a management team with people you trust.

Low profile/Under the radar

Many entrepreneurs like to be pioneers and win accolades from the world's media for their vision. However, businessmen often push the boundaries of what is prudent in China. They try to be the first to bring something to China and convince the authorities to change laws to accommodate their business. Much of this sentiment stems from the concept of "first mover advantage" that US business schools espouse as the key for beating the competition. But in China, where regulations tend to be vague and open to interpretation by local authorities, it is often better to be the second mover. Aside from Chou who emphasizes the advantage of having many years of background in China, the chapter illustrates this point. Bilodeau did not try to trail blaze. He set up factories and simply beat the competition.

It is better to let the first mover struggle to secure official support and convince the domestic market of the need for its products and services.

Second movers can watch the pioneer make mistakes, and then set their own strategies with the support of the government. After a precedent has been set, the next foreign company seeking to invest in a sector will spend far less time and money on approvals.

Who you know or what you know

Many Chinese and foreigners trying to do business in China believe that *guanxi* is the magic pill that ensures business success. They pay supposedly well-connected consultants or relatives of high-ranking government officials under the belief that one needs them to do business in China. Misguided entrepreneurs believe strong government connections can magically wipe out the need for good management teams, viable products, and international-level business practices. While relationships are important in China – as they are anywhere in the world – entrepreneurs should not overestimate the importance of *guanxi* to growing a business in today's China.

The three entrepreneurs in the case studies all understand the importance of cultivating relationships with clients and partner companies. Chou states that, "the basic thing you need is to create networks and be recognized for your expertise." ChinaLOOP found success because it helped clients market effectively to target markets better than other firms can and not through high-level *guanxi*. A reputation for honesty and ability travels a lot farther than bought connections.

Recruiting and retaining the right team

The problem that faces all companies in China is finding and retaining talented employees. China can be a human resources nightmare. Although the applicant pool is huge, it is hard to find qualified talent. As Chou says, "finding associates is one of our biggest challenges."

When building a business in China the first consideration that a company should have is if team members have practical China experience.

Many firms have made the mistake of hiring managers from Hong Kong or Taiwan who speak the language but who do not really understand business practices on the mainland. Another potential mistake is hiring mainlanders who return to China after earning MBAs abroad – they too often lack real experience in Chinese markets and experience worse culture shock than true expatriates when they return to China.

It is much better to hire individuals who have practical experience navigating the business world on the mainland regardless of what their nationality is. Once you find the right people it is important to retain them. Bilodeau has had his GM by his side for over 10 years. Their mutually beneficial relationship has become a win–win situation.

One of the biggest issues that HR faces in China is retaining talent. Once a business finds a Chinese executive who fits the company culture they must show that person that there is no glass ceiling. Klett asserts that money is not the only path to employee retention, and he is right. Chou recommends companies respect their people and "to spend a lot of time training and caring for your team."

If employees are treated with respect and given good opportunities for training and advancement within a company, they will prove to be valuable long-term assets. Too many foreign firms put glass ceilings in place and do not allow Chinese executives to reach the highest levels of the organization. It is especially important for entrepreneurs who are building a business around a core of talent to ensure that Chinese employees know they can grow along with the company. Why would an ambitious Chinese executive want to stay in an organization where career advancement is unforeseeable?

China is an exciting place for entrepreneurs. Many foreigners like to call it the Wild East, as new industries are sprouting up and fortunes are being made in short periods of time. While the business culture is indeed transforming quickly, it is only the well-thought-out entrepreneur that executes a sound business strategy who will make money.

NOTES

1   Richard McGregor, "Fingers Caught in the Presses," *Financial Times*, May 3, 2005.
2   Cameron Wilson, "The China Factor," *EuroBiz*, October 2005, http://www.sinomedia.net/eurobiz/v200510/legal0510.html.
3   The cases were published in 2006. Published with permission.

Index

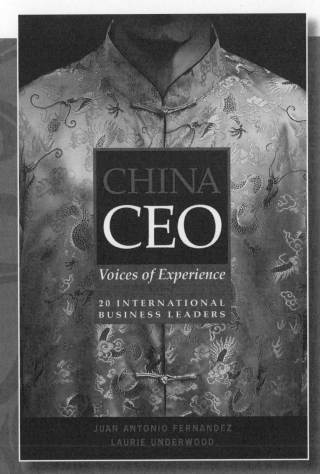